Personnel Management in Recreation and Leisure Services

(Second Edition)

ARNOLD H. GROSSMAN, Ph.D.
Professor
Recreation and Leisure Studies
New York University

i

Author

Arnold H. Grossman, Ph.D., C.S.W., is Professor, Department of Recreation, Leisure, Physical Education and Sport in the School of Education, Health, Nursing, and Arts Professions at New York University. He served as the Department Chairperson for ten years; and he has worked in management positions for over 15 years in social agency and camping programs providing recreation, leisure, and social services.

Contributors

Edith L. Ball, Ed.D., is Professor Emerita, Department of Leisure Studies in the School of Education, Health, Nursing, and Arts Professions at New York University. Dr. Ball has served as the Executive Director of Stuyvesant Neighborhood House, New York, and as a member and President of the Board of Neighborhood House, New York. She has also served on the Board of Trustees of the National Recreation and Park Association and on the Board of Directors of American Youth Hostels.

Doris L. Berryman, Ph.D., is Professor, Department of Recreation, Leisure, Physical Education and Sport in the School of Education, Health, Nursing, and Arts Professions at New York University. She has and continues to conduct, reearch in behavioral assessment, appraisal and evaluation instruments, activity analysis, and prescriptive programming. She has served on the Board of Trustees of the National Recreation and Park Association.

Joan H. Kindy, Ed.D, is Professor Emerita, Department of Counselor Education of the School of Education, Health, Nursing, and Arts Professions at New York University. She served as the Associate Dean for Personnel of the School for five years.

Claudette B. Lefebvre, Ph.D., is Professor and Chair of the Department of Recreation, Leisure, Physical Education and Sport at New York University. She has served as a recreation leader, therapeutic recreation specialist, and department head in a diversity of hospital and institutional settings and as the executive director of residential camps for disabled children and adults.

Marie B. Ray is Director of Girls' Camp, Camp Akiba, Reeders, Pennsylvania; and she has served as the Associate Director of Camp Sun Mountain, Shawnee-on-Delaware, Pennsylvania. In both positions, Ms. Ray has recruited, selected, supervised, and managed camp personnel over a period of 23 years.

Willoughby Anne Walshe, M.S. She is currently managing her own business firm. She has held the position of assistant manager of a large law firm where she obtained first-hand knowledge and experience in complying with occupational safety and health regulations.

Contents

Difficult? Suggested Guidelines for Motivating Employees;
Summary.

Two-Way Streets; Communication; Authority; Responsibility;
Delegation; Techniques of Delegation; Staff Meetings;
Summary.

Normal Stress and Distress; Sources of Stress; Individual
Reactions to Stress; Work-Related Stress and Burn-Out; Stress
Management; Summary.

Time Management; Time Wasters; Procrastination; Open-Door
Policy; Uninvited Visitors; Lack of Planning and Indecision;
Memoitis and Computeritis; Wasting Subordinates' Time;
Integrating Personal Life Goals with Work Goals; More Time
Management Techniques: In Brief; Summary.

Causes of Accidents; Unsafe Conditions; Unsafe Acts;
Principles of Accident Prevention; Occupational Safety and
Health Act; Posting Notices; Recording; Reporting and
Violations; Summary.

Definition of Evaluation; Importance of Evaluation;
Development of an Evaluation Program; Implementing the
Program; Methods of Evaluating Performance; Personnel
Ratings; Willingness to Assume Responsibility; Assessing
Employee Potential; Participative Performance-Oriented
Evaluation; Work Planning and Progress Reviews; Annual
Performance-Review Form and Interview; The Appraisal
Interview; Summary.

Foreword

While there is a growing amount of discretionary time, there are some trends which do not bode well for the non-profit recreation and leisure service agency or association:

- More women are entering the labor force and have less time for voluntary activities.
- Paid employees are increasingly unionizing and demanding salaries comparable to those of public agencies.
- The Internal Revenue Service is increasingly pressuring agencies to leave off advocacy and social action lest they lose their tax exempt status. Thus, the tendency for people to form voluntary groups to do something about problems which have "ever pricked the conscience of righteous people" becomes blunted. These groups have traditionally been "institutions in embryo."
- Welfare programs, such as S.S.I., Aid to Families with Dependent Children, Medicaid, Food Stamps, and eventually a guaranteed annual income, are removing poverty and economic need as forces which cause people to seek services of agencies.
- A declining birth rate is reducing the number of children to be served by agencies. It also reduces the number of children in the family, so there are more resources for the family to provide for its own recreation and leisure pursuits.
- Mass media is competing for the time and attention of people in their leisure. (Try to get people out for a program when the Super Bowl is being played.)

Such trends as these make it ever more urgent that both volunteers and professional staff experience satisfaction and growth from their agency involvement. Whether they get such rewards depends, all out of proportion, on the leadership, management, and supervision they receive. Today there is much study and experiment designed to reduce the "management of men and women" to a science. We are also being pressured to become more accountable, i.e., to be able to prove that we have accomplished what we claim. Both these trends are healthy if not pressed too far.

Increasingly, our private and voluntary agencies are going to be required to have: 1) goals that are of sufficient appeal and urgency to attract people to give of their time and resource to pursue them; 2) goals sufficiently specific and clear that they can be understood and general enough that they can be encompassing; 3) programs to implement these goals which have enough imagination to make them attractive; 4) personnel trained and competent in the skill of effective participation; 5) supervision to keep personnel on track in operating the program and also to make the involvement a growth experience; and 6) a built-in method of evaluation which makes it possible for the total agency to give accountability to its supporters and those it serves.

Dr. Grossman is to be commended for the production of this text to assist in the accomplishment of these goals.

Dan W. Dodson, Ph.D.
Professor Emeritus
New York University

Introduction

Approaches to Managing for Success

Recreation and leisure services are provided through organizations, and managers exist for the explicit purpose of managing these organizations for success. The questions are: what is an organization? and how do managers make these organizations successful?

"An organization is a group of people whose activities are consciously coordinated toward a common objective or objectives."[1] Consequently, the primary function of managers is to manage people so that the objective(s) of the recreation and leisure service organization are achieved. Managers must be able to translate the idea of the organization, i.e., its purpose for existence, into action and to get the work done effectively through other people. Such is success; and there is no simple recipe for achieving it. But we do have the best thinking of theorists and practitioners and the results of management research to guide us. This information is presented in the pursuit of success in the area of personnel management.

This book is concerned with *people* who work in recreation and leisure service organizations. It is directed primarily to the managers of these organizations, whether they be at the top level, e.g., executive or associate directors, superintendents; middle level, e.g., program directors or department heads; and first-line supervisors, e.g., supervisors of programs for youth, teens, aging, or the disabled. It is written also for students in recreation, parks, and leisure studies curricula—the managers of tomorrow.

Management is considered a *process* because the task of reaching the objective(s) of the organization is not a one-time act but a series of ongoing activities. Most of the literature refers to the following functions of management which comprise the management process: planning, organizing, staffing, coordinating, controlling, leading, motivating, communicating, evaluating, and decision making. As a large percentage of the manager's time and effort is directed to managing personnel, the majority of these functions are presented here from that perspective. It is recognized that management functions extend beyond the area of personnel management; however, the discussion of these from the larger perspective is beyond the scope of this book.

Managers, from supervisors of youth programs to superintendents of large departments of parks and recreation, are often envied by people who have never held management positions. The envy stems from the perquisites that accompany the positions. But many managers will indicate that there is another side to the coin: the problems and difficulties. And managerial success depends on how effectively managers reduce their number and handle them when they arise. The basic premise of this book is to provide today's and tomorrow's managers with information on sound personnel management concepts, principles, and techniques to achieve those ends.

In the revised edition of this book, the material is divided into four parts, each of which has a major thrust. Part I, (Chapters 1, 2, and 3) covers making and implementing policies. Chapters 1 and 2 focus on the executive's role in policy-making and developing and implementing personnel policies as the foundation of personnel management. A new Chapter 3, "Guidelines for Managing AIDS in the Workplace," has been added to assist the manager in handling one of the most challenging health, social, economic, and personal phenomena of the decade. Part II (Chapters 4 and 5) is devoted to organizations and individuals at work. It covers the functions of planning and organizing, including approaches to job design and work redesign. Part III (Chapters 6–13) presents concepts, methods, and techniques for managing professional personnel. Three new chapters are included in this part: developing and implementing motivation strategies, managing work-related stress, and managing time. The remaining chapters address the areas of recruitment and selection; training and development; communication, authority, and responsibility as aspects of delegation; employee safety and evaluation. The fourth part (Chapter 14) covers special knowledge, procedures, and techniques related to the management of volunteer personnel, a vital human resource in recreation and leisure service organizations.

It is the author's hope that the revised edition of this book will enable students, practitioners, administrators, and educators to more thoroughly understand and apply the essential functions of personnel management from a humanistic perspective. It is also his hope that the implementation of the personnel practices presented will lead to more effective delivery of recreation and leisure services and will enhance the professionalization of the field.

REFERENCE

1. M.H. Mescon, M. Albert, F. Khedouri (1988). *Management* (3rd ed.). New York: Harper & Row, Publishers, p. 7.

PART ONE
Making and Implementing Policies

The purpose of this chapter is to help the manager answer:

- Who makes policies?
- Who adopts policies?
- Why are there policies, rules and procedures?
- Can the executive and staff make policies?
- Can policies be changed? How?
- Who is responsible for implementing policies?

Chapter 1

Policy-Making: The Executive's Role

Arnold H. Grossman

Executives in recreation and leisure service agencies have continually participated in policy-making; however, the executive's role in the process has been given neither the attention nor the recognition which it deserves. Traditionally, the governing board, i.e., board of directors, trustees, or commission, has made the policies and the executive has implemented them. It is this distinction which has been primarily used to differentiate the roles and function of the board from those of the executive. And, it is this distinction which has forced the executive to perform the policy-making role as a subversive activity.

Recreation and leisure service agencies have traditionally been a part of the social welfare structure in the United States. Historically, the philosophy and practices of social welfare have been to provide charitable services for people who cannot make out for themselves. It has been concerned with the professionalization of staffs of welfare institutions who could provide service to the immigrants and to the impoverished. "The welfare worker . . . was the surrogate of the power order as it sought to sandpaper the deviant to the dimensions of the dominant society."[1]

The Great Society, with its requirement of "maximum feasible participation of the poor," and the civil rights revolution changed the rules of the game, and business as usual could not continue in social agencies. No longer could human rights be denied or human personalities be traumatized because people lacked the power to make their interests felt in communal decision making.[2] Social agencies, of necessity, had to share power with the clientele. The provider of service had to share policy-making with the consumers of the services. It necessitated a restructuring of community relations, and called for providing services *with* people rather than *for* people. It demanded accountability!

The executive director is the agency's professional expert—its top manager. It is the executive who is on the job full time and who is accessible to clients. Clients present their interests and demands to the executive, and the executive must transmit these needs to the board or commission along with plans and recommendations for board action. The executive has the professional expertise, the necessary information, the agency as central concern, and is the one whom the constituency of the agency holds accountable.

The changing structure of society has caused the executive's role in policy-making to be recognized by the board, the clients and the executive, and has also secured its legitimation. Furthermore, it has required that the executive devote a larger percentage of time and energies to the policy-making role.

POLICIES FOR THE MAKING

A policy is a plan of action adopted by the board of directors or commission of an agency. Taking into consideration the short-range and long-range objectives of the agency, the board or commission has the legal obligation to determine the general principles and practices which are to guide the courses of action. Policies provide the structural framework of an agency. Generally, they are adopted after careful study or extensive experience to indicate the limiting boundaries for courses of action and to exclude those courses of action that are unacceptable. Policies are the agency's guideposts.

Not all of the agency's policies originate within the organization. Local, state and federal public regulations often dictate policies, especially if the agency is receiving funds from any of these sources. Two examples for illustrative purposes would be a non-discrimination policy, i.e., non-discrimination in terms of sex, age, race, religion, color, nationality in selection of personnel and clients; and a full accessibility policy, i.e., accessibility of handicapped persons to facilities, programs, and employment opportunities. Other funding sources, such as private foundations, often are among the principal policy makers for agencies today.[3]

There is often confusion between policy statements, procedures, and rules. As the executive director, staff members, and volunteers make operating decisions each day which actually reflect agency policy, procedures and rules are established to handle specific situations.

"A procedure describes what action is to be taken in a specific situation."[4] The establishment of procedures avoids repeating a trial-and-error process and alleviates the burden of repetitive decision-making. Established procedures provide the acceptable process in executing the agency's policies. They indicate the how, who, when, and where in everyday practice by enumerating a step-by-step sequence. A rule, on the other hand, "specifies exactly what is to be done in a specific, single situation. Rules differ from procedures in that they deal with specific and limited issues. Procedures cope with situations that involve a sequence of several related actions."[5]

Although legislators create public recreation and park commissions and departments, the board establishes the legal or corporate existence of voluntary non-profit recreation and leisure service organizations and formulates their general purpose or goals. Within this framework, policies are adopted regarding: financial procedures, including the provision and expenditure of funds; organizational structure, including positions and lines of authority; personnel practices and conditions of work, including the selection and evaluation of the executive; programming, including content, scope, quality, and procedures for evaluation; coordination and integration of the agency's work with other services in the community; and procedures for periodic evaluation of the agency's operations. Adopting policies in these areas, among others, is a continuing responsibility of the board. While policies may be based on logical thinking and intelligent decision-making when adopted, some policies become obsolete as time passes. Policies are not engraved in marble; consequently, they should be modified or retracted if they no longer serve to help the agency meet its purpose or goals.

BOARD AND THE EXECUTIVE: A SHARED POWER RELATIONSHIP

An individual or group "has power when it has the capacity to make its interests felt as an impact in communal decision-making processes."[6] Only when the board of directors as a group and the executive have a relationship in which they both have power can effective policies be formulated and adopted to meet the agency's objectives; in other words, the agency is doing that for which it exists. There are numerous factors which determine the viability of such a relationship. One manner in which these factors can be examined is by exploring the distinguishing characteristics of the board and of the executive and by discussing the implications of the incumbents in these positions.

The board or commission of a recreation and leisure service agency is its legal governing body. As a corporate body, it has the ultimate responsibility of the agency internally as well as to external authorities and groups, e.g., legal, regulatory, or a source of finances. The board is a continuous entity of the agency, even though its individual members usually function on a part-time basis and customarily have tenured terms. In addition, its members are typically lay people who represent the constituency or the community served by the agency and who have little, if any, expertise in the areas of recreation and leisure services. A final distinguishing characteristic is that the board takes group action, i.e., it acts as a single unit on the collective decision of its members.

The executive director is the full-time head of the agency, who was selected by the board and holds the position at the pleasure of the board. The executive is the professional expert of the agency with direct responsibility for its operation. He or she is identified with the agency and represents it to the community, to other organizations, and to the recreation and leisure service professions. The executive is an individual and exercises singular authority in carrying forward the work of the agency.

The shared power relationship between the executive and the board of directors exists when they can come together as peers in the policy-making process with neither in a compromising position. There are numerous blocks which may prevent this type of relationship from developing:

- There is role confusion between the executive and the board (or its members) with either or both attempting to execute the role functions which are rightfully the prerogative of the other.
- The executive is incompetent and cannot fulfill the obligations as the head of the agency.
- The members of the board or commission are weak, incompetent, uncommitted, or lack an understanding of the agency's objectives and progress.
- There is a philosophical or professional conflict between the board and the executive due to a lack of, or differences in, professional training, standards, and in ethics or age, race, sex, and social class.
- There is a communication gap between the executive and the board because the board members do not comprehend the agency's purpose or functions, its role in the community, or are inconsistent in their attendance at board meetings. On the other hand, the executive may lack skills in effective communication; conse-

quently, an accurate picture of the agency's status or problems is not presented to the board.

It should be pointed out that a shared power relationship between the executive and the board does not necessarily mean one in which there is only consensus and an absence of conflict. Conflict is one of the normal ways through which people interact with each other. In any communal decision-making process, differences will exist; consequently, there will be group-alignment on one side or another and conflict is bound to ensue. The problem lies in dealing with conflict in a creative manner so that it does not become stultifying and destructive. The task is to direct the conflict toward socially constructive ends—effective policies for the agency to grow and to achieve its objectives.

THE POLICY-MAKING PROCESS AND THE EXECUTIVE'S RESPONSIBILITIES

There are five major steps in the policy-making process:

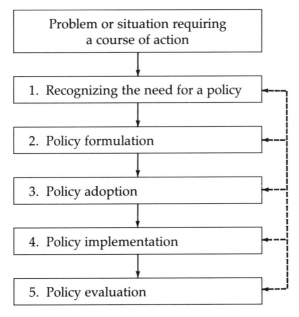

Policies are not made in a vacuum. They are made because a particular situation exists or a problem arises that demands a course of action. The problem or situation can arise in connection with the consumers of the services, the staff, the executive, the board members, or as a result of an external authority. The first step in the process is to *recognize there exists a need for a policy.* The executive has the responsibility of recognizing his or her needs for policy statements as well as those of the clients, the staff, and possibly with regard to external authorities. It is the executive who is on the job full time and is most likely to become aware of problems or situations which require a stated policy for effective decision-making. Meetings with clients, observations of programs and activities, and the making of daily decisions, as well as regularly scheduled staff meetings and supervisory conferences, provide the executive with a myriad of opportunities to recognize the lack of guideposts which result in ambiguous or inconsistent decisions. In many instances, the need for a policy is not recognized and continuing trial-and-error processes take place or a policy is implemented by day-to-day practice. In some instances, the policy is adopted after the fact as the agency has inadvertently committed itself to a course of action determined by the agency's executive or staff member(s).

The second step in the policy-making process is *policy formulation.* Once a need for a policy is recognized, planning and research must be undertaken to examine alternative courses of action. The projected effects of each course of action on the various parts of the agency, as well as the congruency of each with the agency's long-and-short-range objectives, must be determined. Planning and research may be the responsibility of the executive and the staff, a committee of the board, or a combination of the above with representatives from the agency's clients. The potential contribution of staff members, who are on the front lines, and of the clients to the process of policy formulation should not be underestimated. Outside experts or consultants may be contracted to work with the established commission or its committees for major projects. A written policy or policy statement is prepared for board approval based on the research findings. In practice, the majority of the policies presented to the board for consideration are drafted by the executive.

The third step in the policy-making process is *policy adoption.* This is the responsibility of the board or commission arising from its legal status as the governing entity of the agency. The board, however, is usually advised by the executive before it makes its decision. When a matter is taken to the board for a decision, the executive usually recommends a course of action; however, if the matter is presented by a committee, commission or consultant, the board usually asks the executive for advice. Through these processes the executive guides the thinking of the board in the area of policy adoption, but the final decision resides with the board.

The fourth step in the policy-making process is *policy implementation*. This is the responsibility of the executive and the staff. It involves developing procedures to implement the adopted policy. The executive's role as liaison between staff and the board assumes primary importance in this step of the process. The policy must not only be communicated to the staff, but each member of the staff must understand why the policy was adopted and its significance to the agency's operations and purposes. The executive's concept of management on the authoritative/participative scale as well as his or her relationship to the staff as an entity is crucial for effective implementation of policies. The executive is more likely to gain the staff's support of a policy if the decision-making processes regarding the development of procedures are shared with its members, rather than distributed as an authoritative order. Although others, such as staff members, board members and volunteers, may participate in the implementation process, the ultimate responsibility for policy implementation remains with the executive.

An underlying assumption is that the executive will be committed to all policies adopted by the board or commission, even if he or she happens not to agree with some of them. In the event that such a situation arises, the executive has the right and responsibility to inform the board of his or her thinking on the policy in a rational and logical manner. If the executive feels that the policy is in conflict with his or her professional or moral values, or that the policy is taking the agency on a course of action with which he or she does not wish to be associated, the executive can attempt to negotiate a compromise or submit a letter of resignation. If the policy can be lived with, the executive can request that the policy be adopted and implemented for a designated period of time, after which its effectiveness would be reviewed.

The fifth step in the policy-making process, and one that is often overlooked, is *policy evaluation*. This step, as the model indicates, provides feedback to the other four steps. In fact, it is more than a step; it is a continuous process. If the evaluation demonstrates that the established policy, as formulated, adopted and implemented provides a satisfactory course of action to the indicated problem or situation, then nothing but its continued implementation is necessary at the present time. This, however, does not mean that the policy should not be evaluated at a specified time in the future. If, on the other hand, the established policy is not providing a satisfactory course of action for the indicated problem or situation, then one has to investigate the previous steps in the process to determine where the fault lies. Is it in the method of implementation? Is it in the policy statement as adopted? Is it in the manner in which the policy was formulated? Was there a need for a policy to meet the problem or situation in the first place? Policy evaluation is the responsibility of the executive and the staff as part of the overall program evaluation process of the agency. Recommendations for modification, retraction, or further research of agency policies should be included in the executive's yearly report to the board unless more immediate action is called for during the year. Of course, policies relating only to the board as an entity must be evaluated by it under the leadership of the president or chairperson of the board, with an ensuing appropriate course of action.

SUMMARY

This chapter covered the executive's role in policy-making in the context of power. It has been assumed that effective policy-making in recreation and leisure service agencies requires that both the executive director and the board of directors (or commission members) must have the capacity to make their interests felt as an impact in the communal decision-making process. As the social engineer in the relationship between the staff and the board, the executive's role in recognizing the need for policies, policy formulation, adoption, implementation, and evaluation must be recognized and legitimatized. In this role, the executive must facilitate the making of effective policies so that the agency can achieve its stated purpose and objectives as well as maintain its accountability to clients. The executive must enable the board members to learn group skills for communal decision-making. They must learn skills of "caucus, confrontation, negotiation, arbitration, dialogue and compromise."[7] On the other hand, the board has the right to expect that the executive will accept full responsibility in the policy-making process and will utilize professional knowledge and skills in enabling the agency to establish and maintain the most effective policies and procedures to accomplish its stated mission.

NOTES AND REFERENCES

1. Dan W. Dodson, "Looking Ahead in Health and Welfare," (Center for Human Relations, New York University, 1962), p. 1
2. Ibid.
3. Winslow Carlton, "Agency Policy—Who Makes It—Who Controls It," **Twenty-Fifth Board Members' Institute.** (New York: Federation of Protestant Welfare Agencies, 1967), p. 2.

4. M.H. Mescon, M. Albert, F. Khedouri, **Management,** 3rd ed. (New York: Harper & Row, Publishers, 1988), p. 302.
5. Ibid, p. 303.
6. Dan W. Dodson, "Power as a Dimension of Education," **Power, Conflict and Community Organizations.** (New York: Council for American Unity, 1967), p. 7.
7. Dan W. Dodson, **New Challenges to Social Agency Leadership,** edited and compiled by Arnold H. Grossman. (South Plainfield, New Jersey: Groupwork Today, Inc., 1976), p. 71.

The purpose of this chapter is to help the manager answer:

- Why are personnel policies needed?
- Who develops personnel policies?
- When do personnel policies need to be developed?
- When do personnel policies need to be changed?
- What is the difference between personnel policies and procedures?
- What happens when established policies and procedures are not followed?

Chapter 2

Developing and Implementing Personnel Policies

Joan H. Kindy

Within each organization, there are goals and purposes to be accomplished. These purposes are carried out by people, without whom organizations would not exist. The life of an organization is not dependent upon specific individuals, but upon some persons performing certain tasks. People are psychosocial beings with psychosocial needs. An organization can ignore neither the tasks to be performed nor the needs of the persons performing them. Personnel policies define, in a formal manner, the expectations of the organization with regard to the roles various persons must assume in order for the organization to accomplish its goals and purposes.

This chapter is concerned with the development and implementation of personnel policies. The contextual framework lies within role theory which will be discussed first. Then, the questions of why personnel policies are needed, who develops them, and when they need to be developed and changed will be addressed. Finally, specific personnel policies and procedures will be suggested.

CONTEXTUAL FRAMEWORK FOR PERSONNEL POLICIES: ROLE THEORY

Roles are expectations and define the activity of individuals within organizations. Scholars from the disciplines of psychology, sociology, anthropology, and the applied fields of education and business have studied the concept of role and have developed various terms to connote the aspects of their specific theories. A comprehensive description and analysis of the work of these "role scholars" can be found in Lonsdale's chapter in **The Sixty-third Yearbook of the National Society for the Study of Education,** entitled "Maintaining the Organization in Dynamic Equilibrium."[1]

Regardless of the terms used to explain the theory, writers agree that organizations are hierarchical in nature, i.e., that there are superordinates and subordinates within the organization. They also agree that persons within the organization function within the parameters of role definitions and role perceptions. Furthermore, they agree that the performance of roles is dependent upon personality, e.g., needs. One of these needs is defined by Murray and Kluckhohn as the "need for roleship." They define this need as "the need to become and to remain an accepted and respected, differentiated and integrated, part of a congenial, functioning group, the collective purposes of which are congruent with the individual's ideals." They go on to say that "so long as the individual feels this way about the group he has joined, he will try to abide, as best he can, by its *schedule* of role functions."[2]

This schedule of role functions is sometimes communicated by means of an organizational chart, which depicts the line and staff authority of certain positions within the organization. Another means for communicating role expectations and activities is found in clearly articulated personnel policies and procedures, the essence of this chapter.

WHY ARE PERSONNEL POLICIES NEEDED?

Personnel policies and procedures are essential to the smooth functioning of an organization. The members of the organization function best when they can *know* the limits of their authority; when they can *know* the limits of the authority of their superordinates and subordinates; when they can *know* the principles and procedures for promotion, for increases in salary, for appealing decisions, for securing benefits and vacations, and the like. The word *know* is emphasized to stress that without written policies, the rights, responsibilities, and perquisites of an individual can only be inferred. The resulting lack of security leads to inefficiency, confusion, non-productive interpersonal relationships, absenteeism, and attrition.

WHO DEVELOPS PERSONNEL POLICIES?

Personnel policies and procedures are usually developed by the management of the organization, and are approved by the board of directors. The degree of consultation with non-management personnel in the development of these policies and procedures depends upon the nature of the organization, its philosophy of management, and the various ways in which non-management personnel are organized. That is, in an organization in which the professional employees are unionized, there is a different relationship between management and non-management than in a non-union organization.

The issue of non-management involvement in policy-making is a very sensitive one. One philosophy is stated in the following quotation:

> . . . one of the great resources available to an organization trying to improve its effectiveness is its own people. By encouraging people to become involved, concerned participants rather than making them feel powerless and manipulated by unseen and inscrutible forces, the organization can draw ever-increasing strength, vitality, and creativity from its people.[3]

As the old saying goes, however, a camel is a horse put together by a committee. It is the responsibility of the organization's executive director, who is responsible to the board, to assume the responsibility and accountability for personnel policies which are consistent with the ideals of the organization and with its financial limitations. Thus, for the manager, it becomes a matter of a delicate balance between, on the one hand, exercising the necessary authority and assuming the responsibility for policy development and, on the other, involving the professionals and volunteers within the organization to such a degree that they feel important to the organization.

WHEN ARE PERSONNEL POLICIES DEVELOPED AND CHANGED?

Personnel policies and procedures are usually developed when organizational and individual needs demand. The absence of a policy and the resulting confusion produce a lack of equilibrium within the organization. People spend more time discussing, for example, "I wonder why I did not get promoted," than in performing those tasks necessary for the functioning of the organization. Other times, policies are developed from practices which have "history" within the organization. As Simon points out,

> . . . there are to be found in almost every organization a large number of "practices" which have not been established as orders or regulations, and which are not enforced by sanctions, but which are nevertheless observed in the organization by force of custom or for other reasons. Often the line between policy and practice is not sharp unless the organization follows the "practice" (or "policy") of putting all its policies in writing.[4]

Changes in policy often come about because of changes in practices or changes in the organization itself. For example, let us say that an organization has a policy that all salary increases are determined according to merit. Merit assumes that people perform differentially and that the performance of one person is better (or worse) than that of another. Within this organization, however, the practice has arisen whereby the differentiation is not recognized or measurable and all are rewarded according to a like formula. If this practice continues, the policy must be changed. Likewise, should the employees become unionized or should the organization not have any money for salary increases, the policy concerning merit salary increases would have to be changed.

When practices change but policy statements do not, the trust-gap between management and employees widens. The roles to be performed by these mistrusting employees are performed with less enthusiasm, less often, and less competently. The "need for roleship" is not satisfied within the individual; the organization suffers, and so do its clients.

Competent managers are alert to changes in practice which should result in policy changes. Policies do not always have to be changed; sometimes, procedures have to be clarified. Following through with the foregoing example of a merit salary increase policy, suppose that the practice has been that those employees who are judged to be of the lowest merit do not receive increases. In a certain year, however, due to increases in cost of living, it is determined that all employees will receive some increase, even those in the least meritorious group. There still exists a merit increase policy; the *procedure* has changed. Changes in procedure should be clarified in writing, just as should changes in policy.

PERSONNEL POLICIES AND PROCEDURES

The purpose of this section is to suggest policy statements and some possible procedures in essential personnel areas. Some policies are applicable only to professional employees; others are applicable also to volunteers. The following policy statements concern:

- Recruitment and appointment;
- Responsibilities and expectations;
- Reward system;
- Fringe benefits;
- Termination;
- Grievance.

Recruitment and Appointment: Recruitment policy is most often visible in advertisements which say, "The Boy Scouts of America is an equal opportunity, affirmative action employer. B.S.A. has a long history of guarding against job discrimination in any form and it continues to encourage the appointment of women and members of minority groups to its staff. At present, there is in effect an affirmative action plan to assure full implementation of this policy."

The reader is directed to federal literature on Executive Order 11246, which mandates nondiscrimination and affirmative action in public and non-public institutions which receive federal monies over a specified amount.* However, the basic philosophy of most leisure and social service organizations reflects the principles of affirmative action and equal access to employment for all, regardless of sources of funding.

Procedures in recruitment involve the following:

a. Development of a specific position description, which includes qualifications for the position, application procedures, and deadline date;

b. Dissemination of the position description to the many agencies, institutions of higher education, and individuals who could be expected to inform qualified persons of the opening;

c. Advertisement in professional journals and newspapers;

d. Acknowledgment of applications, follow-up of references/ recommendations;

e. Selection interview;

f. Action by a selection committee and/or the supervisor of the position and agency director.

Appointment policy would most likely include a statement such as: "Appointment is based on consideration of educational qualifications and demonstrated achievement in the field of _____ in relation to the goals of the _____ agency and the position to be filled. In making recommendations for appointment to the board or commission, the executive takes into account the judgments of professional peers." Inherent in this policy are certain procedures, which include assessment of an individual's educational background and past achievements, recommendations to the executive by a selection committee, and the executive's recommendation to the board. Whether or not the applicant is interviewed at each level depends upon the

---

*For a further discussion of nondiscrimination and affirmative action, see Chapter 6.

complexity and size of the agency and upon the level of responsibility and accountability of the position.

Appointment is a two-way street. The person is selected by the agency, and the agency is selected by the person. Thus, commitments are made by both parties, each to the other. The formalization of these commitments sometimes takes the form of a contract or a letter of agreement, signed by both parties. The board or commission usually delegates the authority to the executive to sign the contract or agreement letter for the agency, except in the case of the executive, whose contract or agreement letter is signed by the board's chairperson or president.

The use of a written contract or letter of agreement is recommended so that the obligations of the employer-employee relationship are explicitly stated. The contract or letter agreement should be developed in consultation with the agency's legal counsel. In most recreation and leisure service agencies, the terms of contract for full-time employees are oral and written. The written parts may be found in correspondence, (see Figure 3.1 for a sample letter of appointment), personnel policies, position descriptions or collective bargaining agreements. A written agreement signed by both parties is more often used with part-time or seasonal employees. (See Figures 2.2 and 2.3.)

Responsibilities and Expectations: The basic policy statement of responsibilities and expectations is found in the position description. All professionals and volunteers should have position descriptions and should have access to the descriptions of positions other than their own. The description is a specific statement of duties and responsibilities and to whom the incumbent reports. It defines the organizational roles which the incumbent is to assume and provides the basis for evaluation.* (Two examples of position descriptions are found in Figures 2.4 and 2.5.)

Policies concerning responsibilities and expectations common to specific groups of employees or volunteers are found in the personnel policies handbook and relate to such matters as the "duty period," ethical practices, and evaluation.

With regard to the "duty period," policy statements might read as follows:

- "Members of the professional staff are expected to be engaged in activities directly related to their position descriptions on all work

---

*For further discussion of position descriptions, see Chapter 6.

SAMPLE LETTER OF APPOINTMENT

Mr. John Doe
Box 100
Hometown, New Year 12345

Dear Mr. Doe:

I am pleased to advise you of your appointment as Director of the Teen Division of the (agency). The conditions of employment, which were discussed with you, are now confirmed as follows:

1. You will assume your position as a member of the staff on (date).
2. Your salary, beginning (date), will be at the rate of $_____ per year, payable every two weeks by check. Your salary will remain at this level on the personnel scale through (date).
3. Your employment will be continuous throughout the year.
4. You will work 35 hours per week, Monday through Friday, as scheduled by the (agency).
5. Sixty days after commencing employment you will be eligible to be included in the Group Health Insurance Plan of the (agency). A booklet describing this Plan will be made available to you.
6. The (agency) participates in the ABC Pension Trust Fund. When eligible for participation in this Fund, you will be given the opportunity to participate under the same conditions as other staff people.
7. You will be allowed a two-week vacation, with pay, each year for the first three years of your employment.
8. You will be expected to take part in regularly scheduled staff meetings, in-service training programs and any other programs deemed advisable by the (agency) for your professional growth.
9. You will appear, as scheduled, at the DEF Institute for a physical examination. It is understood that your health condition must be acceptable to us as a final requisite for employment with the (agency).
10. It is understood that you will not engage in outside employment while a member of the staff of the (agency).

On behalf of the staff of the (agency), I welcome you to our team. We look forward to a happy and rewarding association and one long in duration.

Very truly yours,

Andrew Klein
Executive Director

cc: Program Director
    Personnel Department
    Bookkeeper

Figure 2.1 Sample letter of appointment for full-time employee.

LETTER OF AGREEMENT

This is an agreement between _____

_____

(Social Security No. _____), who resides at

_____

_____

_____

(Zip Code) _____Telephone (_____)_____, herein called the
"Employee," and the Leisure Service Agency, 1100 Hooray Street, Fun-
town, New York 10000, herein called the "LSA."

This agreement is effective _____ and expires _____ .

Either party to this agreement may terminate it by notifying the other
party in writing of the intent to terminate on one month's notice.

The LSA agrees to pay the Employee on the following basis:

_____

_____

_____

The Employee agrees to execute the duties and responsibilities of (title
of position) as described in the (year) revision of the attached Position
Description with specific duties and responsibilities in the (program
area/department).

In addition, the Employee agrees to attend regularly scheduled staff
meetings of the (program/department/division), regularly scheduled
orientation and training sessions, regularly scheduled supervisory conferences and evaluation conferences, and comply with "Personnel Policies and Procedures of the LSA."

It is agreed that the Employee is eligible for all the benefits listed in
the "Personnel Policies and Procedures of the LSA" for part-time
employees.

It is agreed that under the terms of this employee agreement that LSA
will withhold City, State, and Federal taxes and will deduct and make
FICA payments.

I have read the above statement and accept the terms of this agreement.

_____   _____
(Employee's Signature)   (date)

For the LSA

_____   _____
(Supervisor/Director)   (date)

Distribution: Employee; Supervisor/Director, Personnel Office

---

Figure 2.2 Sample letter of agreement for part-time employees.

CAMP STAFF AGREEMENT

CAMP _____ and _____

The signing of this Agreement by the Camp Director and the above named Staff Member binds them to the following terms:

1. The Staff Member agrees to serve the Camp to the best of his/her ability in the capacity of _____

_____.

2. The dates of agreed employment are from _____ to _____.

3. The salary to be paid by the Camp to the Staff Member for the above period is _____.

IN ADDITION to the above salary, the Camp agrees to provide:

_____

_____

_____

4. The Staff Member agrees to abide by the Personnel Policies and Practices as attached, and to the following special conditions:

_____

_____

This agreement shall be deemed to have been executed in the State in which the Camp is located.

ACCEPTED according to the above Terms and Conditions
Signed: _____   Signed: _____
CAMP _____   STAFF MEMBER _____
By _____   Address _____
Address _____   _____
_____   Telephone _____
Date: _____   Date: _____

(Two copies are submitted; retain one copy and return the other.)

Figure 2.3 Suggested Camp Staff Agreement developed by the American Camping Association. (Reprinted with permission.)

ABC RECREATION AGENCY

POSITION DESCRIPTION

TITLE: Assistant Program Director
INCUMBENT: _____
REPORTS TO: Program Director
ASSOCIATION: New York City
BRANCH: Aloe Branch
DEPARTMENT: Program
DATE: _____

GENERAL FUNCTION

Under supervision of the Program Director, the Assistant Program Director administers policy and program for youth related to the Aloe Branch.

KNOW-HOW

The Assistant Program Director must have the planning, organizational and management ability to implement those programs for youth which are vital to the community interest and consistent with objectives and priorities of the Association, Aloe Board and its committees. The incumbent must have a thorough understanding and keen sensitivity of people; educational training and/or experience necessary for effective development and implementation of quality programs for youth and families; be able to relate effectively with a heterogeneous community and staff; recruit, train, and supervise volunteer leaders and employees; and manage facilities and equipment designated for these functions and use by youth constituents. The incumbent should be able to clearly communicate the goals and needs of the program to community and organization to qualitatively affect end results.

PRINCIPLE ACTIVITIES

1. *Guides* the appropriate volunteer committee and councils in development of program priorities and policies.
2. *Plans and organizes* with appropriate co-workers youth programs which meet specific community needs.

3. *Recruits and trains* employees and volunteer leaders to carry out program segments.
4. *Supervises and leads* program activities.
5. *Prepares and administers* budgets, reports, payroll, requisitions, membership and participation records, work orders, and correspondence necessary to operation of a youth program.
6. *Evaluates* program and leadership effectiveness.
7. *Promotes membership, activity, and camp enrollments.*
8. *Establishes* facilitating relationships with other community youth workers and youth serving organizations.
9. *Shares* as a member of the Aloe Program staff team in Branch and Association activities, training and projects.
10. *Leads* task groups, general capital and special fund raising efforts.

EFFECT ON END RESULTS:

Effectiveness of the incumbent's fulfillment of this position will be measured against these objectives:

1. There is a well-balanced program of high quality for boys and girls, ages 3 through 17, reflecting community need and ABC priorities and objectives.
2. There is effective collaboration between youth and physical education staffs, Chalset Committee recreation workers, and other Aloe co-workers.
4. Day camps are well enrolled and resident camps strongly supported.
5. Improved and new program models are developed to meet expanding and changing constituent needs.
6. There is a regular flow of accurate information reflecting membership needs and trends and program effectiveness.
7. Youth workers and office staffs (employees and volunteers) are informed about programs and helpfully advise constituents.
8. Program and facilities are responsibly administered and fiscal management maintains budgeted income-expense ratios.
9. Youth activities of the Branch are regularly featured in community public media.
10. There is involved an active group of volunteers related to the youth program.

Figure 2.4 Sample position description for a full-time staff person.

XYZ RECREATION DEPARTMENT
POSITION DESCRIPTION

RECREATION SUPERVISOR

GENERAL STATEMENT OF DUTIES:

Under general supervision of the Director, is responsible for the organization and administration of specified recreation services; does related work as required.

DISTINGUISHING FEATURES OF THE POSITION

The assignment of Recreation Supervisor is a third line position in the Recreation Department. The position involves responsibility for planning, organizing, and supervising major segments of the community recreation program. There is a general responsibility for planning, promoting and publicizing assigned programs in close cooperation with the Director of Recreation. Supervision, either direct or general, is exercised over subordinate level employees.

EXAMPLES OF WORK: (illustrative only)

1. Assists, consults, advises, and gives appropriate direction in planning for activities as assigned.
2. Plans, organizes, and promotes special activities or events.
3. May be called upon to give instruction in one or more specialized fields of activity.
4. Develops detailed schedules for leagues and tournaments.
5. Meets with volunteer organizations interested in recreation projects and plans with volunteers.
6. Assists with the control and assignment of supplies and equipment necessary for the conduct of the program.
7. Assists leaders with development of program content and leadership techniques necessary for the successful operation of the program.
8. Assumes a leadership role in various activities when necessary.
9. Supervises the maintenance of facilities and the construction and repair of program equipment.
10. Prepares publicity and news releases for an assigned portion of the recreation program.

11. Supervises and evaluates all subordinate staff personnel in his assigned area of responsibility.
12. Maintains records and makes reports.
13. Attends staff meetings and makes recommendations for improvements and modifications of program.

REQUIRED KNOWLEDGE, SKILLS, AND ABILITIES

A knowledge of recreation administration theory and procedures, and supervisory skills; some knowledge of public administration; ability to promote, plan and organize recreation activities, and to work with groups of people of all ages, ability to speak before a group; and ability to write clearly and concisely.

COMPENSATION

The Recreation Supervisor is a professional member of the XYZ Recreation Department. The position is based upon a twelve-month assignment including one month's vacation, with a salary range from $ _____ to $ _____ .

The one-month of leave time is to be arrived at with the approval of the Director of Recreation.

The Recreation Supervisor will be a member of the XYZ Recreation Department's Retirement Plan and will derive full benefits offered by the department to its professional staff.

ASSIGNMENT SCHEDULE

Generally speaking, the Recreation Supervisor's work schedule will include a five-day week with assignments for weekdays and evenings, although these hours depend upon the time of year and the programs in progress. Programs are conducted as a rule during school vacation periods but generally not on legal holidays.

ACCEPTABLE TRAINING AND EXPERIENCE

Graduation from an accredited college or university with a Master's Degree in Recreation or Leisure Studies.

Figure 2.5 Sample position description for a full-time staff person.
(Additional samples of position descriptions for staff members can be found in Chapter 6. Position descriptions for volunteers are located in Chapter 14.)

days, with the exception of official agency holidays and earned vacation days."

- "Members of the volunteer staff are expected to perform agreed upon responsibilities during those days and hours to which the volunteer has committed him/herself to the agency."

Note that the preceding policy statements do not include specific hours, such as from 9 a.m. to 5 p.m., during which times offices are usually open. Such a statement would appear in a section on procedures, if it is appropriate to the particular agency.

Procedures would include the details concerning holidays and vacations. For example:

- The agency recognizes legal holidays of the United States of America and of the State of New York, i.e., New Year's Day, Martin Luther King, Jr.'s Birthday, Lincoln's Birthday, Washington's Birthday, Memorial Day, Independence Day, Labor Day, Columbus Day, Election Day, Veterans Day, Thanksgiving Day, and Christmas Day.
- A specific holiday schedule is distributed to all staff by the executive at the beginning of every calendar year.
- In addition to official holidays, professional staff members are paid for vacation of no more than 20 work days per annum. Professional staff should arrange with their supervisors for the taking of vacation. When the desired period for vacation is for five days or more at one time, the request must be made at least one month in advance.

The supervisor takes into account the needs of the agency when approving the vacation schedule for an individual. When two staff members are seeking vacation for the same period, seniority will be considered in granting the vacation request, if agency needs make it inadvisable for both to be away simultaneously.

All vacation authorizations are subject to the approval of the executive, and vacation time may not be carried over from one calendar year to the next.

Procedural statements regarding illness and emergency should also be developed. Such statements would be as follows:

- Should a staff member, professional, or volunteer, not be able to carry out his/her responsibilities due to illness or other personal emergency, the supervisor should be notified by telephone. Written notification should also be given to the supervisor.
- Refer to the section on fringe benefits for a statement of the agency's policy concerning illness and personal leave.

A policy regarding the ethical principles to which the agency ascribes is another important aspect of policies concerning responsibilities and expectations. Most professional organizations have published statements of ethical principles, and a reference to such a statement or statements would be sufficient for purposes of the agency's personnel policies handbook. An example of such a policy follows:

"The Senior Citizens of Port Washington adheres to the Revised Ethical Standards of the American Psychological Association[5] and expects its professional and volunteer staffs to follow those principles in the performance of their responsibilities."

Subsequent procedural statements would include methods for knowing the standards and for reporting and documenting violations:

- All staff are expected to know the content of the "Revised Ethical Standards for Psychologists," reprinted by permission of the American Psychological Association in the Appendix of this handbook. The title "psychologist," as used in the Standards, should be interpreted as applying to staff members of this agency.
- When a staff member has knowledge of a violation of any ethical standard on the part of another staff member, it is incumbent on that person to inform the executive of the alleged violation. The executive will expect written documentation of the alleged violation, either prior to or subsequent to a conference with the staff member alleging the violation.
- An extension of Principle 1, "Responsibility," for the staff of the Senior Citizens of Port Washington makes it essential that staff members accept no personal or monetary gifts from clients.

Evaluation of performance is also a policy matter and is one of the most important of personnel policies. Evaluation leads to rewards in the forms of salary increments and promotion, as well as to termination. It provides guidance for growth and development of the staff member as an individual and as a group member. It provides data to the administration and the Board for assessment of the health of the organization. Staff members need to know what is being evaluated, by whom, how often, and the results of the evaluation.

A policy statement for an organization which has a merit increase system for professional staff would read as follows:

"In order to encourage consistently the highest levels of professional performance, annual increments for professional staff are based upon criteria of merit. Judgments of merit each year are based upon an annual self-report and an annual supervisor's report and become part of the individual's permanent record. These records are also used for such purposes as career counseling and professional advancement."

A similar policy statement should be developed for volunteer staffs, since evaluation of performance is also important for them. However, the result of a highly positive evaluation is not a salary increase; it may be promotion, or it may be a certificate of meritorious service.

Procedures for implementing such a policy would include the development of an evaluation instrument, specific to the individual's role in the organization, which the individual and the supervisor use to evaluate the year's performance of responsibilities. A statement of procedures would include the dates for submission of the evaluation to the agency director. Depending on the size and administrative philosophy of the agency, the supervisor may consult with the individual about his/her self evaluation before writing his/her supervisor's evaluation, or they may be sent independently to the director. It is essential that the individual receive feedback and respond to the feedback soon after the evaluation process. Obviously, evaluation is the basis for the reward system.

Reward System: Rewards, whether intrinsic or extrinsic, are essential to the maintenance of the organization. People need to feel that their efforts are appreciated, or they will seek appreciation elsewhere. Intrinsic rewards are personal satisfactions felt by an individual who says to him/herself, "I know I am doing a good job." The intrinsic reward is feeling good about oneself. Extrinsic rewards, on the other hand, are tangible, provided by the agency.

For the professional staff member, salary increases and promotional opportunities are the most tangible rewards for meritorious service. Policies should state clearly the bases for such rewards.

A policy statement regarding salary determination would read as follows:

"The specific salary of a professional staff member for a given calendar year is determined by the executive, subject to the approval of the board of directors, on the basis of the indicated merit of the individual."

Obviously, the implementation of such a policy refers to the evaluation policy and procedures. Procedures for salary determination would also include statements concerning the roles of the supervisor, executive and board in the implementation of the policy.

Promotion depends upon the organization of the agency and the particular roles needed to carry out its purposes. Of course, it is necessary to avoid the "Peter Principle"; that is, promoting employees until they reach a "level of incompetence." For example, a person who is an excellent group leader may not be an excellent supervisor.[6]

Promotion may depend upon the number of openings available in a given year, merit of the individual, projected success in the new position, or possible expansion of programs. The policy should include a statement of basic criteria for promotion to each position.

Where promotion is not available, either for professionals or volunteers, the rewards for meritorious service could include payment for attendance at conferences, special recognition at annual dinners, or newspaper recognition.

The latter are especially applicable to volunteers, since salary is not at issue; however, promotion to supervisory positions applies to volunteers as well as professionals.

Fringe Benefits: It is essential that a fringe benefits program be established for all agency personnel. Fringe benefits typically include group health insurance, group life insurance, disability insurance, retirement programs, contributions to Social Security, leaves of absence for various reasons, vacations, and holidays. They may also include tuition assistance for advanced education.

Of the benefits mentioned, leaves of absence need clarification. The basic types are for illness, personal emergency, and jury duty. They may also include leaves for purposes of educational advancement.

In agencies where persons are performing strenuous work or are in constant close contact with others, annual health examinations should be required and should be a part of the fringe benefits package. Fringe benefits for volunteers could be a way in which recognition for meritorious service can be given.

A policy statement could be as follows:

"In order to enhance the performance of staff members toward the achievement of the goals of the Community Recreation Association, the agency provides certain fringe benefits designed to assure their security and professional development."

The policy should be followed by a statement of criteria for specific fringe benefits, the amount of support provided by the agency, the amount of contribution expected by the staff member, and procedures for securing such benefits.

For example, most agencies have affiliations with group health and hospital insurance and require the staff member to share a small part of the cost for such participation. The explanatory statement in the policies and procedures handbook might read as follows:

• The Community Recreation Association has a contract with Blue Cross/Blue Shield of the State of New York, which provides partial reimbursement for physician and hospital expenses. A schedule of reimbursements is available from the executive and is issued to each new staff member at the time of appointment. Enrollment, while voluntary, usually begins on the first day of affiliation with the Association and terminates 30 days after the staff member leaves the Association. Cost to the staff member depends upon annual salary, the schedule of costs being available in the office of the executive. Payroll deductions are made monthly for participants. The executive assists the staff member in securing benefits when needed.

Termination: As was stated previously, a person chooses to accept a position in an organization, and the organization chooses that person to perform certain tasks necessary to its functioning. Termination, like appointment, is a two-way street: the person may choose to leave the agency—or, the agency may decide that the person must leave. Whichever the case, policies and procedures must be established.

When an individual is considering terminating his/her affiliation with the organization, he/she should be able to turn to a policy such as:

"All personnel are expected to give due notice, in writing, of intention to leave The Crestwood Recreation Association, whether by resignation or retirement. Due notice is construed as not less than four months for supervisory personnel and three months for all other personnel."

Procedures would include an indication of the persons to whom written notice should be sent and statements regarding turning over such things as records, reports, and equipment.

For example, notice should be given in writing to the executive, with a copy to the supervisor, indicating intended date of severance and reasons therefor.

Likewise, a policy concerning termination of affiliation by the organization is necessary and is, indeed, one of the most sensitive of personnel policies. The policy might read as follows:

"Termination of staff members is based upon consideration of quality of performance in relation to the achievement of the goals of The Crestwood Recreation Association. The judgments of peers and supervisors are taken into account by the executive when recommending terminations to the board."

Procedures must be especially clear with regard to termination by the organization. In terms of the suggested policy statement, procedures would state how quality of performance is considered, the roles of peers and supervisors, when notice is given, how notice is given, and severance pay, if any. It is essential, with regard to an individual's constitutional right to due process, that procedures include a written statement to the person being terminated concerning the specific reasons for the termination.

Grievance: One aspect of due process is the right of the individual to appeal a decision made about him/her with which he/she disagrees. This aspect is usually covered by a policy on grievance and provides detailed procedures of implementation. It should be the intent of the policy and procedures to resolve differences at the lowest level of professional relationship and as informally as possible. A sample of a grievance policy and procedures has been suggested by Grossman:[7]

The policy of the North Shore Youth Agency is to assure all employees fair and equitable treatment. Dissatisfactions and complaints should be voiced when they occur. When desired changes cannot be or are not made informally, a formal grievance procedure is available.

Step 1. If an employee feels unjustly or unfairly treated or disciplined, the employee must first take up the complaint with the immediate supervisor. The supervisor must reply to the employee's complaint within five (5) days.

Step 2. If no mutually satisfactory settlement of the complaint results from Step 1, a meeting of the department head, supervisor, and aggrieved employee shall take place no later than three (3) working days following the referral of the complaint to Step 2. The department head must reply to the employee's complaint within five (5) working days.

Step 3. If the grievance has not been satisfactorily resolved at Step 2, the aggrieved employee and a representative, if desired, will be granted the opportunity to meet with the appropriate administrative official and the director of employee relations or designees. In grievances involving questions relating to allegations of discrimination because of sex, sexual orientation, age, disability, creed, race, or national origin, the manager of affirmative action will participate in a fact-finding and advisory capacity with the director of employee relations or a designee. This meeting should take place no later than five (5) working days following the referral of the grievance to Step 3. The director of employee relations will reply to the employee's grievance within five (5) working days.

Step 4. Should the grievance fail to be resolved at Step 3, the employee may request its referral to the executive of the North Shore Youth Agency for review and final disposition.

It is important for supervisors to know how to deal with complaints and grievances non-emotionally and fairly. An excellent discussion of these important skills appears in the International City Management Association's Bulletin 10, in an article entitled "Employee Complaints and Grievances."[8]

SUMMARY

This chapter covered personnel policy development and policy implementation in the context of role theory. It assumed that the individual helps the organization attain its purposes and that the organization assists the individual in meeting his/her psychosocial needs.

Policies and procedures, however, are not sufficient unto themselves. There must exist an attitude of flexibility within the organization, both for exceptions to policy when circumstances so warrant and change in policy when the exceptions become the rule. A competent management can anticipate such circumstances.

A competent management also provides counseling for staff members when individual and organizational needs arise. Counseling, in this context, may be defined as assistance in decision making, problem solving, and conflict resolution. Since personnel policies involve such matters as survival (salary), fulfillment of achievement needs (promotion), the need for roleship (the appropriate position within the organization), and human dignity (opportunity for grievance), the individual's needs and perceptions are sometimes in conflict with those of the organization. Counseling can help to maintain healthier individuals and, therefore, healthier organizations.

NOTES AND REFERENCES

1. Richard C. Lonsdale, "Maintaining Dynamic Equilibrium," in **Behavioral Science and Educational Administration: The Sixtythird Yearbook of the National Society for the Study of Education,** Part II, chapter VII, edited by Daniel E. Griffiths. (Chicago, Illinois: The National Society for the Study of Education, 1964.)
2. Henry A. Murray and Clyde Kluckhohn, "Outline of a Conception of Personality," in **Personality in Nature, Society, and Culture,** (2nd ed.), chapter 1, p. 19. Edited by Clyde Kluckhohn and Henry A. Murray, with the collaboration of David M. Schneider. (New York: Alfred A. Knopf, 1953.)
3. Robert G. Owens and Carl R. Steinhoff, **Administering Change in Schools.** (Englewood Cliffs, New Jersey: Prentice Hall, Inc., 1976), p. 103.
4. Herbert A. Simon, **Administrative Behavior.** (2nd ed.). (New York: The Free Press, 1957, p. 59.)
5. American Psychological Association, Revised Ethical Standards of Psychologists, in APA **Monitor,** March 1977, pp. 22 and 23.
6. For discussion of the "Peter Principle," see Dr. Laurence J. Peter

and Raymon Hull, **The Peter Principle.** (New York: William Morrow and Co., Inc., 1969.)

7. Arnold H. Grossman, "Sample Policy Statement for Grievance Procedure," class material from course, "Supervision of Recreation
and Leisure Services," Department of Leisure Studies, New York
University.

8. International City Management Association, "Employee Com-
plaints and Grievances" (Bulletin 10), in **Effective Supervisory
Practices.** (Washington, D.C.: International City Management
Association, 1965), pp. 1–6.

The purpose of this chapter is to help the manager answer:

- Why is the workplace an important setting for AIDS education and training?

- What principles can I use as guidelines for managing HIV infection and AIDS in the workplace?

- What personnel policies should I be concerned with regarding HIV infection and AIDS?

- Why is there a need for HIV training and education programs in the workplace?

- What are the components of an HIV and AIDS education and training program for all employees?

- What are the additional components of an HIV and AIDS education and training program for employees who provide recreation and leisure services?

- What are the mandatory components of an HIV and AIDS education and training program for employees who work in health-care settings and may require unplanned exposure to blood, body fluids, or tissues?

- What equipment and supplies must I provide for workers in health-care settings to reduce the risk of infection with HIV and other blood-borne pathogens?

- What are effective approaches and strategies for HIV and AIDS education and training?

Chapter 3

Guidelines for Managing AIDS in the Workplace

Arnold H. Grossman

With no vaccine or cure in sight, AIDS will become more prevalent throughout the workplace, from the assembly line to the executive suite. Employers who face their discomfort about discussing sex and drugs and who plan a rational response to AIDS in advance, are likely to avoid the far more traumatic and embarrassing experience of trying to calm a work force stampeding for the exits in retreat from a real or imagined case of AIDS on the job.[1]

The World Health Organization (WHO) projects that 500,000 to 3 million new AIDS cases may occur from 1987–1991 among persons already infected by the Human Immunodeficiency Virus (HIV), and that a vaccine to protect against HIV and suitable for widespread use will probably not be available for five to ten years.[2] The Centers for Disease Control estimates that there are currently 1 million to 1.5 million infected people in the United States;[3] and the U.S. Public Health Service predicts that 450,000 cases will have been diagnosed by the end of 1993.[4] These figures suggest that nearly every manager will have to deal with someone in his or her organization who has AIDS, whether it is an employee or a client.

It is important to note that the figures cited above are estimates of those already infected with the HIV and, therefore, are based on the assumption that no new infections take place. In order to make this assumption a truism, education that changes attitudes and behavior is the only weapon of society. And the workplace is one of the most effective places in which this education can take place. This idea is reinforced by the U.S. Surgeon General, C. Everett Koop, who declared: "Worksites in particular can serve as effective settings in which to provide AIDS education. And the ideal time to educate your employees about AIDS is *before* your corporation has its first AIDS case."[5]

PRINCIPLES FOR THE WORKPLACE

The Citizens Commission on AIDS for New York City and Northern New Jersey has developed a statement which can assist managers in designing effective guidelines regarding AIDS in the workplace. Developed and disseminated in February 1988, "Responding to AIDS: Ten Principles for the Workplace" addresses rights, policies, laws and regulations, education, confidentiality, and infection control procedures.[6]

The "Ten Principles" and selected comments as developed by the Citizens Commission on AIDS are as follows:

1. **People with AIDS or HIV (Human Immunodeficiency Virus) infection are entitled to the same rights and opportunities as people with other serious or life-threatening illnesses.**

An employee who is diagnosed with a catastrophic illness faces potentially devastating consequences. While the threats of death or prolonged suffering are paramount, just as damaging are concerns about one's ability to *live* with the illness—to continue working, to receive health benefits, and to experience the emotional support and assistance of friends and colleagues. Employment is more than a means to earn a living; it defines an essential part of the lives of most people.

When the catastrophic illness is a stigmatized one—as cancer used to be and AIDS is today—the employee faces even greater obstacles. The stigma surrounding AIDS is inimical to the interests of the affected individuals, to employers, and society. There is no relevant difference between the way employers should treat employees with lung cancer or kidney disease and the way they should treat people with AIDS or HIV infection.

All employees with serious or life-threatening illness that do not endanger others in the workplace should, if they choose, continue to work to the fullest degree possible. . . . If it becomes necessary to modify their job assignments because of increasing disability, all reasonable efforts to make suitable accommodations should be undertaken. These accommodations might include more flexible hours, time off for medical appointments, reduction in workload, "telecommuting" (working at home using computer communication), or other adjustments that do not require a fundamental restructuring of the workplace or excessive costs. Because health care benefits are so closely tied to employment in our insurance system and because AIDS (like other catastrophic illnesses) is costly, employees with AIDS or HIV infections should receive promptly all health care and other benefits to which they are entitled. Employers and unions should support counseling and Employee Assistance Programs for employees with disabilities and should consider developing techniques of case management.

2. **Employment policies must, at a minimum, comply with federal, state, and local laws and regulations.**

The attitudes and actions that embody a policy of fair and equal treatment for people with AIDS or HIV infection, as expressed in Principle 1, are not only compassionate—they are required by law. New York and New Jersey, like most states, have statutes that prohibit discrimination in employment, both public and private, on the basis of a person's "disability." New York City also has such a law.[7]

Under this principle, workers may not lose their jobs, or be treated differently from fellow workers merely because they have AIDS, test positive for antibodies to HIV, or are thought to be at special risk for illness. They may be accorded different treatment, however, if they are unable adequately to perform the duties of the job or have an active, untreated contagious infection that presents a probable risk to other employees through workplace contact.

The federal government also forbids discrimination in employment on this basis, but its statute covers only the government itself and employers receiving federal money, such as hospitals and schools. The Supreme Court made clear in March 1987 that the federal statute, known as the Rehabilitation Act of 1973, includes contagious conditions as well as other kinds of "handicaps," paving the way for future interpretations explicitly concerning AIDS.

In addition, employers who discriminate may be liable under tort law for invasion of privacy, defamation, intentional infliction of emotional distress, or assault and battery (for forced testing).

3. **Employment policies should be based on the scientific and epidemiological evidence that people with AIDS or HIV infection do not pose a risk of transmission of the virus to coworkers through ordinary workplace contact.**

Because AIDS is a new infectious disease, it is natural that there should be concern about methods of transmission. Although much remains to be learned about AIDS, this aspect has been well studied.

In the Surgeon General's Report on Acquired Immune Deficiency Syndrome, Dr. C. Everett Koop declared:

> AIDS is an infectious disease. It is contagious, but it cannot be spread in the same manner as a common cold or measles or chicken pox. It is contagious in the same way that sexually transmitted diseases, such as syphilis and gonorrhea, are contagious. AIDS can also be spread through the sharing of intravenous drug needles and syringes used for injecting illicit drugs.
>
> AIDS is *not* spread by common everyday contact but by sexual contact. . . . Yet there is great misunderstanding resulting in unfounded fear that AIDS can be spread by casual, non-sexual contact. The first cases of AIDS were reported in this country in 1981. We would know now if AIDS were passed by casual, non-sexual contact.

4. **The highest levels of management and union leadership should unequivocally endorse nondiscriminatory employment policies and educational programs about AIDS.**

Because of the fear and stigma surrounding AIDS, it is imperative that those in positions of leadership—the CEO of the organization and the head of the union or other employee organization—respond to workers' needs and concerns. That level of response is critical because it establishes the seriousness with which the company and the union are addressing AIDS. It also makes it more likely that policies and programs will be implemented consistently.

5. **Employers and unions should communicate their support of these policies to workers in simple, clear, and unambiguous terms.**

Policies and programs developed at the highest levels must be communicated to all employees in language and formats that are meaningful and understandable. Different management and supervisory levels will require different educational efforts. For example, supervisors and managers need to be informed about their obligations and options when an employee becomes ill. They may need explanations and interpretations of company policies concerning medical benefits and so on. They need advice on dealing with fearful workers and crisis management.

All employees should be given full information about the company policy—whether it is a specific AIDS policy or a policy that applies to all catastrophic disease, including AIDS. There should be no room for doubt about the company's commitment to the health and welfare of its employees, and to the principle of nondiscrimination.

6. **Employers should provide employees with sensitive, accurate, and up-to-date education about risk reduction in their personal lives.**

Employers' concern with health promotion, and with reducing health care costs, has been manifest in recent years. Corporate wellness programs, including information and education about smoking, hypertension, exercise, nutrition, cancer, and other health concerns have become well established. AIDS is a new disease requiring special attention. Such education should be incorporated into existing health promotion programs, but it can also be provided on an ad hoc basis.

Most people learn about AIDS from the media—an important but often incomplete and confusing source. The workplace is well-suited for AIDS education; it offers the potential of more comprehensive, targeted, and ongoing education for groups and individuals. Most important, it offers the potential of interaction with knowledgeable health educators who can sort out myths and misinformation and reassure employees about groundless fears while providing them with responsible information to reduce their risk in their private lives.

7. Employers have a duty to protect the confidentiality of employee's medical information.

Information about an employee's medical history is confidential; it must not be shared with third parties, including coworkers, except where there is a justifiable need to know, and only with the employee's consent.

This general rule has special pertinence to AIDS because of the potentially dire consequences to the individual of a breach of confidentiality. Employees should have control over the personal information collected about them in the course of filing claims for medical benefits, applying for medical leave, or in the course of discussing their health status with supervisors.

There are well-established exceptions to the general rule that confidentiality must be maintained. These generally occur when an employee signs a consent form giving permission for an insurance company to investigate claims for reimbursement. Those who have access to this information as part of their jobs—as physicians or supervisors or claims clerks—have an obligation to prevent its further disclosure. Employers who fail to uphold this standard are potentially liable for claims of invasion of privacy, defamation, and intentional or negligent infliction of emotional distress.

Some employees may wish to disclose their condition voluntarily to their coworkers. This may open avenues of support and assistance. However, they should be under no obligation to do so.

8. To prevent work disruption and rejection by coworkers of an employee with AIDS and HIV infection, employers and unions

should undertake education for all employees before such an incident occurs and as needed thereafter.

The experiences, both positive and negative, of dealing with AIDS in the workplace so far have reinforced the concept that education for all employees before any case of AIDS occurs is the most prudent approach.

Education cannot always prevent work disruption, but it can alleviate and shorten the ill effects. The absence of education, on the other hand, is almost certain to create a more lasting and damaging impact.

9. Employers should not require HIV screening as part of general pre-employment or workplace physical examinations.

This principle concerns the use of antibody or other blood tests to determine whether a person has been infected with HIV. Because there is no evidence of risk of AIDS transmission through ordinary contact (Principle 3), knowledge of an employee's serostatus has no relation to workplace safety. For this reason the U.S. Public Health Service does not recommend routine workplace screening (see CDC Guidelines of November 1985).

In some states and cities, employers are prohibited by law from requiring HIV antibody tests for job applicants or employees. Even if an employer may legally test, if the results are used to make a decision concerning the employee's hiring or promotion, the employer may be liable for discrimination claims.

Testing to eliminate people with HIV infection to reduce future health benefits costs is also suspect. Statutes and regulations concerning protection of handicapped people also prohibit making employment decisions on this basis.

Another argument against routine workplace screening concerns the accuracy of the current tests and the high cost of identifying a few truly positive individuals.

10. In those special occupational settings where there may be a potential risk of exposure to HIV (for example, in health care, where workers may be exposed to blood or blood products), employers should provide specific, ongoing education and training, as well as the necessary equipment, to reinforce appropriate infection control procedures and ensure that they are implemented.

The previous principles apply to the workplace generally; the final principle applies to those special occupational settings where, because of the potential for transmission through exposure to contaminated blood, employers have special obligations. Although the trigger for these concerns is AIDS, the target should be all blood-borne infectious agents, especially hepatitis B virus. According to Dr. James O. Mason, head of the Centers for Disease Control:

> Hepatitis B is spread in ways similar to AIDS; however, when the two are compared, the hepatitis B virus is hardier than the AIDS virus; there is more of it than of the AIDS virus in the bloodstream; and hepatitis B is far easier than AIDS to catch. . . . The risk of infection to a health care worker following a needle stick from a carrier of the hepatitis B virus, for example, is between 6 and 30 percent, far in excess of the documented risk of infection to a health care worker following a needle stick involving a patient infected with the AIDS virus—a risk that is much less than 1 percent.

The risk, however small in comparison with other occupational risks, must be addressed. Employers must provide the necessary training and retraining to guard against HIV and other blood-borne infections. This training must be specific and ongoing, emphasizing the need for appropriate, consistent levels of protection. It should give due weight to the risks, but not overemphasize them. Furthermore, the materials employees in these situations need to protect themselves—for example, protective gloves or masks, glasses, containers for disposed needles, mouthpieces that protect those who perform cardiopulmonary resuscitation—must be readily and consistently available. The Centers for Disease Control has issued recommendations for prevention of HIV transmission in health-care settings (August 21, 1987); these are the most authoritative guide.

Throughout this process, employers should require employees to adopt the most stringent infection control measures and not to use shortcuts. Because of the impossibility of knowing (even with testing) whether a person's blood is truly infected, the only safe course is to treat all blood as potentially infectious.

EDUCATION AND TRAINING

As stated and discussed briefly above, Principles 6 and 10 of the Citizens Commission on AIDS call for employers to provide employees in general with "sensitive, accurate and up-to-date education about risk reduction in their personal lives," and those in health care settings with "specific, ongoing education and training, . . . to reinforce appropriate infection control procedures and ensure that they are implemented." As education and training are components of the role of managers in recreation and leisure settings, these will be further elaborated in this section.

The Need for Education and Training: Children have been denied the right to attend school; parents and children have marched in picket lines around schools; adults have lost their jobs; families have asked lovers of sick men to leave their bedsides; and a family's house has been firebombed because the parents of three boys with hemophilia who tested seropositive wanted to keep them in school. Why?

Siegel gives us the answer to the question in one sentence: "From the onset of the AIDS epidemic, the disease has been repeatedly referred to as a 'medical mystery'."[8] The media has tended to highlight the scientific uncertainties surrounding a number of issues related to HIV-related diseases. This has led the public to "the conclusion that it is wise to err on the side of extreme precaution, even if such a position adversely affects the civil rights of certain groups."[9] This has been further exacerbated by the fact that the scientific community has not developed an efficacious treatment for HIV infection or AIDS, or a vaccine to contain the spread of the virus. In addition, the media has continued to speculate on the transmissibility of the virus through casual contact, non-intimate sexual contact, and through work or school exposure to infected individuals. Other issues related to public fear are the increasing number of diagnosed cases and fatalities, the long incubation period which has led to the discovery of HIV acquired through transfused blood, and the continued perception that the virus can be spread by casual social contact to individuals who do not or have not engaged in high-risk behaviors. The latter is based on the continued misunderstanding of the modes of transmission of HIV.[10]

HIV related disease is not only contagious, it is associated with sex, drugs, and death. It is a disease that has been transmitted most frequently by sexual contact between sexually active male homosexuals/bisexuals and by the sharing of needles between intravenous drug users (IVDUs): two segments of the population which society has not only had difficulty in accepting, but has attempted to segregate. And since AIDS was first diagnosed in the homosexual population and initially labelled "GRID" (Gay Related Immune Deficiency Syndrome) and attributed to "fast lane sex," the general population believes that all persons with HIV (homosexual or heterosexual) belong to these stereotypic populations. ("Although subsequent research has revealed significant within and between group diversity in the sexual behavior of gay individuals with AIDS, ARC, and those infected with HIV and currently asymptomatic, this initial stereotype persists."[11])

There is another side of the coin concerning the stereotypes created about gay men and IVDUs. That side says that HIV is a gay or IVDU disease; consequently, it is not a peril to the general population.

As HIV is a sexually transmitted disease, the public is also responding to it and HIV-infected persons as it responds to others who acquire sexually transmitted diseases. As Siegel states: "This is a significant factor in the public's response to this illness. Sexually transmitted diseases are widely regarded as the outcome of sexual excess and low moral character." She continues, ". . . those who suffer from a STD have commonly been viewed as depraved. Once the patient is so judged, his suffering is met with much less concern or compassion."[12]

These as well as other issues underscore the importance of education and training in recreation and leisure settings. Not only will managers be providing education and training directly to supervisors and employees, they will indirectly be educating the employees' families and friends and the public—as these individuals will transmit this information to the consumers in leisure settings.

Education and Training Programs: The content and format of education and training programs should vary according to the target population. Effective programs are those which employees see as valuable and meeting their needs and, therefore, attend voluntarily. However, in those health care settings where employees may be exposed to blood, blood products or other bodily fluids, the education and training programs may be mandatory to meet the federal guidelines for employers to provide effective education and training.

The basic content for training all employees in recreation, park, and leisure service settings should include: a description of the disease and the spectrum of manifestations from HIV infection to AIDS, how HIV is spread, how it is not spread, behaviors that put one at risk, methods of prevention, and information about voluntary HIV antibody counseling and testing. Employees should also be informed that there is no risk to the donor in donating blood.

Training for individuals providing recreation and leisure services should be more comprehensive. Included in this training should be psychosocial factors related to individuals who are HIV-infected, or have AIDS Related Complex (ARC), or AIDS. Some of these factors are: social isolation, alteration in quality of life, drop in self esteem, intensity of emotion, issues of control and dependency, denial, financial stressors.[13] The psychosocial issues related to professionals working with persons who are HIV-infected, or have ARC, or AIDS should also be presented. Some of these factors are: fear of contagion, fear of the unknown, fear of death and dying, denial of helplessness, fear of homosexuality, anger, overidentification, need for professional omnipotence,[14] and fear of intravenous drug users.

Other topics to be included in the education and training of recreation and leisure professionals are: 1) psychosocial issues related to homosexual men and women, heterosexual men and women, substance abusers, adolescents, and minority populations; 2) stress and coping; 3) death and dying, including bereavement, mourning and grief; and 4) neuropsychiatric manifestations, including AIDS Dementia Complex (ADC). Price, a neurologist at Memorial Sloan-Kettering Center, N.Y.C., estimates that 90 percent of people with AIDS may suffer from ADC.[15] This is a term that Price and his colleagues coined to describe the loss of intellectual abilities which interfere with social and occupational functioning and are possible consequences of HIV. Those intellectual functions most frequently cited as impaired in AIDS are memory and concentration,[16] confusion,[17] and mental slowing.[18]

As indicated in Principle 10, employers in health care settings have special obligations regarding the establishment of policies and education and training for the protection of all employees. The **Morbidity and Mortality Weekly Report** of August 21, 1987, states these under the title "Implementation of Recommended Precautions," as follows:

1. Initial orientation and continuing education and training of all health-care workers—including students and trainees—on the epidemiology, modes of transmission, and prevention of HIV and other blood-borne infections and the need for routine use of universal blood and body-fluid precautions for all patients.
2. Provision of equipment and supplies necessary to minimize the risk of infection with HIV and other blood-borne pathogens.
3. Monitoring adherence to recommended protective measures. When monitoring reveals a failure to follow recommended precautions, counseling, education, and/or re-training should be provided, and if necessary, appropriate disciplinary action should be considered.[19]

The *Federal Register* (October 30, 1987) elaborates on these recommendations. It states: "The employer should establish an initial and periodic training program for all employees who perform Category I [Tasks That Involve Exposure to Blood, Body Fluids or Tissues] and II tasks [Tasks That Involve No Exposure to Blood, Body Fluids or Tissues But Employment May Require Unplanned Category I Tasks]. No worker should engage in any Category I or II task before receiving training pertaining to the SOPs [Standard Operating Procedures], work practices, and protective equipment required for that task."[20] The specific components of that training program are beyond the scope of the current work; and managers so responsible are referred to the *Federal Register*. In addition, managers in these settings are referred to the "PHS Recommendations for Preventing Transmission of Infection with HTLV-III/LAV in the Workplace" (November 15, 1985)[21] and its subsequent updates.

Approaches to Education and Training: HIV training and education can be incorporated into ongoing in-service or development training programs or established as a special training program. Whichever approach is used, the content and specific educational strategies should be designed for the target audience.

As individuals learn best by using a variety of their senses, a combination of strategies and approaches should be used. Some information is best communicated by lectures, overhead transparencies, and written materials, e.g., the spectrum of HIV infection; while other information is best communicated through the use of well prepared videotapes or movies, e.g., attitudes towards persons with AIDS.

Some organizations have recruited outside experts to design and instruct HIV education and training programs. Others have sent human resource personnel or those responsible for in-service and developmental training to conferences, workshops, and train-the-trainer programs so that they can provide training for employees. Whoever the trainers may be, they should be credible and have the trust of the employees.

The Health Services and Resources Administration of the U.S. Office of Public Health has established 13 AIDS Regional Education and Training Centers, covering the United States. The mandate of these Centers is to provide HIV education and training at central locations or onsite for health care professionals. In addition, the National Institute of Mental Health, under its Health Care Provider AIDS Education Program, has established 21 projects to address the neuropsychiatric manifestations and psychosocial sequelae of HIV infection and AIDS on a regional and national basis. These federal programs are additional resources which managers can use to ensure appropriate training for their employees.

Whatever venue of education and training is used, there should be opportunities for follow-up. This may take the form of a private discussion with a qualified counselor, or access to a hotline, or referral to another agency for additional information and ongoing confidential assistance.

SUMMARY

"No other medical event in recent history has produced the degree of public fear and private response that the AIDS epidemic has produced. With the recognition that perhaps . . . [1 to 1.5 million people] are already infected with a virus that represents a ticking time bomb, there has been a dramatic increase in the second epidemic, the epidemic of fear," writes Ostrow—a pioneer in researching psychiatric and psychosocial consequences of AIDS. "This fear, whether it be of death, contamination, or just passivity in the face of a mortal threat, may well be the driving force behind all behavioral responses to AIDS."[22] The purposes of this chapter were: 1) to provide guidelines for HIV education and training programs in the workplace to reduce or eliminate this fear; and 2) to elaborate principles for establishing policies to treat employees who are HIV-infected or have AIDS with fairness and equality.

"Responding to AIDS; Ten Principles for the Workplace," developed by the Citizens Commission on AIDS, were presented with selected comments from the Commission's report regarding each principle. The principles address rights, policies, laws and regulations, education, confidentiality and infection control procedures.

The need for educating and training in the workplace was discussed. This was addressed in terms of the "epidemic of fear" (using Dr. Ostrow's terminology); the fact that the scientific community has not developed an efficacious treatment for HIV infection or AIDS, or a vaccine to contain the spread of the virus; the increasing number of diagnosed cases and fatalities; continued misunderstanding of the modes of transmission; and the association of HIV-related diseases with drugs and sex (especially homosexuality)—taboo subjects for many.

The content of education and training programs was then presented. First, the content with which all employees must become knowledgeable: a description of the disease, the spectrum of manifestations from HIV infection to AIDS, how HIV is spread, how it is not spread, behaviors that put one at risk, methods of prevention, and information about voluntary HIV antibody testing.

Second, additional information which individuals providing recreation and leisure services must know: psychosocial factors related to individuals who are HIV infected, have ARC or AIDS; psychosocial issues related to professionals working with these individuals; psychosocial factors related to groups of individuals at various levels of risk for HIV infection; stress and coping; death and dying; and neuropsychiatric manifestations, including AIDS Dementia Complex.

Third, the special obligations of managers in health-care settings regarding the establishment of policies and education and training for the protection of all employees, including: the epidemiology, modes of transmission, and prevention of HIV and other blood-borne infections and the need for routine use of universal blood and body-fluid precautions for all patients. Along with this education, managers are responsible for: provision of equipment and supplies necessary to reduce the risk of infection with HIV and other blood-borne pathogens; and monitoring adherence to recommended protective measures.

Approaches to education and training were discussed. It was recommended that a combination of approaches be used including: written materials, videotapes, movies, lectures with transparencies, outside speakers, and specially trained personnel responsible for inservice and development training. Whatever venues are used, there should be opportunities for follow-up, e.g., counseling, referral; and the trainers must be credible and have the trust of the employees. It was noted that two federal agencies have established projects which managers may find useful as resources for HIV training and education: the Health and Resources Administration and the National Institute of Mental Health.

NOTES AND REFERENCES

1. Sam B. Puckett, "When A Worker Gets AIDS," **Psychology Today,** (January 1988), p. 27.
2. United Nations Development Programme, Division of Information, "Development in Action Newsletter," (September 1987), p. 3.
3. Bruce Lambert, "Number of AIDS Cases in New York Still Varies," **The New York Times** (September 23, 1988), p. B3.
4. Harvey V. Fineberg, "The Social Dimensions of AIDS," **Scientific American,** Vol. 239, No. 4 (October 1988), p. 133.
5. U.S. Public Health Service, Department of Health and Human Services, "Surgeon General's Report on Acquired Immune Deficiency Syndrome," (1987).
6. Single one-page copies of "Responding to AIDS: Ten Principles for the Workplace," as well as the "Principles" with commentaries in report form, are available from the Citizens Commission on AIDS for New York City and Northern New Jersey, 51 Madison Avenue, Room 3008, New York, N.Y. 10010.
7. J.J. Bannon, Jr. and Lauren B. Bannon, ("Legal Commentary," **Management Strategy,** Vol. 11, No. 3, Fall 1987, p. 3ff), state that "At least 38 states, including Connecticut, Florida, Illinois, Maine, Massachusetts, Michigan, Minnesota, Missouri, New Mexico, New Jersey, New York, Oregon, Pennsylvania, Rhode Island, Washington and Wisconsin have laws which prohibit discrimination

against the handicapped, and these states have determined that persons with AIDS are handicapped."

8. Karolynn Siegel, "AIDS: The Social Dimension," **Psychiatric Annals,** Vol. 16, No. 3, (March 1985), p. 168.

9. Ibid, p. 169.

10. Ibid.

11. Ibid, 170.

12. Ibid.

13. Ken Wein and Diego Lopez, "Overview of Psychological Issues Concerning AIDS." (New Jersey: State Department of Health, July 1987), pp. 1–2.

14. Joan Denkel and Shellie Hatfield, "Countertransference Issues in Working with Persons with AIDS," **Social Work,** (March–April 1986), pp. 114–117.

15. Christopher Joyce, "Assault on the Brain," **Psychology Today,** (March 1988), pp. 38–42.

16. J.C. McArthur, "Neurologic Manifestations of AIDS," **Medicine,** Vol. 66, (1987), p. 407; and B.A. Navia, et al., "The AIDS Dementia Complex," **Annals of Neurology,** Vol. 19, (1986), p. 517.

17. Navia, Ibid.

18. Navia, Ibid; and R.W. Price, et al., "The Brain In AIDS: Central Nervous System HIV-1 Infection and AIDS Dementia Complex," **Science,** No. 239, (1988), p. 586.

19. U.S. Public Health Service, **Morbidity and Mortality Weekly Report,** (August 21, 1987), p. 12S.

20. **Federal Register,** Vol. 52, No. 210, (October 30, 1987), Notices, p. 41821.

21. U.S. Public Health Service, **Morbidity and Mortality Weekly Report,** (November 15, 1985), pp. 681–695.

22. David G. Ostrow, "Models for Understanding the Psychiatric Consequences of AIDS," **Psychological, Neuropsychiatric and Substance Abuse Aspects of AIDS,** T. Peter Bridge, et al., eds. (New York: Ravens Press, 1988), p. 85.

PART TWO

Organizations and Individuals at Work

The purpose of this chapter is to help managers answer:

- Is planning a waste of time?
- Are planning and scheduling the same thing?
- When plans are written, why are they not carried out?
- No one can predict the future, so why engage in long-range planning?
- What are performance objectives?
- Why is there duplication, overlap, and confusion among employees?
- Why develop an organizational chart?
- How many employees should one person supervise?
- Is it good practice for an employee to have two supervisors?

Chapter 4

Planning and Organizing Work for Recreation and Leisure Services

Arnold H. Grossman

Most managers in the recreation and leisure services field are not trained in planning and organizing work. Managers are usually promoted because of high performance ratings based on knowledge and skills as recreation or group leaders providing direct service to clients in a leisure service agency. Technical competence is important, but it is only one of the skills needed by managers. As one climbs the management ladder, technical skills become less important, while human relations skills and conceptual skills gain in importance. Figure 4.1 illustrates the relative proportion of the three areas of skill needed by managers at the various levels.[1]

As previously noted, most managers have the technical skills needed. In the field of recreation and leisure services these are: program scheduling, activity leadership skills, knowledge of group process, knowledge of a wide range of activities, budget processes and procedures, purchasing and use of equipment and supplies, planning and conducting special events, activity skills, recording skills and knowledge, and skill in program evaluation. Managers who do not have these technical skills present a pathetic sight as they try to cover up their incompetence. Employees seem to have a particular knack for exposing technically incompetent managers, and they do not respect or follow them.

Recreation and leisure services are human services, and most managers have basic skills in human relations; however, these are often

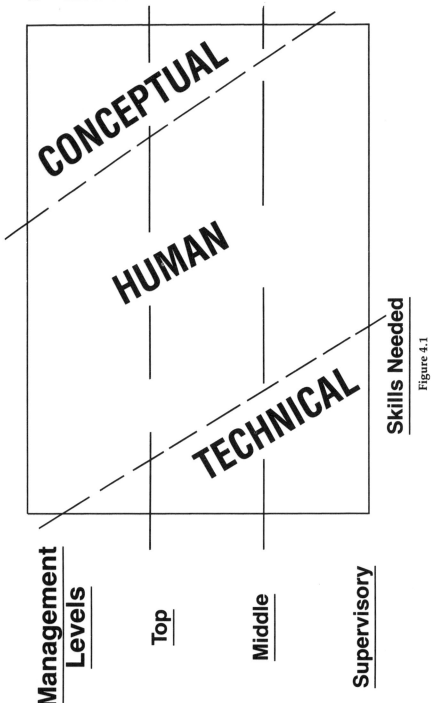

Figure 4.1

narrowly developed in the area of direct service. Interpersonal skills developed in working with the consumers of a service are different from those required of a manager working with employees through whom one has to achieve results. For example, motivating an employee to perform adequately in all aspects of work is different from that of motivating a consumer of the service to participate in an activity.

The third area of skills needed by managers are conceptual skills. Managers must be able to conceptualize the work for which they are responsible, identify the parts, see these parts in various combinations and arrangements, recognize how the various functions depend on one another, visualize the relationship of the service to the community, and formulate the components into an integrated whole. This chapter is concerned with the conceptual skills of planning and organizing.

THE PLANNING PROCESS

Planning is advance decision-making about the work for which the manager is responsible. It enables one to become the master of the work rather than a slave who is constantly responding to crises. As defined by Mescon, et al, "The *planning function* involves deciding what the organization's objectives should be and what its members should do to attain them." They indicate that the planning function seeks answers to three fundamental questions: Where are we now? Where do we want to go? How are we going to get there? "Through planning, management seeks to establish guidelines for channeling effort and decision making that will create unity of purpose within the organizations' membership. In other words, planning is one of the ways in which management gets all of its people pulling in the same direction—toward the organization's objectives."[2]

When recreation and leisure service managers plan, they make things happen instead of having them happen. In essence, planning is a process in which managers ask the questions why, what, when, where, who, and how? In answering these questions, one engages in scheduling, i.e., translating the answers into sequential steps. Unfortunately, many managers schedule without planning. This can produce misunderstandings on the part of the employees and consumers, poor coordination, role confusion among employees, dissatisfaction among employees, waste of resources, poor programming, and disappointed consumers whose needs and expectations are not met. Good planning, on the other hand, produces the opposite results: effective coordination and delegation, economical use of resources, satisfied personnel and consumers, as well as more effective control of operations and program components.

As indicated previously, planning is a process in which the recreation and leisure service manager asks the questions why, what, when, where, who, and how? When the manager has asked each of these questions and has supplied detailed answers, the results will be a comprehensive plan with a schedule for its implementation. An exploration of the factors to be considered under each of these questions will provide more definitive guidelines to the planning process.

- *Why?* Why is the recreation or leisure service being provided? In other words, what is the stated purpose or mission of the agency or service for which one is planning. The answer to this question provides the foundation and framework for the remainder of the planning process.
- *What?* What is to be accomplished? In accordance with the stated purpose of the agency or service, the manager must establish the objectives to be achieved by the service, project, or program. The objectives provide direction to the manager's efforts as well as a means of control. They provide the yardstick against which the manager can measure the results of the plan and the schedule. Consequently, clearly stated objectives are vital to the planning process.

The objectives should be written in terms of expected performance and should include the result to be achieved, the action to be taken to achieve that result, and the time period after which the result can be expected. For example, objectives of a new recreation program serving children who are developmentally disabled in a leisure services agency might be:

1. Within two months of initiation, to recruit 40 individuals for the program.

2. Within four months of initiation, to assess the leisure skills of 100 percent of the children recruited.

3. Within six months of initiation, to develop a recreation program that will teach four new leisure skills to 75 percent of the children.

4. After one year, to integrate 50 percent of the 40 individuals into the regular recreation program of the center.

In addition to the three components of an objective stated above, i.e., the result to be achieved, the action to be taken, and the time period after which the result can be expected, the objective may include who is responsible for taking the action. For example, objectives of a September to June program for aging persons might be:

1. For the current officers to design and execute procedures for the nomination and election of a new president, vice president, secretary, treasurer, and the eight members of the advisory committee by October 15.

2. For the new officers to establish a committee structure, including a program committee, a membership committee, a newsletter committee, a trip committee, and a special events committee by November 1.

3. For the trip committee to plan, organize, and conduct six one-day trips and two weekend trips during the program year.

4. For the newsletter committee to gather material, write, print, and distribute five newsletters (one every other month) during the program year.

- *When?* A time framework is an essential ingredient of every plan. The manager has to ask: When is the recreation or leisure service, project, or program to start? When are the various phases to be implemented? When are the objectives expected to be achieved? The answer to the last question should be included in the statement of the objectives, as in the illustrations above.

- *Where?* Where should the recreation or leisure service, project or program be implemented? Should it be implemented in one leisure service center or park—or should it be implemented in a number of different facilities?

- *Who?* Who will implement the service, project or program? Who will provide the best leadership? Who is most qualified to achieve the desired results? Who will gain needed experience or training by working in the service, project or program? If these questions are not adequately answered in advance, the manager's opportunities for delegation will be curtailed as each of the employees under his or her supervision will assume additional responsibilities in the intervening time period; consequently, the manager will have to assume the added responsibilities.

- *How?* How will the service, project, or program be implemented? The method chosen to implement the plan is vital in terms of its projected success. Will traditional approaches be used, or is there an opportunity for new and creative approaches? One important question to ask while determining the method of implementation is: How will the service, project, or program be evaluated? More often than not, the method of evaluation is considered only upon completion, when some of the vital information is no longer available; consequently, an evaluation method must be an integral part of the implementation plan.

Although the questions asked in the above discussion of the planning process were limited to areas of planning for a service, program, or project, the recreation and leisure services manager has to ask the same questions in other areas of required planning, such as: planning work schedules of the personnel, maintenance, paper work and reports, training programs, changes in programs or services, special events, budgeting and fund raising.

LONG-RANGE PLANNING

Managers, if they plan at all, usually engage in short-range planning. They continue to act under the assumption that people and situations will remain stable. The appearance of stability, however, masks a multitude of subtle and dynamic changes. According to Toffler, in his book *Future Shock*,[3] the only constants in our pre-cooked, pre-packaged, plastic-wrapped, instant society are growth and change. We are living in a dynamic and progressive society, always on the move.

Managers are not the only people in recreation and leisure service agencies that operate under the assumption of stability. Supervisors, leaders, and consumers also maintain an attitude of stability. When situations remain constant people know what to expect, how to respond, and feel secure. There is a predictability in the present situation, while change brings the "unknown" which often arouses fear, anxiety, and stress. In addition, an individual's status and power are related to the present situation, and change may mean a potential loss. FInally, change may threaten an individual's or group's values, traditions and standards. Notwithstanding these resistances to change and the concomitant difficulties arising from them, managers have to engage in long-range planning. If they do not, the world is likely to pass by them and their agencies. In other words, the agencies will lose their relevance in meeting societal needs and, consequently, their viability as human and leisure service agencies.

While long-range planning follows the essential principles and procedures outlined above, the assessment and fact-finding phase to answer the questions of why and when must be based on long-term trends, and alternative goals and objectives must be established. In addition, a series of phases for implementing the long-range plan should be stated which will permit the plan to be presented and implemented gradually and enable managers to create a climate that is conducive to the change being attempted.

PITFALLS

Some of the common pitfalls managers should avoid in planning are:

- Do not plan to accomplish too much within a short time span.
- Do not assume that a plan will be executed because it is written on paper.
- Do not plan before you gather the necessary data on which the plan is to be based.
- Do not create an unbalanced plan. Make certain that each aspect of the plan gets the attention that it deserves.
- Do not plan alone. Make certain that everyone concerned is involved in the planning process. Developing orderly problem-solving processes will enable the individuals affected by the plan to have an understanding about it and its outcomes.
- Do not ignore the emotional dimension of the individuals involved in, or affected by, the plan. Although individuals cannot be convinced or intimidated out of their fears, anxieties, and resistances, they can be released from some of them if they receive adequate information and their feelings can be expressed and recognized.

ORGANIZATION OF WORK

The primary objective of organizing is to group the work to be performed. As defined by the International City Management Association, "To organize work is to arrange it into interdependent parts; each part has a special relation to the whole. It is the proper arrangement of the parts that make for well-organized work."[4]

The organizing function is related to the planning function. The question of grouping the work must be addressed each time one supplies the answers to the who, where, and when of the planning process. It is being discussed as a separate section of this chapter in order to identify the principles of management, approaches, and processes which must be considered. Specific attention will be directed to the use of the organizational chart as an aid as well as to the different types of authority relationships in an organization.

Creating an Organization Structure: Organizing is the creation of structure. Every recreation and leisure service agency, from the smallest to the largest, has an organization structure. The structure is the framework which has been established so that the operations of the agency can proceed in an orderly manner as the agency seeks to achieve its goals.

As most recreation and leisure service managers are appointed to positions in existing agencies, they inherit an organization structure within which they must work and to which they have to adapt. It is important to understand the structure, its major components, and the principles which underlined its establishment.

Principles of management. Three basic management principles must be considered in establishing any organizational structure: unity of command, logical assignment, and span of control. The International City Management Association enumerates these, among others, as follows:[5]

1. *Unity of command.* This principle states that each individual in an organization should be responsible to only *one* superior. In essence, the principle states that each individual in the organization must have one superior to whom he or she reports and that each manager must know the particular individuals for whom he or she has responsibility. As Koontz and O'Donnell state: "The more completely an individual has a reporting relationship to a single superior, the less the problem of conflict and the greater the feeling of personal responsibility."[6] Adherence to this principle establishes a precise *chain of command* within the organization.

2. *Logical assignment.* This principle states that individuals doing the same work should be grouped together and that the work be planned and scheduled in a logical order. If work is not logically assigned, duplication, overlap, confusion, and poor performance will result.

3. *Span of control.* This principle states that there are limiting factors which must be considered in determining the number of subordinates a manager can effectively supervise. The limiting factors are: *span of control (people), span of control (distance)* and *span of control (time).*

a. *Span of control (people).* It is impossible to state the exact number of individuals that a manager should supervise. The type of work (simple, routine vs. complex, highly specialized) as well as the capacities of the manager must be considered. If too few individuals are assigned to a manager, the agency does not make use of his or her full capabilities; however, if too many individuals are assigned to a manager, managing effectiveness and efficiency will be limited because of an overdemand on the manager's ability, time, and energy.

b. *Span of control (distance).* This aspect of span of control relates to the physical area for which the manager is responsible. The individuals directed by a specific manager should not be situated too close to him or her, as this will result in oversupervision; however, they should not be located too far away, as this will result in undersupervision.

Depending upon the capacities of the individuals and the manager, the resources available, and the goals to be achieved, the most feasible distance should be established.

c. *Span of control (time).* Every manager must be able to allocate time to the different types of work required. There are four main types of work: (1) routine work, most of which may be delegated to subordinates; (2) regular work, that which must be performed by the manager; (3) special work, that which is initiated by the manager or assigned by his or her superior; and (4) creative work, that which is done to improve the quality and quantity of work. No specific guidelines can be stated as the amount of time devoted to each type of work will vary with each recreation and leisure service manager depending on the nature of the work and the time of year or season, among others.

Dividing the work. The ultimate goal of organizing and dividing the work is to establish a method of determining individual tasks and responsibilities of those working in the agency, the distribution of authority, and the processes of delegation. The decisions that a manager makes in regard to this task must reflect consideration of the principles of management previously discussed as well as an individual approach to job design to be discussed in the following chapter.

The major approach to dividing the work is *departmentalization.* It means dividing the work force of the agency into organized units or departments. There are four avenues which a manager can follow in creating departments:

1. *Function.* Workers are grouped into departments according to function, e.g., drama department, music department, physical fitness and sports department, aquatics department, health department, maintenance.

2. *Type of clientele.* Workers are grouped into departments according to the type of clientele served, e.g., pre-school, youth, teenage, adult, senior citizens.

3. *Geographic area.* Workers are grouped into departments according to geographic area, e.g., Southwest Recreation Center, Northeast Playground, Red Eagle Camp.

4. *Process.* Workers are grouped into departments according to the process utilized in providing service, e.g., group process, leadership, instruction, counseling, consultation.

Most managers in recreation and leisure service agencies use a combination of these strategies in creating departments. Consequently, in a single agency, one can find departments such as: Youth Department, Guidance and Counseling Department, Physical Fitness and Sport, and Blueberry Annex. The main criterion guiding the manager's decision must be that of creating those departments which will enable the agency to establish an efficient means of operations to achieve its objectives.

Levels of authority. Once the manager of a recreation and leisure service agency departmentalizes the work, he or she must make a decision regarding *levels of authority.* It is this decision that establishes the formal chain of command within the agency. For example, a number of workers in the youth department may be responsible to one of two supervisors; the supervisor will be responsible to the head of the youth department; the head of the youth department, along with the head of pre-school and teen-age departments, will be responsible to the Director of Youth Services; the Director of Youth Services will be responsible to the Program Director. The Program Director will be responsible to the Associate Director of the agency; and the Associate Director will be responsible to the Executive Director, who in turn is responsible to the Board of Directors.

Authority levels within an agency establish its power structure. Those individuals appointed to positions located on high authority levels have more power; consequently, they have a greater capacity to make their interests felt as an impact in the communal decision-making processes of the agency.[7] In addition, the authority level of the position occupied by an individual usually reflects his or her social status, perception of role in the organization, and choice of associates.

By-passing the chain of command. It should be stated at the outset that this section of the chapter is not advocating the by-passing of the chain of command. One should recognize, however, that an informal organizational structure develops and exists in every agency along with the established formal structure. It is the informal structure which provides for cross-communication, rather than going through the channels. For example, the head of the youth department and the head of the teen-age department may work out a joint problem without referring to the Director of Youth Services. It is this type of cross-communication that enables those with first-hand knowledge of the situation to make the required decisions. If everything within an agency went through the formal chain of command, many of the simple operations of an agency would be impeded. A manager, however, must be discreet as to when he or she can by-pass the chain of command and when it must be followed.

The Organizational Chart: The most common aid utilized to establish and portray the organizational structure of an agency is the *organizational chart,* sometimes called the table of organization or T.O. It is a graphic view of the organization's structure and illustrates the hierarchy, positions, functions, and chains of command established so that the agency can effectively and efficiently accomplish its objectives. (See Figures 4.2 and 4.3)

The development and use of an organizational chart enhances the operations of an agency. It presents a pictorial view of the agency structure to each individual in the organization and it enables the individual to see how he or she fits into the organization. In addition, the chart provides the individual with the opportunity of observing his or her possible line of promotion and progression. On an agency-wide basis, the chart enhances communications and personnel relations as individuals can observe the positions and functions of others in the agency. Last, but not least, the chart provides a mechanism for analyzing the current organization structure with a view toward the future.

The limitations of an organizational chart should be noted. It depicts the skeleton of the agency's structure in a static state; consequently, it only remains accurate as long as the status-quo is maintained. A second limitation is that it does not show precise functions and precise amounts of authority and responsibility, it only depicts these in general terms. The third limitation is that it does not portray the informal relationships which exist. These limitations do not negate the value of an organizational chart, however, one should understand its limitations so that one does not assume it is providing information that it does not contain.

Most organizational charts depict one or two types of authority relationships: line, or line and staff. In the *line organization,* authority flows from the highest level manager down through the chain of command to the lowest position. (See Figure 4.2.) In the *line and staff organization,* staff personnel are incorporated in addition to the line organization. (See Figure 4.3.) Staff personnel are specialists in specific areas, e.g., program development, contractual services, personnel, who assist and advise the line personnel; however, they are not within the chain of command of the line personnel. It should be noted, however, that staff personnel who act in an advisory capacity to line personnel may have individuals responsible to them in a line relationship. For example, the Director of Personnel may be responsible for three individuals who report directly to him or her and who work with specific supervisors. (See Figure 4.4). Line-and-staff organizations are more flexible than line organizations as they permit line personnel to concentrate on the regular work of the agency while delegating special functions to the staff personnel.

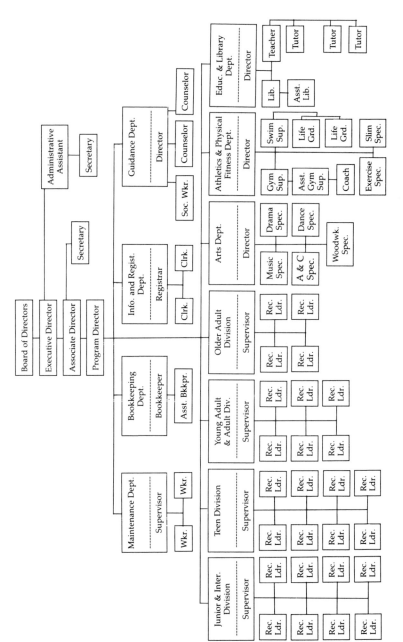

Figure 4.2 Line organizational chart for a hypothetical recreation and leisure service agency.

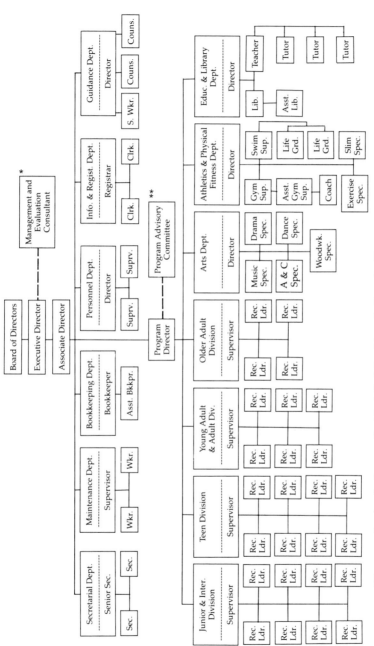

*Management and evaluation consultant in staff relationship to the Executive Director.
**Program Advisory Committee in staff relationship to the Program Director.

Figure 4.3 Line and staff organizational chart for a hypothetical recreation and leisure service agency.

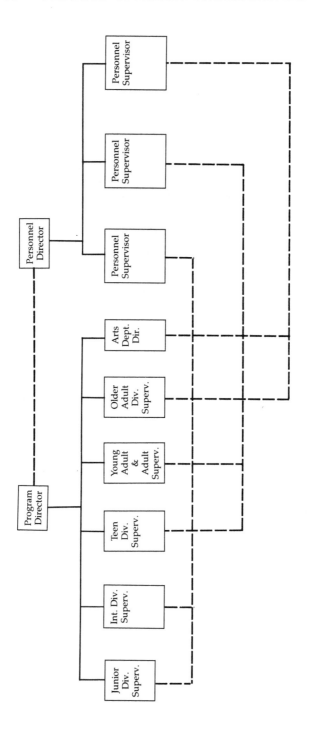

Figure 4.4 Relationship between a staff function and line functions.

The International City Management Association differentiates the functions of line and staff as follows:[8]

Line Functions	Staff Functions
Line directs or orders	Staff advises.
Line has responsibility to carry out activities from beginning to end.	Staff studies, reports, recommends, but does not carry out.
Line follows chain of command.	Staff assists line but is not part of chain.
Line decides when and how to use staff.	Staff always available for line use.
Line is the doing part of the organization.	Staff is the assisting part of the organization.

SUMMARY

This chapter has been devoted to planning and organizing the work in recreation and leisure service agencies. Planning and organizing are interrelated and continuous processes. Effective planning and organizing enable the manager to establish those operations which will help the agency to achieve its goals in an efficient manner. These two functions form the basis upon which the other managerial functions of staffing, directing, and controlling are dependent.

It is important to remember that the recreation and leisure service agency is an organization which was established to serve one or more goals in the area of human services. The organization is an instrument. It is a means to an end, and it should not become an end in itself. Frequently, managers become concerned more with preserving and enhancing the organization itself than with helping it to serve its stated purpose. This is the most common form of goal displacement. "It . . . is the process by which an organization reverses the priority between its goals and means in a way that makes the means a goal and the goal a means."[9] It is a process that can be avoided if the manager provides balance in executing each of his or her functions and keeps the stated goals (objectives) of the agency in the forefront.

NOTES AND REFERENCES

1. Based on the concept developed by Robert L. Katz, "Skills of an Effective Administrator," **Harvard Business Review,** Vol. 33, No. 1, January-February, 1955, pp. 33–42.

2. M. H. Mescon, M. Albert, F. Khedouri, **Management,** 3rd ed. (New York: Harper & Row, Publishers, 1988), pp. 49–51.
3. Alvin Toffler, **Future Shock.** (New York: Random House, 1970).
4. International City Management Association, "Planning and Organizing the Work," Bulletin 4 in a series on **Effective Supervisory Practices.** (Washington, D.C.: International City Management Association, 1965), p. 1.
5. International City Management Association, "Basic Concepts of Organization, Bulletin 3 in a series on **Effective Supervisory Practices,** pp. 2–3.
6. Harold Koontz and Cyril O'Donnell, **Management: A Systems and Contingency Analysis of Managerial Functions,** 6th ed. (New York: McGraw Hill, 1976), p. 444.
7. Dan W. Dodson, "Power as a Dimension of Education," **Power, Conflict and Community Organizations.** (New York: Council for American Unity, 1967), p. 7.
8. International City Management Association, "Basic Concepts of Organization," p. 5.
9. Amitai Etzioni, **Modern Organizations.** (Englewood Cliffs, New Jersey: Prentice-Hall, Inc., 1964), p. 10.

The purpose of this chapter is to help the manager answer questions such as:

- What are current trends and issues which impact on the way personnel services are managed?

- What is job design and what are its implications for personnel management?

- What are job task components, position descriptions, job descriptions, and job specifications?

- What is job analysis; how and why are job analyses conducted?

- What is work redesign and what forms can it take?

- What are the potential benefits and drawbacks of various approaches to work redesign such as: work simplification; job enlargement; job enrichment; job rotation; career management; flextime arrangements; job sharing; and, MBO?

- What are the implications of various job design, job analysis, and work redesign strategies for the personnel manager in recreation and leisure service delivery systems?

Chapter 5

Approaches to Job Design

Claudette B. Lefebvre

Leisure service delivery systems and their managers are increasingly confronting a diversity of rapid changes in society so aptly described as "future shock" by Toffler[1] almost 20 years ago. Coping effectively with change necessitates anticipating it, and, as Toffler notes, "the problem is not . . . to suppress change, which cannot be done, but to manage it."[2] Recreation agencies (like many other human service organizations) must be viewed as relatively open systems which currently exist and function in a somewhat uncertain environment[3] wherein achievement of the primary social goals of the agency must often be accomplished with increasingly diminishing resources.

There is little question that "staff are the critical ingredient in human service organizations"[4] and "modern leisure-service management is deeply concerned with ways of promoting the maximum productivity and commitment on the part of its employees."[5] As personnel are such a significant factor in achieving agency objectives, the incidence of staff burnout, apathy, dissatisfaction, absenteeism, or addictive substance abuse not only proves costly to the individual and agency as a whole but also acts to seriously disrupt service delivery to clients. It is increasingly being recognized that "maximizing productivity through people requires concentration of effort, and the pursuit and use of well-formulated program or service technology."[6] Results and analyses of research and evaluation data clearly demonstrate that: 1) "the way in which we manage agency personnel can greatly influence worker productivity and program effectiveness"[7]; 2) "productivity is maximized through careful selection of staff, attention to performance appraisal, and commitment to staff training"[8]; 3) supervision and management practices must reflect "changes associated with worker demands for more equality, participation, and recognition[9]; and, 4) supervisory and management personnel must increasingly consider "working with employees in different work settings to bring out their fullest energies and creative abilities"[10] and to "achieve a climate of highly motivated participation in the work of the organization."[11] This chapter explores various approaches to significant personnel management strategies—job design, job analysis, and job redesign—within the contextual framework of leisure service delivery systems and their organizational environments.

MANAGERS AND THEIR ORGANIZATIONAL ENVIRONMENTS

Management personnel serve in a unique stewardship capacity for the effective and efficient allocation of each agency's human, capital, and financial assets[12] as they seek to meet the organization's primary social obligation of responding to the needs and expectations of diverse constituencies.[13] One view of organizational excellence focuses on maximizing organizational performance in four distinct but interrelated areas including: 1) enhanced and efficient service delivery output to intended recipients; 2) the effective utilization and acquisition of resources from within the agency's own environment to maintain and expand requisite services; 3) adoption of supervisory practices which encourage involvement of all agency personnel in such a way that worker satisfaction and productivity are maximized while absenteeism, burnout, and staff turnover are minimized; and, 4) assurance of service effectiveness as measured by constituency and user satisfaction, change, and quality determination.[14]

Management planning, decision-making, and strategy implementation are always influenced, to some extent, by prevailing trends and issues. Current issues which might warrant consideration by recreation managers include, among others:

- the variability and frequent instability in the availability of economic funding to support human resource and social service systems—especially those in the leisure services and recreation sectors;
- increased demands for accountability (i.e., demonstrated proof of the effectiveness and efficiency of existing and projected services) from multiple and diverse constituencies[15];
- growing demands for involvement and participation in the determination of service and work objectives, priorities, and program

implementation procedures at all levels of the service delivery system;

- significant shifts in the number and type of qualified personnel available and needed at any time to meet the continually changing needs of diverse client constituencies;
- rapid acceleration in the introduction and enforcement of governmental and regulatory policies, guidelines, and procedures affecting employment practices in all sectors; and,
- significant alterations in individual and societal values specific to work, leisure, personal satisfaction, individuality and creativity, and adopted life-styles;[16]

Leisure service agencies currently function in a somewhat uncertain milieu in which social and organizational environments are rapidly being restructured. As organizational environments change, individual agencies and organizations too must alter themselves to meet rapidly changing needs, priorities, and objectives.[17] In order to effectively respond to changing environmental needs, agencies and organizations must engage in on-going research and evaluation activities to assess which of many indicators may be most useful in determining priorities, establishing objectives, and implementing alternative strategies.[18]

The feasibility of implementing diverse alternative service delivery strategies is ultimately determined by the availability and accessibility of each agency's human, capital, and financial resources. Rarely does any individual leisure service agency have the comprehensive resources to meet all of the unique and complex needs of its diverse current or potential constituencies.[19] As agencies seek to maximize dwindling resources, consideration should be given not only to the adoption of permanent, but also transitional and temporary organizational structures and functioning groups to implement approaches and strategies adopted.[20]

Resolution of strategy selection dilemmas are, in part, dependent on the specificity of stated agency objectives and priorities. As agency mission statements often prove to be overgeneralized, somewhat nebulous, or intangible[21], it may be necessary to reconsider and revise these in order that agency goals and operational objectives may be more realistically derived. Once operational priorities have been delineated, implementation strategies can be developed which maintain and support the agency's integrity and viability so that it can continue to effectively and efficiently serve its diverse constituencies.

Willingness to change is a key factor in making organizational change but, in order to be effective, willingness must be accompanied by 1) a corresponding commitment to enhanced participation in the establishment of objectives, priorities, and implementation strategies at all levels of the service delivery system[22] and 2) the development and enhancement of requisite knowledge, skills, and competencies among all individuals who will be expected to implement alternative operating strategies adopted.[23] Achievement of a climate of highly motivated employee participation requires the use of diverse, creative strategies designed to assure that staff can ultimately share in "a common vision of practice and a deep commitment to the agency and its clients."[24]

JOB DESIGN: A PERSONNEL MANAGEMENT STRATEGY

Ideally, every employer seeks a working environment in which jobs are so designed that the needs and objectives of the individual, the agency, and society would be perfectly suited; however, this is rarely ever achieved in practice.[25] In general, two types of hiring errors most frequently occur. In the first instance, individuals may be placed on jobs where they experience failure, while in the second instance individuals may not be placed on jobs where they can experience success. In either case, the human and financial outcomes, for both the individual and the agency, may prove costly.[26]

Design and allocation of job tasks and staffing is one of several components of the personnel management process.[27] Yet, many agencies lack a systematic approach to and practices for the basic personnel function called employment. In practice, employment must be viewed as an on-going process in which "planning before recruitment is a must."[28] Job design is a dynamic, comprehensive, future- as well as historically-oriented process which utilizes systematic, analytic methods designed to provide the manager with necessary information to appropriately: 1) identify the specific task components of positions and jobs within the agency or department; 2) develop and implement operationally effective position descriptions; 3) develop meaningful job descriptions and job titles; and, 4) determine relevant job specifications or required job qualifications for jobs, positions, and job title clusters.[29]

Task components are generally defined as the distinct and unique activities that constitute essential and logical steps in the performance of work by an employee. *Position descriptions* describe the comprehensive collection of tasks which make up the total work assignment of each individual worker. In essence, it would be appropriate to say that there are, in effect, as many position descriptions as there are individuals employed. While position descriptions define the work assignments of individuals, *job descriptions and titles* are designed to accurately depict a cluster of representative positions (e.g., department head, program specialist, recreation leader, therapist,) which are significantly alike in regard to major job tasks to justify their being covered by a single job analysis).[30]

"In all types of leisure-service agencies, classification and standardization of job titles are essential to effective organization."[31] Standardization of job titles and descriptions within an agency provides the basis for: 1) clearly defining job responsibilities at various levels in the organizations; 2) establishing comparable salary levels for similar job demands and requisite qualifications; and, 3) establishing a meaningful career ladder with opportunity for employee promotion within the system.[32]

Job specifications generally set forth the personal attributes, knowledge, skills, competencies, education, experience, and special requirements expected of prospective candidates for a given job.[33] It is essential to note that job specifications must always: 1) be directly related to actual job requirements; 2) reflect nondiscriminatory and equal opportunity orientations; and, 3) be consistent with governmental and regulatory body policies and guidelines. Job specifications or required qualifications may never reflect arbitrary or capricious desires or preferences on the part of the managers or governing bodies. "A carefully designed employee selection system should be directed toward hiring the best qualified individuals in a fair and equitable manner."[34]

JOB ANALYSIS

As noted earlier, employment processes really must begin prior to recruitment and "one of the most critical elements is developing a systematic job analysis procedure."[35] It is generally agreed that "there is no one best way to conduct a job analysis."[36] Often conducted by a job analyst, the ongoing process of job analysis remains an integral managerial function. Major components of the job analysis process broadly include: 1) determining the historical antecedents of the job; 2) identifying the current status of the job; and, 3) noting trends and projections for future needs assessment.

The first step in a job analysis process "is to determine the key factors which relate to virtually all jobs"[37] including such elements as: the job title; basic job responsibilities; to whom the employee is responsible; task functions in each of several domain categories (e.g., board relations, personnel, program evaluation) which are rank ordered in relation to the percentage of time spent in each task; knowledge, skills and abilities required; desired education and experience; and, essential special requirements (e.g., certification, registration, or licensure).[38]

Data needed for answering basic questions in the job analysis process are generally gathered through systematic reviews of historical and written materials in addition to observations of and interviews with job incumbents and related personnel. Specific areas of focus include, among others:[39]

- What the worker *does* on the job as described by active verbs. Job analysis procedures "must be *behavior centered*, focusing on the actual behaviors needed for effective on-the-job performance, and *reliable*, in the sense that different job analysts will agree on their components."[40]
- What equipment, modalities, and techniques the worker utilizes in performing tasks;
- What specific knowledge and skills a worker must have in order to perform job tasks effectively;
- The degree of responsibility held by the worker and the potential effects of misjudgments or error on client safety and satisfaction or on the effectiveness and efficiency of service delivery;
- The physical and human environmental working conditions in which the employee routinely carries out job tasks; and,
- Extant relationships between the position under analysis with other positions within the agency and the broader community and society.

The ultimate purpose of conducting comprehensive job analyses is to collect information about jobs "that will provide the basis for making decisions not only related to recruitment and selection but to training, supervision, promotion, compensation and other personnel functions."[41] Job design is a dynamic, on-going process necessitating the periodic review and regular updating of job analyses data[42] as it is recognized that jobs themselves are relatively impermanent, changing over time even when their incumbents remain the same.[43] Changes in jobs and their requirements are mediated by numerous factors including, among others: seasonal or situational needs; budgetary considerations, constraints, and fiscal crises; variables in the physical environment; employee-determined alterations resulting from the accrual of worker experience;[44] and, the working climate established by varying interaction patterns between and among coworkers, supervisors, and subordinates.[45]

Job design and work redesign approaches (to be discussed in the following section) are primarily concerned with restructuring worker tasks and functions by manipulating variables inherent in each of two interrelated concepts—job scope and depth. *Job scope* broadly refers to the number of different tasks, functions, and operations an individual usually performs in the course of work and to how often these tasks are repeated. By definition, an individual who regularly performs a limited number of tasks with considerable frequency would be viewed as a worker with a narrow job scope; an individual who regularly performs many diverse tasks but who does so with limited frequency, by contrast, would be viewed as a worker with a wide job scope.[46] *Job depth* refers to "the relative amount of influence a worker has over the job itself and the work environment."[47] Job depth generally includes such factors as: autonomy in planning and carrying out tasks; setting a working pace; and, participating in decision-making processes.[48]

Work Redesign Approaches: Implications for Personnel Management

Over time, the quest for quality work-life environments has spurred the development of numerous work redesign approaches ultimately intended to enhance productivity by improving worker motivation and job satisfaction and by reducing costs associated with absenteeism, turnover, and poor work quality.[49]

Although there is not, as yet, enough research evidence available to draw firm conclusions about the effectiveness of specific work redesign approaches, "studies do show that work redesign generally results in improved job satisfaction, lower absenteeism and turnover, and improved product quality," although productivity has not been found to have been significantly enhanced in most of the cases cited.[50] Following is a brief overview of selected work redesign approaches with implications drawn for managerial consideration.

Work Simplification: This approach is concerned with dividing units of work to be accomplished into their most fundamental or component parts and tasks. Work simplification approaches generally support the concept of employee specialization and the development of worker proficiency in highly selected tasks. Toffler notes that, in a broad context, work specialization tends to increase the number of different occupations while technological innovation concomitantly acts to reduce the average life span of emerging occupations.[51]

Work simplification approaches have largely paralleled the growth of mass production, increased technology, and automation.[52] Early management thinking viewed specialization approaches as a means for generating specific benefits in industrial settings, including "less employee training, increased skill levels at each specialized job, separation of skilled and unskilled tasks with lower wage costs for unskilled jobs, and increased opportunities to use special purpose machines."[53] It should be noted that work specialization frequently resulted in oversimplification of repetitive work tasks and, over time, it became apparent that "increasing numbers of people began to find highly specialized, repetitive tasks boring and demotivating."[54]

Research conducted in the social sciences suggests that most people exert their best efforts when they feel competent to complete required tasks. However, decision making concerning the degree of work specialization to be adopted by an agency or department should include consideration of the demonstrated disadvantages of this approach. Potential drawbacks to work simplification have been found to include, among others, "reduced flexibility to shift work assignments, less sense of accomplishment by workers, and increased worker boredom and absenteeism."[55] This approach may have a more specific limitation in leisure service systems wherein it is generally accepted that "recreation leaders and therapists deal with a variety of tasks and challenges and must work creatively to succeed."[56]

Job Enlargement: This approach focuses on redesigning work patterns by increasing job scope—the number of specific tasks a staff member will be expected to regularly complete. In job enlargement approaches, alternatively termed "horizontal job loading," jobs may be continually restructured so that related additional activities or tasks are systematically added to the worker's current job requirements.

Job enlargement approaches provide a diametric contrast to those of job simplification or work specialization, and they generally appeal to differently motivated constituencies. Job enlargement appears to be most effective with employees who are readily challenged or motivated to complete increasingly broader units of work and to participate in an increasingly wider scope of activities. It must be recognized, however, that job enlargement may be interpreted by some employees as "job overload," and that in such instances, it is possible that attempts at job enlargement might actually result in diminished employee productivity. Job enlargement often occurs adventitiously when supervisors seek out their most productive staff members to increasingly take on unanticipated tasks or projects or to fill in during periods of fiscal crisis.

Job Enrichment: Job enlargement generally seeks to enhance the scope of tasks performed by an individual worker; job enrichment, on the other hand, focuses on the enhancement of job depth by augmenting the individual's responsibility for and autonomy in planning, work performance, and decision making. Often referred to as "vertical job loading," job enrichment approaches generally are concerned with adding employee-valued tasks and responsibilities to the worker's currently existing work requirements. "Research has shown that those individuals with strong needs for growth, achievement, and esteem usually respond favorably to job enrichment."[57]

While job enrichment might seem to present the potential for an ideal working environment for employees and managers alike, consideration should be given to a number of pragmatic issues in the implementation of these approaches. The effectiveness of job enrichment approaches is ultimately dependent upon the mutual willingness and ability of 1) the employee to be challenged and 2) of the manager to offer appropriate work restructuring opportunities to meet perceived employee challenges which are subject to change over time. The manager must be prepared, therefore, to be engaged in a process of continuous and dynamic job restructuring if changing worker needs and interests are to be met effectively. Needless to say, the size of the job group pool involved in job enrichment approaches can further complicate the process. It has been noted that "attempts to enrich jobs are often frustrated by union constraints"[57] through insistence on restrictive job descriptions, tenure requirements, and other work contract terms and conditions.

Job Rotation: This approach to work redesign, which seeks to offset potential job overspecialization and monotony, generally takes one of two major forms. In one instance, specific work functions are systematically rotated among selected groups of workers, while in the second, workers are rotated through various service units, departments, or facilities under the agency's aegis for varying periods of time on some predetermined time schedule. Job rotation has long been recognized as a viable technique for preparing individuals to assume positions of increased responsibility and authority within an agency or organization and it has been recognized as "an important means of developing managers . . . through the work they perform."[58]

The basic intent of job rotation practices is to expose individuals to the wide range of activities and services that are inherent in the organization's make-up and to help them to become increasingly aware of "the various problems of different departments, the need for coordination, the informal organization, and the interrelationships between objectives of different subunits of the organization."[59] There is little doubt that "this knowledge is vital to success in higher-level positions,"[60] and it is becoming increasingly clear that job rotation approaches can have significant implications for personnel at other levels as well. It has been noted, particularly in the arena of leisure service delivery, "a strong case can be made for applying job rotation on all levels of an organization."[61]

One potential drawback to this approach could occur among employees who are rotated on a pre-planned time schedule. They may, under certain conditions, experience limited opportunity to derive the personal satisfaction and group recognition that accompanies completion of specific projects. Implementation of job rotation approaches, however, may be particularly useful for recreation and leisure service delivery systems where job assignment needs may be seasonally, cyclically, or situationally mandated. Additionally, job rotation approaches can provide the leisure service manager with alternative means for: 1) orienting and training personnel; 2) maximizing the knowledge, skill, and competency potentials of full-time personnel by assigning them to different facilities, geographic sites or locales, or population groupings on the basis of anticipated seasonal or situational needs; 3) assuring that special events, projects, and special programs are given appropriate staffing and supervision; and, 4) providing effective leaders with opportunities for supervisory experiences by coordinating programs predominantly staffed by part-time or seasonal personnel.[62]

Career Management: This comprehensive approach to professional development is designed to assist management and personnel at all levels to identify and develop diverse and alternative pathways for the individual's potential growth, development, and career advancement *within* the organization.[63] Career management approaches effectively incorporate diverse components of the job design process, job analysis procedures, and work redesign approaches and strategies as viable and achievable career development and advancement criteria.

Public recreation and leisure service delivery systems have typically organized personnel structures on a three-tier model including: administrators (executive or top level management); supervisors (secondary or middle level management); and, leaders (activity or group leaders, therapists, or specialists).[64] A more recent trend in personnel structuring has been to identify job levels and responsibilities on the basis of a generic functional classification at three different levels of responsibility described as: *managerial* units (including both top and middle management positions); *logistical* units (including staff, support, and resource positions); and, *operational* units (including all line personnel who are directly responsible for carrying out programmatic and plant operation activities).[65]

Career management approaches are ultimately intended and designed to mutually facilitate the organization's use of personnel knowledge, skill, and competencies to the fullest of their potential and to "help individuals to use their capacities to the fullest"[66] in their quest for career development.

Flex-Time Arrangements: Increasingly, agencies and individual personnel face lateness and absenteeism problems arising from the inevitable conflicts which arise between fixed work tours and personal needs relative to family commitments, requisite child care arrangements, commutation schedules, and continuing education activities, among others. One approach to resolving such conflicts has been the adoption of alternative working hour arrangements, variably called "flextime," "flextour," or "gliding time," under which many employees are now "able to fine tune their full-time work hours to better fit their needs."[67]

Flex-time arrangements are generally applicable to full-time employees and are predicated on the work assignment needs of the particular agency and its service delivery programs. While the concept of flex-time arrangements has largely flourished in the insurance, credit, and other information processing industries, some approaches, such as the "four-forty" work week (in which an employee works 10 hours daily for four working days) has become prevalent in such areas as nursing and in numerous institutional settings.

An essential component of implementing effective and efficient flex-time scheduling is the agency's or department's ability to clearly identify those hours of the working day in which the bulk of the anticipated workload is likely to be demanded. While flex-time permits employees to set individual working schedules, these must coincide with the identified "core time" specified by the agency or program. For example, "if core time is designated as 10 a.m. to 3 p.m., one worker might report at 8 a.m. and leave at 4 p.m. Another might start at 10 a.m. and leave at 6 p.m."[68] When considering flex-time arrangements in the recreation and leisure service sector, it is essential that management clearly identify not only specific program and client contact needs, but also related preparation and activity closure time needs.

Job Sharing: While many of the previously described work redesign approaches have had their roots in the industrial sector, job sharing is a phenomenon whose "first inroads were made in the early 1970s when human-service personnel such as social workers, parole officers, and teachers found job sharing to be a way to ward off job burnout."[69] Once established and the benefits to employers and employees alike began to be recognized, job sharing strategies were rapidly adopted for many clerical posts, some professional level positions, and ultimately in private industry.[70] By the beginning of the 1980s, best guesses suggested that thousands of Americans were already engaged in some form of job sharing.[71]

Job sharing is a work redesign approach which effectively provides managers with "an innovative plan that coordinates two part-time workers in a post formerly held by one full-time worker."[72] Job sharing approaches appear to have specific implications for the recreation and leisure service sector which already has a rich tradition of employee part-time and seasonal specialists to meet program needs. Job sharing strategies include scheduling variations ranging from an actual half-time division of the work day to split-week, week on and week off, or other fractional divisions of the workload assignment for any given position. Job sharing is a far more complex concept than simply breaking up one full-time position into two part-time or specialist positions. The position in question continues to be viewed as a single job with alternative incumbents and time arrangements for its fulfillment. It is imperative, therefore, that careful attention be paid to recruiting and hiring two job-share team members who can demonstrate the compatibility necessary to maintain the established integrity and viability of the shared position. There is little question that, in the case of mismatched or poor pairings, the ultimate effectiveness of job sharing efforts could be undercut.[73] Another important point for consideration is the establishment and maintenance of an effective communication system between and among job-share team members, co-workers, and management. "Though hours may vary greatly from team to team, all job sharers must work out ways to make the work transaction as smooth as possible."[74] Some tested alternatives include: building into the respective time schedules some brief overlap time; the regular use of logs or journals; and, regular telephone conferences to facilitate better communications and "to help tie up loose ends, monitor current projects, and plan for the future."[75]

While job sharing approaches may require additional paper work, processing time, and the allocation of additional funds for increased employee benefits of each job sharer, Grossman states: "Some employers have found a number of clear-cut benefits to supporting and encouraging this new work pattern,"[76] including, among others:

- a drop in absenteeism as individual employees are better able to manage and schedule personal and family commitments;
- increased ability to retain experienced employees when their life-status and family needs undergo change;
- decreased need to bring in inexperienced personnel as "built into

most job-sharing arrangements is the understanding that should the scheduled member of the team fall ill, the other will pinch hit"[77].

- reports of increased productivity predicated on the perception that, in general, "on the days they report, job sharers are full of fire and vigor. They give you full measure."[78] Additionally, "job sharing underscores an old maxim: Two heads are better than one."[79] One observer notes that, in general, "two people brainstorming and problem solving [can] be more beneficial than one . . . and two people are more likely to catch possible errors"[80];

- an effective recruitment tool for attracting entry-level professionals and for retaining or returning to the work force skilled retirees. "Many companies now view job sharing as a sound way to protect a major investment: their employees"[81]; and,

- a means for accomplishing the nearly impossible task of staffing the same job in two places at the same time during peak periods.[82]

Job-share approaches provide specific benefits not only to employers and managers but, they offer current and potential employees considerable opportunities for planning variations in their work patterns as personal and family commitments and needs change over time. It is not surprising that "many working mothers, two-career couples, students, and retirees on fixed incomes" have already discovered "that part-time, shared jobs are an appealing way to balance budgets, career and family concerns, and the emotional need to work with the longing for free time."[83]

While the job share options appear to have many potential benefits to management and employees alike, some consideration should be given to selected potential drawbacks in the implementation of such strategies. The first of these relates to the potential for managerial abuse of the approach. For example, while it has been found that "many employers are prorating benefits for job sharers—splitting health and dental packages and vacation time—others provide almost no fringes."[84] Other observers, most notably union officials, share the concern that "some employers may use job sharing to get overtime hours without paying overtime wages."[85] The second point for consideration is based in the "part-time stigma that job sharers sometimes suffer."[86] Societal and organizational stereotypes, prejudices, and preconceptions surrounding part-time workers and their presumed undercommitment to work often serves as deterrent for organizations and potential job-share employees to derive the full potential benefits of this approach.

Management by Objectives (MBO): Generally defined, MBO is a systematic, broadly based participatory management process for setting organizational goals, determining priorities, developing operational objectives, and implementing strategies to achieve the agency's primary social goal of meeting diverse constituency expectations. MBO processes are generally predicated on the assumptions that: (1) human behavior is rational, (2) individuals feel greater commitment to meeting objectives when they participate in the planning as well as implementation aspects of a job, and (3) devolution of authority to the smallest units in the work process is both viable and desirable.

Work redesign approaches utilizing MBO strategies generally seek to relate and integrate required employee tasks and responsibilities with the specific units of work determined to be necessary in achieving predetermined agency objectives. Such an approach demands considerable employee and management flexibility. However, by virtue of the broad-based participatory involvement required of personnel at all levels, it has generally been found to be an effective restructuring approach.

MBO process includes several essential, interacting components; the absence of any one of the components serving to render the system inoperative. Significant components of the process are briefly described as follows[87]:

- *Objectives.* These should be described in precise and measurable terms. Specific questions to be addressed include: (1) What will be done?; (2) When will it be done?; and (3) Who will do it?
- *Plans.* Having established objectives and having considered a diversity of possible alternative strategies, selection decisions are enacted at the appropriate managerial levels and a step-by-step action plan or "blueprint" is drawn. Plans established should include: (1) justification for assumptions made and for alternatives selected, (2) a time referenced agenda for the completion of specific tasks, and (3) criterion-referenced measures to assess whether or not predetermined objectives have been met as planned.
- *Managerial direction and action.* This component is concerned with the implementation phase of the process. It refers to the establishment and practice of appropriate managerial direction and guidance strategies to assure the effective completion of tasks undertaken. The manager's functions are, of necessity, broad and include: (1) organizing, (2) communicating, (3) motivating, (4) coordinating, and (5) developing and enhancing requisite skills among personnel assigned to predetermined tasks. It should be noted that the manager in MBO systems generally serves as "a director of processes rather than as boss of operations."[88]

- *Control and Monitoring.* This component is specific to each aspect of the MBO process. Consideration of monitoring and control methods to be utilized should begin at the initial step of objectives-setting and should continue throughout the process. Specific evaluation concerns generally include: (1) the feasibility of priorities established, (2) the viability of objectives to be achieved, (3) specific quantitative and qualitative criteria which will be used to determine the degree to which objectives have been achieved, (4) the establishment of appropriate time frames for evaluation; (5) assignment of specific personnel who will assume responsibility for completion of tasks identified; and, (6) determination of to whom evaluation data and results or analyses will be directed and communicated.
- *Feedback.* Like evaluation, feedback should be an ongoing activity throughout the MBO process. It is concerned with the communication of information at each step of the process in order to check the validity of priorities and objectives and to permit alteration or modification of strategies as deemed necessary or appropriate.

By virtue of its broad-based participatory process, MBO approaches can offer an effective base for the establishment of "mini-contracts" between managers and employees for the completion of expected work tasks and for the conduct of ongoing progress and evaluation meetings. As it provides specific quantitative and qualitative criteria for assessment of employee performance within specified periods of time, the MBO process can serve as a means of supplanting often unwieldy merit systems for conducting employee evaluations.[89] MBO processes generally permit and encourage, and, in actuality, demand that employees exert variable levels of control or experience different degrees of freedom in determining and carrying out implementation strategies adopted to meet the predetermined objectives. Given increased control of the immediate working environment, each employee is effectively encouraged to consistently monitor his or her performance in relation to the predetermined time frames and quantitative and qualitative criteria established. Work environments operating under MBO systems, additionally, tend to reduce direct supervisory or "surveillance" time required of managers and to support cooperative team efforts among coworkers.

SUMMARY

Adoption and implementation of appropriate job design, job analysis, and work redesign strategies have significant implications for recreation and leisure service managers who must 1) assume responsibility for the effective and efficient allocation of their agency's unique human resources and 2) continually strive to attain the ideal goal of tailoring "the supply of workers to fit the exact need of the job situation, day by day and week by week."[90] It is anticipated that by adopting and implementing appropriate approaches, managers will be able to more effectively:

- identify changing needs with regard to the number and type of personnel required and their appropriate allocation and assignment;
- plan for assignment of personnel to tasks which may variably be considered as relatively permanent, transitional, or temporary in nature;
- identify specific employee assets or limitations in the completion of required tasks and to identify which employees may be considered "key" personnel at various stages of the service delivery process;
- identify personnel training and development needs and to determine their priority in relationship to stated agency objectives;
- enhance employee commitment to agency goals and objectives and to the effective and efficient delivery of service to designated clients and respective constituencies;
- provide ample opportunity to delegate appropriate authority, responsibility, decision-making, and monitoring functions to varied individuals at the most immediate points of action at the time of occurrence of those actions;
- provide effective measures for assessing employee performance in a diversity of tasks utilizing appropriate predetermined quantitative and qualitative criteria;
- enhance employee job satisfaction through meaningful participation in the objective-setting, implementation, and monitoring phases of the service delivery process;
- plan for the accommodation of both individual and agency needs with regard to work tasks and scheduling in the changing organizational environment; and,
- facilitate development of increasingly needed "multi-specialists," (persons skilled and knowledgeable in a given area who will be able to transfer these skills into other areas as required), rather than to proliferate the development of "mono-specialists" (whose specializations may become obsolete at any given time).[91]

Recreation and leisure service delivery systems function in rapidly changing and frequently unstable social and organizational environments which challenge managers to develop increased sensitivity and skill in carrying out their mandated responsibilities. As Toffler has so aptly noted: "The problem is not . . . to suppress change, which cannot be done, but to manage it."[92]

NOTES AND REFERENCES

1. Alvin Toffler, **Future Shock.** (New York: Bantam Books, 1971).
2. Ibid., p. 379.
3. Edgar H. Schein, **Process Consultation: Its Role in Organizational Development.** (Reading, Massachusetts: Addison-Wesley Publishing Co., 1969), pp. 10–11.
4. Peter J. Pecora and Michael J. Austin, **Managing Human Services Personnel. Sage Human Services Guides, Volume 48.** (Newbury Park, California: Sage Publications, 1987), p. 12.
5. Richard G. Kraus and Joseph E. Curtis, **Creative Management in Recreation, Park, and Leisure Services.** Fourth edition. (St. Louis, Missouri: 1986), p. 143.
6. Pecora and Austin, p. 10.
7. Ibid., p. 12.
8. Ibid.
9. Ibid., p. 8.
10. Kraus and Curtis, p. 143.
11. Ibid.
12. Dale D. McConkey, **MBO for Nonprofit Organizations.** (New York: AMACON, 1975), p. 6.
13. Jong S. Jun, "A Symposium: Management by Objectives in the Public Sector," **Public Administration Review** (January/February, 1976), p. 6.
14. Pecora and Austin, pp. 8–9.
15. McConkey, p. 4.
16. Toffler, passim.
17. Jun, p. 4.
18. Ibid.
19. Peter F. Drucker, "A Symposium: What Results Should You Expect? A User's Guide to MBO," **Public Administration Review** (January/February, 1976), p. 14.
20. Schein, pp. 10–11.
21. Drucker, p. 16.
22. Ibid., p. 18.
23. Schein, p. 126.
24. Pecora and Austin, p. 10.

25. Marvin D. Dunnette, **Personnel Selection and Placement.** (Belmont, California: Brooks/Cole Publishing Co., 1966), p. 2.
26. Ibid., p. 7.
27. Pecora and Austin, p. 13.
28. D. James Brademas and George Lowrey, **Conducting a Job Analysis: A Systematic Procedure. Management Briefs.** (Champaign, Illinois: Management Learning Laboratories, 1984), p. 3.
29. Dale Yoder and Herbert G. Heneman, Jr., eds. **ASPA Handbook of Personnel and Industrial Relations—Volume I: Staffing Policies and Strategies.** (Washington, DC: The Bureau of National Affairs, Inc., 1974), pp. 4–39.
30. Ibid.
31. Kraus and Curtis, p. 111.
32. Ibid.
33. Yoder and Heneman, pp. 4–72.
34. Brademas and Lowery, p. 2.
35. Ibid., p. 3.
36. Ibid., p. 4.
37. Ibid.
38. Ibid.
39. Yoder and Heneman, pp. 4–72.
40. Kraus and Curtis, p. 114.
41. Brademas and Lowery, p. 5.
42. Kraus and Curtis, p. 114.
43. Dunnette, p. 70.
44. Ibid., pp. 70–71.
45. Ibid., pp. 71–72.
46. Michael H. Mescon, Michael Albert, and Franklin Khedouri, **Management.** Third edition. (New York: Harper & Row Publishers, 1988), p. 636.
47. Ibid.
48. Ibid.
49. Ibid.
50. Ibid., p. 639.
51. Toffler, p. 94.
52. Mescon, Albert, and Khedouri, p. 636.
53. Ibid., p. 673.
54. Ibid., p. 636.
55. Ibid., p. 673.
56. Kraus and Curtis, p. 143.
57. Mescon, Albert, and Khedouri, p. 639.
58. Ibid., p. 632.
59. Ibid., pp. 631–632.

60. Mescon, Albert, and Khedouri, p. 632.
61. Kraus and Curtis, p. 150.
62. Ibid.
63. Mescon, Albert, and Khedouri, p. 632.
64. Kraus and Curtis, p. 112.
65. Ibid., p. 114.
66. Mescon, Albert, and Khedouri, p. 632.
67. John Grossman, "Working in Tandem," **American Way**. (April, 1982), p. 39.
68. Management Learning Laboratories, **Management Strategy**. (Fall 1988, Vol. 12, No. 3), p. 6.
69. Grossman, p. 39.
70. Ibid.
71. Ibid.
72. Ibid., p. 37.
73. Ibid., p. 45.
74. Ibid.
75. Ibid.
76. Ibid., p. 39.
77. Ibid., p. 41.
78. Ibid.
79. Ibid.
80. Ibid.
81. Ibid., pp. 41–43.
82. Ibid., p. 41.
83. Ibid., p. 39.
84. Ibid., p. 47.
85. Ibid.
86. Ibid.
87. McConkey, pp. 13–16.
88. Harry E. Moore, Jr., "Management by Objectives," **Social Agency Management, I** (July, 1975), p. 8.
89. McConkey, pp. 27–28.
90. Kraus and Curtis, p. 151.
91. Toffler, p. 288.
92. Ibid., p. 379.

PART THREE
Managing Professional Personnel

The purpose of this chapter is to help the manager answer:

- When a position becomes vacant should it just be filled?
- Why waste time writing position descriptions?
- What is included in a position description?
- Where does one recruit prospective employees?
- Are nondiscrimination and affirmative action the same?
- What is, and what is not, discriminatory in the selection process?
- What tools are available for screening and selection?
- How does one conduct a selection interview?
- Why make reference checks?
- Can the panel interview, the group selection interview, and the personnel assessment center be of value in selecting employees?
- What constitutes sexual harassment in the workplace?
- Are pregnancy and childbirth considered disabilities in terms of an agency's benefit plan?

Chapter 6

Recruiting and Selecting Professional Personnel

Arnold H. Grossman
and Marie B. Ray

Human resources are the most valuable assets of recreation and leisure service agencies. Without competent professional personnel, even the best funded and equipped agency cannot provide the quality of service the consumers have a right to expect and receive.

The recruitment and selection of professional personnel are two aspects of personnel management that are performed inadequately by executives and supervisors. The problem appears to be related to the "people factor" involved and to the resulting lack of ability to develop an infallible set of procedures to accomplish the tasks. Consequently, managers come to assume that personal judgment and intuition are sufficient. Personal traits, an arbitrarily set educational level and number of years of previous experience, or scores on a test, become meaningful determinants for filling a position to which they have limited, if any, relevance.

The purpose of this chapter is to provide a discussion of the factors and techniques that can serve as guidelines to managers for ascertaining personnel needs, recruiting, and selecting professional personnel in recreation and leisure service agencies. The chapter includes the following topics: determining personnel needs, establishing position descriptions, recruitment techniques, affirmative action considerations, tools and methods for screening, the selection process, and nondiscrimination in the workplace.

DETERMINING PERSONNEL NEEDS

Most recreation and leisure service agencies have determined work tasks that have to be carried out to achieve their essential purposes. These tasks are clustered into relatively homogeneous jobs and positions are created for people who can carry out the work tasks of a job. The positions are grouped and placed in a hierarchical order to create an organizational structure commonly depicted in an organizational chart. (See Chapter 4 for discussion of organizational structures and charts.)

When a position becomes vacant, a manager should explore certain factors before attempting to select a person to fill the vacancy: Are the job functions of this position essential to the agency or department? Can these job functions be carried by existing personnel without detriment to their current functions? Could the agency continue providing needed services if the position were not filled? If the manager answers the first question in the affirmative and the second and third questions in the negative, he or she should review the job's functions and skill requirements. The duties of the job, the expected performance level, the skills and other qualifications should be presented in a new or revised position description. (See Chapter 5 for a discussion of job design and analysis.)

Position Descriptions: Position descriptions assist the manager in recruiting and selecting the right persons to carry out particular job tasks. If one knows what he or she expects of a person who will fill a position, it becomes easier to decide on the sources of recruitment and on the right person from among the applicants. In addition, a position description will help to inform applicants what is expected of them. Over and over again one hears the classical statement, "If I had known what this was all about, I would never have taken this job." Uncertainty about job requirements is a major source of job dissatisfaction. A written position description can avoid this; and, it will bring an understanding of the job to the employee, the manager, and other personnel in the agency. Verbal descriptions, on the other hand, often lead to misunderstandings, confusion, and an overlapping of effort.

Position descriptions are useful in other ways: (1) They assure prospective employee applicants that the agency is efficiently administered and that concern for its personnel is uppermost in its thinking; (2) they give status to the position and assist in building pride in the employee toward his or her job; (3) they provide the manager and the employee with a readily available reminder of the work tasks for which the employee is responsible; (4) they provide a blueprint for planning future personnel needs; (5) they provide a manual for interpreting the whole personnel picture to the board of directors, to the consumers of the service, and to the community at large; and (6) they serve as an objective basis for staff appraisal.[*1]

Position descriptions should contain six major informational areas:

1. Title of position.
2. To whom employee is responsible.
3. General responsibilities, including for whom the employee is responsible.
4. Specific duties or examples of work to be performed.
5. Qualifications, e.g., education, specific skills and knowledge, experience required.
6. The relationship of the position to others in the department and the total agency, e.g., one of five Program Supervisors reporting to the Program Director. A seventh area is included on the position descriptions of some agencies. It has been titled "Effect on End Results" or "Objectives to Be Achieved," growing out of the concept of management by objectives.[**] This area of the position description is written each year and provides concrete criteria for the appraisal of the employee. The task of writing this section yearly allows the manager and the employee to review and to change, if necessary, the general and specific duties included in the description so that the description remains a viable and useful tool. (See Figures 6.1, 6.2, and 6.3 for sample position descriptions.)

The previous discussion assumed that the recreation and leisure service agency had position descriptions or was filling a vacancy. Some agencies, however, do not have position descriptions for the current employees. If such is not the case, the executive officer needs to implement the process of job design and analysis (as discussed in Chapter 5).

Part-time and seasonal employees: In determining personnel needs, the manager should decide which work tasks can be clustered into jobs that can be accomplished by part-time employees. Traditionally, in recreation and leisure service agencies these include: group leaders and assistants; activity specialists in music, dance, drama, arts, crafts

---

*For a further discussion of the use of position descriptions for staff appraisal, see Chapter 13.

**For a further discussion of management by objectives, see Chapter 5.

PQR RECREATION AGENCY

POSITION DESCRIPTION

POSITION TITLE: Recreation Leader, Specialist, or Instructor
REPORTS TO: Supervisor or Assistant Supervisor where appro-
                   priate in youth, pre-teen, or teen programs
SUPERVISES: None, except volunteers as assigned
DEPARTMENT: Youth and teen
JOB SUMMARY: Under supervision of a supervisor or an assistant
                   supervisor, plans and organizes the recreation
                   program for the area to which he or she is assigned.
                   Responsible for leading all recreation activities.

PRINCIPAL DUTIES AND RESPONSIBILITIES

1. Plans and organizes the recreation program for assigned area.
2. Leads recreation activities, group discussions, encourages participation, and/or teaches leisure activity skills.
3. Supervises and assigns volunteers to assist in activities.
4. Responsible for the advising and counseling of individual clients
   or client groups.
5. Works with other recreation staff in assessing clients' needs and
   interests as a basis for program planning.
6. Responsible for reporting the progress of clients and records
   the progress in the appropriate case record.
7. Assists in developing a plan for and is responsible for evaluating
   all recreation activities or instructional courses.
8. Assists in maintaining orderly and clean areas after activities.
9. Responsible for demonstrating and operating all recreation
   equipment and supplies.
10. Responsible for orientation to, and safety in, program areas.
11. Assists in the administration of the recreation program for
    assigned area.

REQUIREMENTS

1. Bachelor's Degree in recreation, leisure studies, or related field.
2. Knowledge of, and skills in, recreation programming, activities,
   and leadership, with a minimum of two years full-time recreation experience.
3. Possess the necessary certifications where indicated by activi-

ties, e.g., water safety instructor, registered therapeutic recreation specialist.

4. Degree may be waived for part-time instructors only if individuals can demonstrate appropriate skill levels in recreation as well as possessing the experience that can be documented in their field of specialization.

Figure 6.1. Sample position description for full- or part-time staff persons.

---

and sports; life guards; tutors; and program aids in game-room or lounge activities. A common pitfall is assuming that position descriptions need not be written for these jobs. The same positive aspects or negative factors will result from having or not having position descriptions, respectively, for these jobs as for full-time employees. In fact, the negative results might be more devastating as the part-time personnel are just that, part time; and, their limited time at the agency limits their perspective of the day-to-day, as well as overall, operation of the agency and their relation to it and the other employees.

The nature of the service provided by recreation and leisure service agencies shifts with the seasons. Generally, there is a greater demand for service during the summer months with school vacations and more adults on their annual vacation leaves. The addition of annual summer programs, such as play streets and day and resident camps; special programs, such as outings, picnics, weekend and week-long trips; and outdoor recreation programs, such as swimming, boating, and sports leagues require additional personnel. Managers often fall into the trap of assuming that the right employees will come along as the summer approaches and that they can be selected without position descriptions on the basis of personal judgment. "It's only for the summer" becomes the rationale. Many an established and respected program has turned into a disaster because of this thinking, with resulting loss of reputation of the program and the manager.

Volunteers: Many work tasks in recreation and leisure service agencies have been carried by volunteers. In fact, many services of some agencies would have to be eliminated if it were not for the use of volunteers. Managers have to determine the specific work tasks that can be accomplished by volunteers. A volunteer service program can be initiated.*

---

*For further discussion of volunteer programs, see Chapter 14.

ABD RECREATION AGENCY

POSITION DESCRIPTION

TITLE: Group Worker
INCUMBENT: _____
REPORTS TO: Program Director
ASSOCIATION: New York City
BRANCH: Misty Branch
DATE: _____

GENERAL FUNCTION

Under supervision of the Program Director, the Group Worker provides leadership, supervision, and instruction using group work process for specific rostered, age-graded youths.

KNOW HOW

The incumbent must have knowledge of and/or experience in group work process: knowledge of needs of children, peer relationships, and dynamics of family life. A knowledge of community resources, identifying and establishing working relationships with families and referral agencies and ability to work in unstructured situations are required. Experience in, or knowledge of, basic program planning and leading recreation activities for children (ages 8 to 17) is necessary.

PRINCIPAL ACTIVITIES

Recruits member youth from membership of United Committee, ABD, and community making use of natural groupings wherever possible from ABD building, schools, community service organizations, streets, and playgrounds.

Organizes youth into cohesive groups which will meet regularly with worker (once weekly) and have two additional contacts weekly.

Plans, organizes, implements with the groups and supervisor, within framework of program objectives, a variety of meaningful regular ongoing recreation activities tailored to specific needs of each group.

Refers youth to appropriate persons and services for assistance.

Records, and provides a record of, group activities, interactions, and worker activities, as directed.

Instructs and leads activities and classes for United program participants.

Participates and attends, as a member of the United Committee staff, those staff meetings and training events of the United Committee and ABD agency.

EFFECT ON END RESULTS

1. There are 15 or more youth enrolled in each group with regular participation by all and having one group and two additional weekly meetings with all group members. (Full-time workers, 4 groups each; part-time workers, 2 groups each.)
2. There is a meaningful variety of regularly scheduled, well-planned events, classes, and recreation activities for each group.
3. The individual group members are counseled, referred, and helped as needs require.
4. Referral services are followed up to successful conclusion.
5. Recordings are of good quality and timely.
6. Group Worker functions in helping co-workers and cooperates with other staff and organization associates.
7. Worker establishes facilitating relationships with community organizations, families, and professionals within the ABD organization.

Figure 6.2 Sample position description for a full-time staff person.

RECRUITMENT AND SELECTION

Recruiting and selecting are the first steps in the manager's attempt to build a team of competent employees to provide the services of the recreation and leisure service agency. The manager has to develop a plan to recruit and select employees with the long-term objectives of the department or agency in mind. In order to accomplish this, the manager has to consider the previous experience, age, years of service, promotability, pay scales, and job development of the current employees as he or she recruits and selects new employees. If employees are too similar in the above noted factors, the manager has not ensured the long-term health of the department or agency.[2]

Recruitment: The recruitment plan begins with the writing of the position description. The next step is to write an abbreviated position description or position specifications, which can be used for the mass media, bulletin boards, and fliers. The position specification should include: (1) the title of the position, (2) a general description of the

KLM RECREATION AGENCY

POSITION DESCRIPTION

POSITION TITLE: Recreation Assistant
REPORTS TO: Supervisors or Assistant supervisor, where appropriate, in youth, pre-teen, or senior center programs.
SUPERVISES: None.
DEPARTMENTS: Youth and teen or senior center
JOB SUMMARY: Assists Recreation Instructor, Leader, Specialist, or Assistant Supervisor in conducting recreation activities as directed by the Program Supervisor.

PRINCIPAL DUTIES AND RESPONSIBILITIES

1. Assists in the planning and the implementation of the recreation program for an assigned area.
2. Assists in leading recreation activities and group discussions and encourages client participation.
3. Assists in developing a plan and in evaluating all recreation activities with other recreation staff and/or other agency staff.
4. Assists in maintaining orderly and clean activity areas.
5. Responsible for demonstration and operation of recreation equipment and the proper utilization of supplies.

REQUIREMENTS

1. Associate Arts Degree (2 year degree) in recreation, leisure studies, or related field.
2. One year of experience assisting in the instruction and leading of recreation activities.

Figure 6.3 Sample position for a full-time staff person.

duties and responsibilities, (3) the qualifications required, (4) the starting salary or salary range, (5) the expected date of employment, and (6) to whom one addresses inquiries regarding the position.

The manager must then identify those sources where potential applicants for the position can be made aware of its availability. In large organizations, personnel departments advertise and screen applicants for available positions; however, in small agencies the executive and managers must assume these tasks. The following have proven to be beneficial sources for recruiting professional employees by personnel departments and managers alike:

- Referral and employment agencies, public and private.
- Colleges' and universities' placement services and bulletin boards in departments of recreation, leisure studies, social work, music, dance.
- Professional journals and newsletters.
- Job marts at professional conventions.
- Local newspapers.
- National newspapers.
- Employee referrals.
- Cooperative fieldwork, internship, or work study programs with colleges and universities.

Nondiscrimination and affirmative action.[3] It is at this point in the recruitment and selection process that nondiscrimination and affirmative action requirements must be considered.

The Civil Rights Act of 1964 was designed as a national statement against discrimination in occupations, voting, use of public facilities, and public education on the basis of race, color, religion, sex, or national origin. Title VII of the Civil Rights Act of 1964 regarding nondiscrimination in employment was amended by the Equal Employment Opportunity Act of 1972, which extended the coverage of the act, created the Equal Employment Opportunity Commission, and stated additional rules, regulations, and enforcement procedures. The main concept embodied in these acts is that of nondiscrimination.

Nondiscrimination requires the elimination of all existing discriminatory conditions, whether purposeful or inadvertent. Employers, employment organizations, training programs, and labor organizations must carefully and systematically examine all of their employment policies to be sure that they do not, if implemented as stated, operate to the detriment of any persons on grounds of race, color, religion, sex, or national origin. These organizations must also ensure that the practices of those responsible in matters of employment, including all supervisors, are nondiscriminatory. These requirements apply to all persons, whether or not the individual is a member of a conventionally defined minority group. In other words, *no individual* may be denied employment or related benefits on the grounds of his or her race, color, religion, sex, or national origin.

The Age Discrimination in Employment Act of 1967, as amended in 1978, prohibits discrimination against workers between 40 and 70 years of age. This act applies to local, state, and federal governments and to employers with 20 or more employees. In addition it eliminates mandatory retirement for federal employees.[4]

Executive Order 11246, as signed by President Johnson on September 24, 1965, and as subsequently amended (Executive Order 11375), imposes equal employment opportunity requirements and affirmative action requirements on those signing federal government contracts or subcontracts. The Vocational Rehabilitation Act of 1973, and as subsequently amended in 1974, extended these protections to "handicapped individuals," and the Vietnam-era Veterans Readjustment Assistance Act of 1974 did the same with regard to such veterans.[5] Consequently, these embody the concept of nondiscrimination, as described above, and the concept of affirmative action.

Affirmative action requires the contractor to do more than ensure employment neutrality with regard to race, color, religion, sex, and national origin. It requires employing organizations to make additional efforts to recruit, employ, and promote qualified members of groups formerly excluded, even if that exclusion cannot be traced to particular discriminatory actions on the part of the employer. In essence, affirmative action is designed to further employment opportunities for women, minorities, and those in legally protected groups. The premise of the affirmative action concept is that unless positive action is undertaken to overcome the effects of systemic institutional forms of exclusion and discrimination, a benign neutrality in employment practices will tend to perpetuate the *status quo ante* indefinitely.

It is important to note that no attempt is being made to indicate the specific details of the Acts and the Executive Order and to whom their coverage applies. The coverage, rules, and regulations differ according to such aspects as organization auspices (public and nonpublic), size of work force, size of contract, and are changed periodically by amendment or court decision. Consequently, it is suggested that each executive or manager of a recreation and leisure service agency investigate and become informed of the legal obligations regarding his or her specific operation.

It is advocated that every recreation and leisure service agency establish personnel policies and practices which adhere to the concepts of nondiscrimination and affirmative action whether it is public or nonpublic, whether it has a small or large number of employees, whether or not it has a government contract. The nature of such organizations should dictate a humanistic approach to service which would be violated if the concepts of nondiscrimination and affirmative action were not embodied.

Screening: The five traditional tools used in screening applicants for a position are: the application, the resume, the interview, the reference check, and employment tests. Each of these will be discussed in the following sections.

The application. The application for employment is used to request basic information about the applicant. Consequently, it should include sections on personal data, including medical history, educational background, previous employment record (including the names and addresses of past and present employers), personal references, and hobbies, interests, and activities. The application should be attractive in appearance, concise, clearly indicate the information which is requested, and provide ample space for the information to be recorded. In designing an application, one must be cognizant of avoiding questions which may lead to discrimination, e.g., date of birth or age; maiden name; Mr., Ms., Miss, or Mrs.; religion, date of marriage, sex. If, however, this information is needed for a bona fide occupational qualification, national security laws or other legally permissible reasons, it may be requested. It becomes incumbent upon the employer to provide the justification and supporting data which clearly indicate that the information requested is for a *bona fide occupational qualification.* (Bona fide occupational qualifications may relate to sex, religion, national origin, age or handicap. Race and color are not permissible exceptions under law.) A suggested format for an application which meets the legal requirements with regard to nondiscrimination is illustrated in Figure 6.4.

The resume. Some recreation and leisure service agencies request that a resume be enclosed with the application for employment, while others request such when they desire to obtain additional information on an applicant in whom they are interested. Some agencies use the resume as the initial screening form and send an application to those who meet the basic requirements for the position according to their resume. Whatever the sequence, if a resume is requested, it is suggested that agencies develop a list of items which are to be included in the resume. A sample list of items and their suggested sequence is illustrated in Figure 6.5. Again, one must be certain to avoid any items which may lead to discrimination unless a bona fide qualification for employment can be established in relation to the item.

APPLICATION FOR EMPLOYMENT

PERSONAL DATA (Please print clearly)

Name_____Date_____
       Last   First   Middle

Address _____
        Street   City   State   Zip

Telephone _____ Social Security # _____

Are you under 18 years of age or over 70 years of age?

_____

How were you referred to (name of agency)?

_____

Have you previously applied to (name of agency)? _____

If yes: When? _____ Where? _____

Person to be notified in case of emergency.

Name _____

Address _____
        Street   City   State   Zip

Telephone _____

Have you been hospitalized or treated by a doctor during the last five years? _____

If yes, where and for what reason? _____

_____

How much time have you lost from work or school because of illness during the past two years? _____

_____

Are you presently under a doctor's care or have any physical defects which preclude you from performing certain kinds of work? _____

If yes, explain. _____

_____

Position or type of work desired _____

Salary expected _____

EDUCATION

Type of School	Name and Address	No. of Years	Did You Graduate	Course(s)/Major	Degree Rec'd
High School					
College					
Post Graduate					
Business or Trade					
Other					

Latest Scholastic Standing: Grade average _____

Rank in class _____ out of _____ .

Scholastic Honors (Honor Societies, Prizes, Scholarships, etc.)

_____

_____

Hobbies, Interests and Activities

_____

_____

EMPLOYMENT RECORD

Former Employers (List below last five employers, starting with last one first.)

Date Mo. & Yr.		Name and Address	Supervisor's Name	Major Duties	Reason for Leaving
From	To				
From	To				
From	To				
From	To				
From	To				

Have you ever been discharged from employment, or have you ever resigned after official notice that:

(A)   Your conduct was not satisfactory?   (Yes or No)

(B)   Your work was not satisfactory?   (Yes or No)

Have you ever been convicted by any court in any jurisdiction? _____
If yes, answer in detail under remarks.

Have you ever served in the U.S. Military?   (Yes or No)

PERSONAL REFERENCES

List two persons, not relatives or former employers, who are well acquainted with you.

Name	Address	Occupation	Years Known

REMARKS

Use this space to record any explanations or supplementary information you may wish to submit.

_____

_____

_____

_____

I authorize (name of agency) to investigate all statements in this application and to contact all employers and references. I understand that false or misleading statements in this application will be sufficient cause for dismissal if employed.

Date	Signature of Applicant

Figure 6.4 Sample application for employment which meets nondiscrimination requirements.[6]

OUTLINE FOR RESUME

I. *Personal Data*

Name
Address—include zip codes
Telephone number—include area code

II. *Education and Training* (most recent first)

A. University(s) and college(s)—include various curricula, major and minor(s), and degree(s) received.

B. High school(s) name, address, major and minor subjects, diploma received.

C. Workshops, institutes, in-service training programs attended within the last five years—include names, location, dates.

D. List scholarships, honors, awards, or professional registrations or certifications.

E. List school/campus activities (student government, interest groups, clubs, offices held, etc.)

III. *Professional Experience* (most recent first)

List all full-time and part-time professional work within the last 10 years, including both paid and volunteer. Include name of agency, address, name and title of immediate supervisor, and dates of work.

IV. *Other Work Experience* (most recent first)

List all other work experience within the last 10 years, both full time and part-time. Include name and type of firm and dates of work.

V. *Professional Memberships*

List memberships in professional organizations. Include offices held, committee memberships, and dates.

VI. *Publications* (oldest publications first)

Provide an orderly chronological bibliography of any books, articles, monographs, reports, or other publications written by you.

VII. *Interests and Activities*

Special skills (music, art, athletic), interests, hobbies, clubs, organizations. Include unusual experiences or accomplishments.

VIII. *References*

List two persons who are well acquainted with you. Do not include relatives or former employees. List full names, addresses, telephone numbers, and the number of years they have known you.

Figure 6.5 List of items and suggested sequences for a resume.

Although some of the items requested in the resume duplicate those in the application form for employment, when it is utilized as a first screening device, the organization and presentation of the resume can provide important clues about the applicant. For example, is the resume typed neatly or written sloppily on a piece of paper torn out of a notebook? Is the information provided under each item logically organized, or is it listed in a helter-skelter manner? If an application for employment is utilized, is the information in the resume consistent with that provided in the application? Some of these same questions should be raised when one looks at the cover letter which is sent with the resume, if one is included; its absence should also be noted. The absence of a cover letter with a resume is analagous to a manager sending a report, a budget or a proposal without a letter of transmittal.

The interview. Time is one of the most precious commodities of any manager in a recreation or leisure service agency. Consequently, one should only interview those applicants who meet the stated qualifications for the position. A review of the applications and resumes while comparing the qualifications listed with those indicated in the position description will yield a list of potential applicants to be interviewed. Closer scrutiny of their applications and resumes will help to further narrow the list of persons. For example, is the statement of salary expected much too high in comparison to what can be offered? What was the applicant's average length of stay in previous employment? Is there a rapid change of positions? What reasons were given for leaving previous employment?

Once the list of potential applicants to be interviewed has been established, the following sequence of events should take place:

1. Schedule the interviews. This step appears to be simple and procedural; however, one must make certain that the date, time, and place selected will be convenient to the applicant as well as to the manager. In addition, quiet, privacy, freedom from telephone interruptions, and a comfortable setting are prerequisites which are not always easily obtained in recreation and leisure service agencies.

2. Prepare for the interview in advance. The manager should review the position description, the qualifications listed for the position and the applicant's application and resume. An interview plan should be established. In other words, determine the areas in which information is needed, e.g., what did the applicant do the two years for which no education or work history is listed; determine the areas that need further explanation, e.g., what were the specific responsibilities and tasks of a recreation supervisor in XYZ recreation agency; determine the areas which need to be explored, e.g., why is the applicant applying for a position with teenagers at the present time when previous work history indicates many years of working with senior citizens? Finally, determine the method of rating the skills and qualifications of the applicant in comparison to those required by the position.

3. Conducting the interview. Welcome the applicant and try to put him or her at ease. A person coming for a job interview is usually nervous, knowing that the responses given may or may not get him or her the position. The normal courtesies of hanging up a coat, offering coffee or tea, as well as a comfortable chair are the first steps in the correct direction; however, they are not sufficient. The objective should be to help the applicant relax and to establish a rapport with the interviewer. The weather is commonly suggested as a starting place, but is a mundane topic. A more appropriate place to start, especially with an applicant for a position in a recreation or leisure service agency, may be with his or her hobbies, interests or recreation participation. Be specific and start with one of those listed on the application or resume. Such an approach has a number of advantages. It demonstrates to the applicant that the material which he or she submitted has been read and it serves as an "ice breaker" because it is something chosen by and personal to the applicant.

Once the applicant has a chance to relax and to get acquainted with the interviewer, the interviewer should move on to the substance of the interview. If one spends too much time with small talk, the applicant will become uneasy, thinking that serious consideration is not being given to his or her candidacy for the position.

The interview must be a two-way process. The manager has to obtain information about the applicant and the applicant has to receive information about the position; consequently, the interview should involve giving and receiving by both parties. Various strategies have been suggested to accomplish the objectives of job interviews. The following hints based on those provided by Ellis, et. al.[7] are representative:

a. Listen more than you talk. Don't disagree with or criticize the applicant or his or her opinions.
b. Choose your questions carefully. Avoid leading questions which provide the applicant with the expected answers. Use open-ended questions that begin with what, how, when, where, why and who rather than questions that can be answered by "yes" or "no."
c. Observe how statements are made as well as what is said. Nervous gestures or mannerisms, as well as hesitations, may be important clues in assessing the significance of the comments.
d. Try to avoid "halo" and bias effects, i.e., don't let one incident or factor color your assessment of all other factors. A positive halo effect can be an unfair bias to the applicant and to you.
e. Look for patterns of success or failure or for temperamental characteristics of behavior. Whatever a person has done in the past is a good indicator of what he or she will do in the future.
f. Keep note taking to a minimum during the interview. The applicant will not mind, in fact he or she may expect you to make some notes; however, too many notes will take too much of the interviewer's time and will most likely distract the applicant and may cause him or her to talk less.
g. Conclude the interview when you have received the information which you need and the applicant has received the necessary information on the position; however, if it becomes clear that the applicant is unsuitable for the position, end the interview as early as possible. If the applicant has the potential for such a position in the future, make it clear that you would like to see him or her again after obtaining additional education, skills, or experience or for a more suitable position.
h. Watch for closing remarks, even after the formal interview is finished. The applicant is usually completely relaxed at this time and will often say what he or she is really thinking. Some revealing comments may be made by the person upon exiting.
i. Thank the applicant for coming and giving of his or her time, and see the person to the door. Tell the candidate when a decision is likely to be made.

After the interview is over, the manager should reflect on it and expand his or her notes on the applicant. It is further recommended that the manager create a rating form which he or she would complete on each candidate. In this instance, pertinent questions refer to items which are directly related to the job requirements. Objective criteria should be established for rating the responses to these questions. The use of a rating form provides two distinct advantages: (1) it enables the manager to compare applicants for the position in relation to objective criteria; and (2) it provides evidence in the event an applicant, who is not selected, decides to litigate the manager on discriminatory practices.

The reference check. John Doe secured a position as a supervisor in a child care agency in Pennsylvania. He was not liked or respected by his colleagues and was considered a bit odd. After questionable job-related decisions were made by him, the administration of the agency instituted a job review. As part of the review, the administration ascertained that Mr. Doe was indeed at the local state hospital, which he listed on his application; however, he was not a member of the staff, as claimed, but a patient. Indeed, he was a "missing" patient! This factual anecdote indicates the necessity of making reference checks.

All reference checks should be in writing. A standardized form mailed to the person listed is the appropriate method. Never make a reference check with an applicant's present organization without his or her permission in writing. The details of any interview with the organization considering the applicant should be kept confidential. It is not ethical to indicate them to the manager of the applicant's present organization, and it may damage the person's career if he or she is not subsequently selected.

All references should be checked. Previous employers can verify the applicant's work record as well as the person's performance and accomplishments. *Never accept unreservedly either the positive or negative reference of one previous employer.* The professional reference, on the other hand, is the key to the applicant's professional being. Professional colleagues of the applicant provide information regarding his or her standing in, and commitment to, the recreation and leisure service profession. Involvement in professional organizations, as well as the candidate's contribution to the field in terms of quality of service and writing, are important attributes, especially as one recruits for higher-level positions. An additional type of reference is the personal reference. This type of reference provides information about the applicant "off-the-job." The person's relation to applicant, e.g., minister, friend, social club member, as well as the length of the relationship, are important factors to consider in weighing the validity of this reference.

Employment tests. Although not prevalent in recreation and leisure service agencies, industry has used various types of tests, i.e., paper and pencil, oral, performance, as screening tools in the selection process with the most prevalent of these being the psychological test. If an employer decides to use a test to predict employee performance on the job, he or she must establish the relevancy of the test to that job.

The U.S. Supreme Court in the 1971 case of *Griggs vs. Duke Power Company* held that the use of test scores and credentials to select employees was a violation of Title VII of the 1964 Civil Rights Act when (a) this selection system resulted in under-representation of minorities and (b) the employer could not show a relationship between test scores or credentials and performance on the job.[8] Employment tests may be useful for managers in hiring some workers. For example, a candidate for the position of recreation leader or a tennis instructor might be asked to conduct an actual session with a group of clients while assessors with rating forms observe the candidate. The ratings forms then should be combined and evaluated.

Personal judgment and subjective criteria. Although not usually mentioned as a criterion for employment or promotion, personal judgment and subjective criteria are usually included in the screening process and affect the final decision. Employers must be certain that such criteria do not lead to discrimination. The United States Supreme Court, on June 29, 1988, issued a ruling related to this topic. It ruled "in Watson v. Fort Worth Bank and Trust . . . that the use of subjective job criteria, even if adopted by the employer without any intent to discriminate, may violate the Federal civil rights laws if the practical impact of the criteria is to deny employment opportunities to certain protected groups."[9] Ms. Watson, a black woman, was denied four promotions to supervisory positions at the bank. Each time a white employee was selected for the promotion by a white supervisor. The bank had relied on the subjective judgment of existing supervisors who had knowledge of the candidates and the nature of the job to be filled. "The Court agreed that subjective considerations which result in unintentional discrimination are no less insidious than their objective counterparts."[10]

The Selection Process: The selection process is as important to the new employee as it is to the manager and the recreation and leisure service agency. It is time to put the pieces of the screening process together, to weigh them with regard to each applicant and to make a decision.

Through the screening procedures, those who lacked the essential qualifications, according to their application or resume, were rejected. Those who were obviously unsuited to the job were rejected at the interview stage. During the reference check, those who displayed poor job progress or the inability to get along with others were disqualified. If an employment test was utilized, those with too low or too high scores were rejected. Consequently, the most qualified have reached the final stage. If one applicant does not emerge as the employee who will fit, i.e., who can and will do the job well, second comprehensive interviews should be held with the most likely candidates. If sufficient information is gathered to make a final choice, a job offer should be made. If accepted, a contract, letter of agreement, or letter of appointment should be issued. If a decision cannot be reached at this time, as none of the applicants will fill the position adequately, it is better to reinstitute the recruitment and selection process rather than employ an individual who will be a liability to the organization, the manager and the consumers of the service.

Alternate Interview Procedures: The most traditional and feasible procedure for interviewing applicants for positions was presented. There are, however, two other types of interview procedures which may be advantageous for use by members of boards of directors, executive directors, and managers in recreation and leisure service agencies. The two alternate procedures are the panel interview and the group selection interview.[11]

The panel interview. This basically is the same as the individual interview, however, the applicant is questioned by a panel—usually three or more people. This method is sometimes used when appointment has to be made by a board of directors or some other group of people. It may save time for the agency and for the applicant who might have to go through a series of interviews, and it may minimize the danger of the ineffectual sole interviewer; however, it is very difficult for the interviewers to establish rapport with the applicant and the interviewing situation is usually artificial.

The group selection interview. In this situation, a number of applicants (numbers may vary from 4 or 5 up to 20) are observed by a selection panel in various group activities, e.g., leaderless group activities, leader-directed activities, committee work, group discussions. The selection panel makes its decision using its observations as well as information gained from other screening devices. Sometimes a group ballot is distributed to the applicants themselves and they indicate whom they think is best for the position, and this becomes additional information for the panel to use in arriving at its decisions. Although this might be a useful technique if a manager or executive is selecting people to fill a number of positions or group leaders, it is administratively cumbersome, time consuming, (usually lasting from one to three days), and may be costly. On the other hand, most applicants enjoy this method more than others and feel they had a fair chance at getting the position. In addition, it finds the most suitable candidates more frequently than any other method.

The Personnel Assessment Center:[12]   The personnel assessment center formalizes and objectifies some of the techniques discussed under the group selection interview. In addition, it is broader in scope as its purposes are not only related to selection but to placement, promotion or development, or some combination of these factors. Brademas states that "the assessment center provides a means of gathering relevant information, under standardized conditions, about an individual's capabilities to perform a job."[13] In essence, it uses In essence, it uses simulation exercises which are designed to measure and identify various management skills, and characteristics, e.g., decision-making, planning, behavior flexibility, written and oral communications, perception, and analytic ability. The exercises, which are developed, are based on a thorough analysis of the job requirements. Ideally, according to Brademas,[14] only six candidates should be assessed at one time; and, they are evaluated by trained assessors who are experienced managers. When the assessment is complete, each assessor writes a comprehensive narrative report on each candidate's performance based on his or her observations, interviews with the candidate, and the results of the paper and pencil tests utilized. The manager utilizes the information contained in the reports to make his or her decision regarding selection, placement, promotion, or development. A feedback session is held with each candidate when appropriate, e.g., placement, development.

NONDISCRIMINATION IN THE WORKPLACE

In addition to the nondiscrimination issues and requirements enumerated earlier (which affect recruitment, selection, training, promotion, and termination), there are two others—primarily related to the protection of women—which must be discussed: sexual harassment and pregnancy. (Another topic which could have been included in this section is HIV infection and Acquired Immune Deficiency Syndrome (AIDS); however, since it has been previously discussed in Chapter 3, the reader is referred to it.)

Sexual Harassment: "Sexual harassment is the imposition of unwanted sexual requirements on a person or persons within the context of an unequal power relationship."[15] It is a form of discrimination and in violation of Title VII of the Civil Rights Act of 1964 as well as guidelines issued in 1980 by the Equal Employment Opportunity Commission (EEOC).

"In terms of the workplace, sexual harassment occurs when a person who is in a position to control, influence, or affect another person's job, career, or grades uses the position's authority to coerce the other person into sexual acts or relations or punishes the person if he or she refuses to comply."[16] Precedents have been established to interpret sexual harassment as a form of sexual discrimination. Although the large majority of the lawsuits related to sexual harassment in the workplace have seen men as the harassers, we should not be blind to the fact that as more women are employed in high management positions, the opposite can occur.

The EEOC established three guidelines for determining sexual harassment in the workplace:

- Submission to the conduct is made either an explicit or implicit condition of employment;
- Submission to or rejection of the conduct is used as the basis for an employment decision affecting the harassed employee;
- The harassment substantially interferes with an employee's work performance or creates an intimidating, hostile, or offensive work environment.[17]

Managers should be proactive in prohibiting sexual harassment in the workplace, especially since the EEOC holds employers responsible for such behavior. They should see that there is a written policy prohibiting sexual harassment in the personnel policies of the agency; and they should make it clear to all employees that the policy exists and the established grievance procedures of the agency would maintain confidentiality if an employee files a complaint against another employee. Every supervisor and manager should be aware that knowledge of sexual harassment without taking corrective action places the agency in violation of the law.

Pregnancy: The Pregnancy Discrimination Act of 1978 was designed to eliminate discrimination against pregnant women. It focuses primarily on employee benefit plans and requires that women employees receive the same disability benefits as any other disability when they are affected by pregnancy, childbirth, or any other related medical condition.[18]

The EEOC, in a policy directive issued October 3, 1988, stated that employers may not fire women or refuse to hire them because of suspicions their exposure to chemicals or radiation on the job may some day cause reproductive or fetal damage. "A policy that expressly excludes women on the basis of pregnancy or capacity to become pregnant on its face discriminates against women on the basis of sex in violation of" an amendment to the Civil Rights Act. To justify such exclusions, the EEOC said, employers must support them with "reputable, objective, scientific evidence" that a hazard adversely affects the potential offspring only through the female parent and not the male.[19]

SUMMARY

Fundamental principles and key tasks were presented on recruiting and selecting professional personnel for recreation and leisure service agencies. A systematic approach was outlined, including: determining personnel needs, writing a position description, establishing a recruitment plan taking affirmative action requirements into consideration, the five tools utilized for screening applicants, and the selection decision. The object of the process is to introduce skilled and competent people into the agency, and it is the responsibility of managers to obtain the right person for the right job under the existing circumstances. There are no pat answers to recruitment and selection, but following the systematic procedures outlined in this chapter should help managers make more knowledgeable hiring decisions.

Managers should continually try to improve their batting averages in the areas of recruitment and selection. They should continually follow up to see whether their assessments of work capability and forecasting have been correct; and, where they have not, they should try to improve on them. Observations regarding employee turnover, performance evaluation interviews, and exit interviews when employees resign can provide important feedback to the recruitment and selection processes. On the positive side, one can examine the applications of the employees who are successful in their positions to analyze and determine those factors that influence job stability and job success. Weighting these items on the applications of prospective employees can help to establish criteria for job success in a particular recreation or leisure service agency.

As part of the recruitment and selection processes, the concepts of nondiscrimination and affirmative action were discussed within the context of the legislation and executive orders which brought them into being. Additionally, two discrimination issues primarily related to the protection of women were discussed: sexual harassment and pregnancy.

NOTES AND REFERENCES

1. Based on "Why Job Descriptions," **Camp Administrative Forms and Suggested Procedures in the Area of Personnel.** (Martinsville, Ind.: The American Camping Association, Inc., 1956), p. 6. (Out of print.)
2. Robert M. Fulmer, **Principles of Professional Management.** (Beverly Hills: Glencoe Press, 1976), p. 220.

3. The basic information was obtained from Dale Yoder and Herbert G. Heneman, Jr., **ASPA Handbook of Personnel and Industrial Relations: Vol. I, Staffing Policies and Strategies.** (Washington, D.C.: Bureau of National Affairs, Inc., 1974), p. 4–8, 4–109; and U.S. Department of Health, Education and Welfare, Office of the Secretary, Office for Civil Rights, **Higher Education Guidelines: Executive Order 11246.** (Washington, D.C.: Office for Civil Rights, Department of Health, Education and Welfare, 1972.)

4. J. Halloran, **Supervision: The Act of Management.** (Englewood Cliffs, N.J.: Prentice-Hall, 1981), p. 307.

5. A. Frakt and J. Rankin, **The Law of Parks, Recreation Resources, and Leisure Services.** (Salt Lake City, Utah: Brighton Publishing Co., 1982), p. 225.

6. Designed by and printed with the permission of Joan Ridolfi, Affirmative Action Coordinator, Chemical Leaman Tank Lines, Inc., Downington, Pennsylvania, 19335.

7. C. R. Ellis, R. E. Taylor and R. S. Rudman, **Personnel Practice: A Guide for Effective Supervision.** (Wellington, New Zealand: Hicks Smith and Sons Limited, 1975), p. 34.

8. See Griggs v. Duke Power Company, 91 USS Ct., 849, (March 1971).

9. J. J. Bannon, Jr. and L. B. Bannon, "Legal Commentary: Employment Discrimination Developments," **Management Strategy,** Vol. 12, No. 3, Fall 1988, p. 3.

10. Ibid., p. 4.

11. Presented by C. R. Ellis, et al., p. 36.

12. This section is based on: D. James Brademas, "The Personnel Assessment Center: A Viable Approach When Selecting Recreation and Park Staff," **Management Strategy** 2, Fall 1978, p. 1.

13. Ibid.

14. Ibid., p. 6.

15. D. E. Maypole and R. Skaine, "Sexual Harassment in the Workplace," **Social Work,** September-October 1983, p. 385.

16. Ibid.

17. Equal Employment Opportunity Commission, "Guidelines on Discrimination Because of Sex, Title VII, Sec. 703," **Federal Register,** 45, April 11, 1980, p. 2505.

18. J. Ledvinka, **Federal Regulation of Personnel and Human Resource Management.** Kent Human Resource Management Series, R. W. Beaty, consulting ed. (New York: Van Nostrand Reinhold Company, Inc., 1982), p. 30.

19. "Ruling on Sex Bias Curbs Employers," **The New York Times,** October 4, 1988, p. A25.

The purpose of this chapter is to help the manager answer:

- Is orientation training all there is?
- Is experience the best teacher?
- Do employees get all the training they need at workshops and conferences?
- Can all employees be trained at the same time?
- Are lectures, meetings, and readings sufficient and effective training methods?
- Who is responsible for development training and retraining?
- Are supervisory conferences an effective method of training?
- Does a lack of training cost money?

Chapter 7

Training and Development of Personnel

Arnold H. Grossman

Almost all managers recruit, interview, select and hire the most qualified and capable employees to improve or maintain the quality of their working forces. This alone, however, is not sufficient. They must establish a systematic training and development program. Nevertheless, many managers in recreation and leisure service agencies abdicate this important training responsibility. The underlying reason appears to be related to the lack of knowledge and skills in the area of training, although many rationalizations are given:

- I have hired qualified people and they will learn what they have to know on the job. Experience is the best teacher.
- The agency has a personnel or training department. It is not my job.
- I do not have the time to train new employees. They have to do it on their own. They will either "sink or swim."
- They get better training working with experienced employees, so I assign them to work with John or Jane.
- They get all the training they need at workshops and conferences, so I give them release time to attend.

Those managers who are "forced" by their agencies to conduct training programs usually approach them with a limited or negative view. The training programs conducted by these managers are usually no more than glorified orientation meetings on personnel policies and procedures, (not to say that orientation in this area is not an important part of the training program), or "this is how it is done in this agency." The philosophy underlying the latter approach is similar to that of a lion tamer in the circus: "When I give the signal, I want you to do this in this way!"

A competent and skilled work force is the most important "tool" of a manager as he or she attempts to achieve the objectives of the recreation and leisure service agency. The results that the manager will achieve in relation to quality of service are directly related to the quality of training provided for new employees when they begin their positions and to experienced employees as they develop in their current positions or move to new ones.

"Training is teaching employees skills that will make them more effective in their current jobs. The ultimate objective of training is to ensure that the organization will always have a sufficient number of people with the skills and abilities needed to attain the organization's objective."[1] The primary responsibility for training is the manager's. No person in the agency has a better knowledge of the competencies of the employees, their deficiencies, and their training needs in relation to the job that is to be accomplished than the manager supervising them.

The purpose of this chapter is to present a systematic approach for the training and development of personnel in recreation and leisure agencies. The approach is based on the following tenets:

- Training should be planned, scheduled, and systematically implemented;
- It should be based on the needs of the individual(s) in relation to the demands of the job; and
- The best-known methods of teaching should be selectively used as they may apply.[2]

The chapter will be organized as follows. Some principles of training will be presented. These are to be followed by a discussion of the common errors made in implementing training programs. Then, four types of employee training will be outlined. The chapter will conclude with a discussion on methods of training.

PRINCIPLES OF TRAINING

Van Dersal[3] enumerates six principles of training managers need to know and understand if they are to fulfill their training responsibilities. These principles are:

Principle One: People must be interested in learning before they will accept training.

Principle Two: Training must be suited to the individual needs of those being trained.

Principle Three: Training must be done either by a supervisor or under his direction.

Principle Four: The rate of training should equal the rate at which an individual can learn.

Principle Five: People learn by being told or shown how to do work, but best of all from doing work under guidance.

Principle Six: Training should be planned, scheduled, executed, and evaluated systematically.

Utilizing these principles as the guideposts for designing and implementing all types of employee training programs will enable managers to initiate effective training delivery systems. The "how's" are to be decided by managers depending upon the training requirements of the employees, the objectives of the training, the type of training, and the content of the training. Some of these aspects will be discussed later in the chapter.

COMMON ERRORS IN TRAINING

Some of the "common errors in teaching employees their jobs" outlined by Boyd[4] result from a violation of the principles of training presented above, while others occur because managers or trainers lack the knowledge or skills necessary for effective teaching. Possessing the knowledge and skills necessary to perform a task or fulfill the responsibilities of a position in a highly competent manner does not ensure that one can *teach* them.

The common errors in training are being presented to highlight the pitfalls which every manager should strive to avoid. These are:

- Feeding Too Much at One Time: Presenting too much information or details to employees so fast will result in its not being assimilated. Because managers know the information or the job so well, they think that such can be quickly received by the trainees.
- Telling Without Demonstrating: Words mean different things to people and often present barriers to learning. While trying to understand one concept, the employees have missed the following two or three. Employees not only must receive the word message, but they must be able to visualize what is expected.

- Lack of Patience: Some people learn at a fast pace, while for others it is a slow process. When managers or trainers become impatient with employees, they create tension. Tension slows the learning process, which leads to further impatience. A vicious cycle develops.
- Lack of Preparation: Distractions, inhibition of learning, and confusion are caused by the manager or trainer who has not prepared the presentation in a logical sequence, who has forgotten materials, or who has to backtrack constantly.
- Failure to Build in Feedback: Training requires two-way communication. If managers or trainers do not build in mechanisms for feedback, they know what they presented, but they do not know what the employees learned.
- Failure to Reduce Tension: New employees are anxious resulting from the unknowns of the situation. Anxiety and tension inhibit learning. Managers and trainers must develop techniques to reduce tension. Refreshments, funny stories, learning more about other new employees, the manager, and their co-workers often help trainees to reduce tension.

TYPES OF TRAINING

Four types of employee training are being presented: orientation training, in-service training, development training, and retraining.

Orientation training: Orientation training is a systematic scheme aimed at introducing new employees to the recreation and leisure service agency; its objectives, organization, and policies; the employees' place in the organization; their co-workers; and the role expectations of their positions.

Managers, whether they realize it or not, begin orientation training during the selection process. While managers interview more than one person for each position, the new employee is usually interviewed by only one person in the organization, namely, the manager. The approach to the interview by the manager, as well as the preparation for the interview and method of conducting it, make a certain impression upon the prospective employee, and first impressions carry over for a long time. They may affect an employee's attitude toward the manager, the organization, toward his or her job, and expected job satisfaction. In addition, managers usually provide information regarding the agency's philosophy, objectives, salary structure, and fringe benefits in general terms.

Every new employee in a recreation and leisure service agency should receive orientation training. Whether the person who is selected is a division director, maintenance person, secretary, supervisor, clerk, leader, or typist, he or she is new to the particular organization. New employees are eager to do well in their positions, to establish meaningful working relationships with their supervisors and coworkers, and to learn the expectations of their positions and the importance of their roles in the functioning of the agency. They want to learn about the organization, to become part of it, and to identify with it. They have not only taken a new position with the agency, but have embarked on a career. Consequently, they are attentive, open-minded, and receptive to training.

The important fact for the manager to realize is that employees work for intrinsic as well as extrinsic rewards. Certainly, the pay check, the hospital and disability benefits, social contacts, (extrinsic rewards), are important; however, the sense of achievement and satisfaction, which can be obtained from working in the agency; the appreciation and recognition shown for work done; opportunities for interesting and challenging work and for involvement in decision-making; as well as opportunities for professional growth, (intrinsic rewards), are vital to employees. The orientation training is an opportune occasion for emphasizing the intrinsic as well as extrinsic rewards available to employees.

When persons work for primarily extrinsic rewards, the manager and agency get a fairly consistent level of performance, but not an enthusiastic and committed effort. Additional efforts must be bought by an increase in the extrinsic rewards. When employees work for intrinsic as well as extrinsic rewards, the manager and agency can usually expect a creative work effort accompanied by a high degree of commitment performed in a consistent manner. Too many managers fail to capitalize on the opportunity that the initial training provides for building a creative and committed work force by designing their orientation training focus primarily on the extrinsic factors in the work situation.

The major topics usually discussed in orientation training include:

1. Agency history, structure, services.
2. Area and clients served by the agency.
3. Agency policies and regulations.
4. Relation of managers and personnel department.
5. Rules and regulations regarding:
    a. Wages and wage payment.
    b. Hours of work and overtime.

   c. Safety: accident prevention and contingency procedures.
   d. Holidays and vacations.
   e. Methods of reporting tardiness and absences.
   f. Discipline and grievances.
   g. Uniforms and clothing.
   h. Parking.
   i. Identification badges.
6. Economic and recreational services such as:
   a. Insurance plans.
   b. Pensions.
   c. Recreation services and opportunities and the use of recreation equipment and facilities.
7. Opportunities:
   a. Promotion and growth.
   b. Job stabilization.
   c. Suggestion and decision-making systems.[5]

A "Department Checklist for New Employees" (see Figure 7.1) was developed by one agency as a method of ensuring that the relevant information for that organization's orientation was covered. It is presented as a guide.

In conjunction with the previous discussion regarding intrinsic rewards, it is suggested that the manager might include the following as part of the orientation training:

1. Unique programs or services of the agency.
2. Model programs or services which are being adapted or used by other agencies.
3. Case histories demonstrating success stories.
4. Opportunities for designing and initiating new programs and services.
5. Opportunities for involvement in decision-making.
6. Opportunities for involvement in short- and long-range planning.
7. Opportunities for professional growth.

These suggestions are presented to stimulate thinking in this area of training and to emphasize its importance. Obviously, each agency has to design and develop such topics in relation to its unique situation.

In-service training: In-service training is the planned process of improving the performance of employees in their present jobs. It is aimed at teaching people the necessary knowledge and skills so that they can fulfill the expectations of their positions with the highest degree of competence possible; and, it is aimed at maintaining them at that level.

DEPARTMENT CHECKLIST FOR NEW EMPLOYEES

EMPLOYEE _____ DEPARTMENT _____

FIRST DAY OF WORK _____ DEPARTMENT HEAD _____

POSITION _____

In order to provide complete information and proper orientation of the new employee to your department and agency, you are requested to cover the information on this checklist with him/her, during the first three weeks. Each item should be checked in the space provided at the time discussed before returning to the Personnel Office.

FIRST DAY

- Hours: starting and quitting time, total per week, work schedules. _____
- Lunch period and rest periods. Arrange for someone to go to lunch with him/her. _____
- Pay: every other Friday, date employee will receive first pay check. _____
- Absence and tardiness: Inform employee to call you as early as possible, explaining effects of absence and tardiness on smooth functioning of the department. _____
- Tour of Department. Introduce employee to co-workers, briefly explaining the work they do. _____
- Explanation and use of department time clock, time card rack, sign in books. _____
- Information regarding facilities. Rest room location, work supplies, bulletin boards, locker room and locker assignment, cafeteria. _____
- Uniforms (where applicable). Laundry service and supply center location. _____
- Dress and appearance policy. _____
- Safety. Alert employee to hazards associated with your work area and procedure to follow in event of accident. _____
- Health Service. Procedure if employee becomes ill or is injured while on duty. _____
- Fire and evacuation. Alert employee to his/her responsibilities.

DURING FIRST THREE WEEKS

- Organization of Department and function. Duties and responsibilities of Department Head and Supervisor(s), and the work and services the Department performs.   _____
- Employee's job and how it relates to others in department and agency in general. Review job description with employee.   _____
- Stress open-door policy and importance of discussing and solving problems immediately.   _____
- Review of agency and Department rules and policies. (Refer employee to handbook during discussion.)   _____
- Probationary period. 3 months duration. Explain standards of performance. Stress importance of good work and attitude. _____
- Equipment. Discuss care and proper usage of any equipment employee will work with on the job.   _____
- Discipline. Alert employee to policy.   _____
- Telephone courtesy and limitations on personal calls.   _____
- Courtesy and behavior with clients and visitors.   _____
- Confidential Information. Employee should not discuss client information with co-workers, friends, relatives or strangers.   _____
- Disaster Plan Procedure.   _____
- Detailed job instruction. Follow-up and make corrections when necessary.   _____
- Job-related Problem Solving. Encourage new employee to feel free to chat with you, his Department Head or a member of the Personnel Department about any problems related to his job.   _____
- Employee Handbook. Make sure employee has received it.   _____

BENEFITS (Refer to Employee Handbook)

- Holidays.   _____
- Vacation and eligibility.   _____
- Hospitalization.   _____
- Life Insurance.   _____
- Pension.   _____
- Sick Leave.   _____
- Death in family.   _____
- Jury Duty.   _____
- Recreation program.   _____
- Employee Committee and events planned.   _____
- Educational Assistance Program.   _____

All of the above items have been discussed with the employee.

Department Head _____ Date _____

All of the above items have been discussed with me and are understood.

Employee _____ Date _____

Please return this complete form to the Personnel Department three weeks from the first day your new employee started to work.

Figure 7.1 Suggested checklist for orientation training.[6]

The intent of in-service training is to obtain and maintain a task force of fully productive employees. Van Dersal points out that: "Training costs money. *A completely untrained employee is the most expensive employee on the payroll,* since he is paid for practically no production at all. When he is at last fully trained, he is, as we say *earning* his pay. All during the time he was not producing as fully as a well-trained man should, the cost of what he *did* produce was higher than it would have been with a trained man."[7]

Once employees are trained, the task becomes one of keeping them at peak performance and up to date. Consequently, training opportunities should be provided which review previously learned knowledge and skills and which present new information, ideas, techniques, methods and developments in the recreation and leisure service fields. Also to be considered is motivating employees to continue their own professional growth and development, e.g., advanced education, attendance at professional workshops and conferences.

Development training: Development training is a systematic scheme to improve an employee's promotional opportunities. This kind of training is aimed at enhancing the knowledge, skills, and abilities of employees, so that they may fulfill the role expectations of positions higher in the organization's ladder. In fact, some recreation and leisure service agencies have designed career ladders. Unfortunately, all too often, climbing up the career ladder usually means accepting an administrative position. It is unfortunate, as many highly competent practitioners who dislike administrative duties and responsibilities are forced into administrative positions; and their practitioner skills are lost to the agency, to the employees who would be supervised by them, and to the clients who would be served by them. Consequently, it is suggested that dual career ladders be established, i.e., one track leading to administration and one track leading to increasingly higher levels of professional practice.

Development training programs must reflect the varying nature of the knowledge, skills, and abilities required as one climbs the organization tree; and it becomes necessary for the manager to personalize the development training. Consequently, the manager must know the employee, including his or her interests and ambitions; know the skills, knowledge, and attitudes necessary to undertake the position the employee seeks; appraise the employee's performance, including strengths and deficiencies; and appraise the employee's potential for the position with or without training. If training is required, this training represents the employee's development needs. The last step is to counsel the employee with regard to the above and to establish a plan for development training, which may include self-improvement as well as group and individual training.

Retraining: The impact of rapid technological growth and change in society with its concomitant effect on social engineering has had a tremendous impact on all aspects of life. Although the most radical changes can be observed in the industrial area of society, the impact on recreation and leisure services is also frightening, even though the changes have been more gradual. A few examples should suffice. Because of the discovery of the "pill," the concern for overpopulation, and legalized abortion in some states, the number of children as a proportion of the population has decreased. Consequently, the recreation or leisure service worker with a specialty in early childhood is less in demand. The aging proportion of the population, however, continues to grow as a result of advances in medical sciences, and automation has produced a continually growing number of unemployed adults as well as employed adults with more free time. Consequently, there is a need for the retraining of the youth worker in the knowledge and skills required for effective work with adults and the elderly. In another area, managers who were trained in the latest management skills and techniques now find themselves limited by the fact that computers have arrived on the scene. These managers are responsible for supervising computer operations with regard to registration, programming, budgeting, referral services, and the like. The point is made. There is and will continue to be a need for the retraining of employees.

Managers must accept a large degree of responsibility for retraining workers who have become redundant, (a term used by Ellis, et al., which appears to be preferable to obsolete). As Ellis, et al., point out,

"One of the difficulties in retraining the redundant workers lies in obtaining a satisfactory climate for learning. An employee who has been told that he is redundant will be under considerable stress—even though he may not show it. Therefore, in selecting any redundant worker for retraining, we should take into account not only whether he will benefit from the training we are offering him, (the 'can-do' factor), but also whether he is keen to learn and put his new skills into practice, (the 'will-do' aspect).[8]

Retraining will become an increasingly inherent part of recreation and leisure service agencies' training programs. As technological advances and automation continue to bring inevitable change, more and more recreation and leisure service workers will have to be trained in skills that were never envisaged when they accepted their positions.

METHODS OF TRAINING

Methods in and of themselves do not provide for the effective training of employees. Managers and trainers have to decide which of the following training methods, or which combination of methods, will provide the most effective results in achieving their various training objectives for a specific employee or group of employees.

Classroom training: This is one of the most common types of training. It assumes that a group of employees have the same training needs, which will be met by a single training program. Classroom training may be given within a recreation and leisure service agency if there is a sufficient number of trainees and a suitable room available. An alternative is for the manager to arrange for the employees to attend classroom-type training at another agency, at a coordinating agency, or at a university. The trainers may be managers from other agencies or consultants contracted to provide the training.

The advantages of classroom training are that it enables a large group of employees to receive training provided by a minimum number of instructors, (as compared to one-to-one training). This is also efficient and economical.

The training techniques used in classroom training include: lectures, guided discussion, case method, brainstorming, problem-solving, demonstrations, participative experiences, small-group discussion, film and slide presentations, charts and transparency projections, role playing, and videotaping.

On-the-job training: This type of training is usually conducted by the manager or delegated to a coworker. It is meaningful to the employee(s) as it occurs in the real situation and the manager is present to help and guide the employee(s). It provides the manager with an opportunity to assess the employee(s) and to offer the knowledge, the technical skills, and the encouragement so that the employee(s) can reach the desired standard of performance.

Simulation training: To try to avoid learning-by-exposure inherent in on-the-job training, some large recreation and leisure service agencies set up situations which simulate the real-life situation. These can be set up on an ad-hoc basis or can be part of a Personnel Assessment Center, as discussed in Chapter 6.

Assigned reading and programmed instruction training: Assigned reading is a useful training method to provide knowledge needed for job performance during orientation training. It is also a technique which can be utilized for providing new information and ideas in relation to in-service training, development training, and retraining. It is incumbent on the manager to assess the employees understanding of the material which was read.

Programmed instruction training is aimed primarily at the individual employee, although it can be utilized in groups. In programmed learning, the knowledge is organized in a logical sequence of modules. After reading each module, the employee is required to make a mental or written response which indicates that he or she understood and remembered the information presented. If the response is correct, the employee proceeds to the next module and if the response is incorrect, the employee is directed to return to the preceding module to obtain the correct response. Programs have been written for many areas, including the writing of behavioral objectives for use in designing and evaluating programs, medical terminology for use in working with the disabled, safety training, and others. Self-scoring tests in the areas of communication, use of time, delegation, and human relations training can be used in the same manner.

Supervisory conferences: The traditional supervisory conference is individual in nature. The manager directly responsible for supervising the employee meets with him or her on a regularly scheduled basis. The purpose of the conferences are: to communicate the supervisor's observations of the employee's performance in an on-going manner, to let the employee know the things he or she is doing well and those not done well, to suggest or demonstrate methods of improving performance, to suggest reading to enhance the employee's knowledge in relation to job performance, and to provide feedback whether or not improvement is demonstrated in areas indicated.

The supervisor can obtain information regarding the employee's performance from other than his or her own observation. Some of these include records submitted by the employees in the form of program reports or client assessments and evaluation, reports at staff meetings, and client evaluations of the employee. Conversations or meetings with clients, the employee's coworkers, and other supervisors also provide feedback to the supervisor; however, the validity and reliability of these must be investigated as some of these persons may have axes to grind and the information may prove to be biased or inaccurate.

Alternatives that substitute for or supplement, individual supervisory conferences are of growing interest. Some of these include group supervisory conferences, peer group supervision, team supervision, and the use of consultation.

Evaluation conferences: The evaluation process provides a formal mechanism for measuring an employee's performance against the requirements of his or her position. It is a formal review of the employee's strengths and weaknesses in comparison to performance standards. If the manager has been an effective supervisor during the evaluation period, there should be no surprises at the time of the evaluation conference. The strengths and weaknesses written in the evaluation should be those discussed during the on-going supervisory conferences. The components of the plan for improvement, in terms of improved job performance or development training, should have been discussed previously. The evaluation conference provides the opportunity of stating the plan in a written and formalized manner and provides a time span to measure growth or improvement, i.e., until the following evaluation conference.*

SUMMARY

The chapter emphasized that employees in recreation and leisure service agencies have to be trained in a planned, scheduled, and systematic manner if they are expected to perform up to standard. There is no reason for managers to think that employees will just crawl out from under a rock and be able to perform without any training at all.

Six principles of the training process were presented along with some pitfalls, such as feeding too much information at one time, telling without demonstrating, and failure to build in feedback. Four types of training, i.e., orientation, in-service, development, and retraining were enumerated. A discussion of common training methods, includ-

---

*For further discussion of performance evaluation and the evaluation conference, see Chapter 13.

ing classroom training, on-the-job training, simulation training, and supervisory conferences then followed.

The training of employees is the responsibility of the manager in a recreation and leisure service agency. Effective training produces a work force of employees who understand what it is they are supposed to do, who know how to do it, and who are able to do it. No manager should settle for less.

NOTES AND REFERENCES

1. M. H. Mescon, M. Albert, F. Khedouri, **Management,** 3rd ed. (New York: Harper & Row, Publishers, 1988), p. 625.
2. William R. Van Dersal, **The Successful Supervisor,** (3rd ed.) (New York: Harper and Row Publishers, 1974), p. 93.
3. Ibid., pp. 101–106.
4. Bradford B. Boyd, **Management-Minded Supervision,** (2nd ed.). (New York: McGraw-Hill Book Company, 1976), pp. 173–176.
5. Adapted from: Robert M. Fuller, **Supervision: Principles of Professional Management.** (Beverly Hills: Glencoe Press, 1976), pp. 223–224.
6. The "Department Checklist for New Employees" was submitted by a student as an example tool for orientation training in "Supervision of Recreation and Leisure Services," Department of Leisure Studies, New York University. Originating agency is unknown.
7. Van Dersal, p. 96.
8. C. R. Ellis, R. E. Taylor, R. S. Rudman. **Personnel Practice: A Guide for Effective Supervision,** (Wellington, New Zealand: Hicks Smith and Sons Limited, 1974), p. 84.

The purpose of this chapter is to help the manager answer:

- What is motivation?
- What have Maslow, McClelland, McGregor, Likert, Argyris, and Herzberg contributed to the understanding of motivation?
- What are the expectancy and equity theories of motivation?
- What is the Porter-Lawler model of motivation?
- Why do managers find motivating employees difficult?
- What characteristics do I have to develop as a manager to be effective in motivating employees?
- What do I have to learn about my employees to be effective in motivating them?
- What are some guidelines I can follow as a manager to be effective in motivating the employees who report to me?

Chapter 8

Developing and Implementing Motivation Strategies

Arnold H. Grossman

Suddenly Hopkins whirled and faced him. *"Somebody has to do the big jobs!"* he said passionately. "This world was built by men like me! To really do a job you have to live it, body and soul! You people who just give half of your mind to your work are riding on our backs."
"I know it," Tom said.

— Sloan Wilson, *The Man In The Gray Flannel Suit*

This conversation, or a similar one related to individual motivation, occurs in organizations frequently. Whether the two individuals are top-level managers, first-line supervisors, or a manager and a subordinate makes little difference.

The motivation of individuals in any organization is inherent in the job of every manager. And, unfortunately, most managers approach the task in terms of the "carrot and stick" strategy—with the "carrot" being the reward and the "stick" being fear. This strategy is based on the assumption that individuals are driven primarily by greed and fear, and they can be manipulated. Although much has been written on the subject of human motivation which indicates the fallacy of this approach, most managers continue to use it because it is the one with which they are most familiar (from their previous bosses or their parents); the one which simplifies human behavior (and therefore, makes sense to many); and the one which emanates from the belief that the authority of their positions will "motivate" (manipulate) an individual. Notwithstanding these justifications, the carrot-and-stick approach has only a short-term effect with certain individuals in specific situations. It is an attempt to do something to an employee rather than recognizing that motivation is not something a manager does to a subordinate, but rather a matter of creating an environment in which the employee takes some action on his or her own because of some desire to do so. Motivation comes from within.

Taking the word "motivation" literally, it is the process of arousing movement, or more specifically, behavior. "Motivated behavior is internally activated, but it can be modified by external conditions in an individual's environment."[1] And, in the work situation, "Motivating is the process of moving oneself and others to work toward attainment of individual and organizational objectives."[2] The effective manager is the one who can achieve organizational goals and objectives while providing opportunities for individuals to meet their needs. In a productive work environment, satisfaction of individuals' needs and meeting organizational goals are harmonious. If a manipulative manager tries to get people to meet organizational goals when they are contrary to individual needs, low productivity will result and employee turnover will probably be high. On the other hand, if a manager meets primarily individual needs to the detriment of organizational goals, the organization is doomed. Therefore, in a work situation, the manager attempts to create a motivating environment in which opportunities and appropriate goals are established to meet the needs of individual employees and which are directed simultaneously at accomplishing or meeting organizational goals.

Before we proceed with a discussion of the theories and models of motivation, there is an important point related to the use of the word "motivate" which needs to be clarified. Robinson et al. state it as follows:

> Since we have said that motivated behavior is internally activated, and that motivation comes from "within" in response to clues "outside" in the environment, it somehow seems contradictory to say that we "motivate" someone. However, "motivate" is a very convenient term, and we can use it if we operationally define it. When we "motivate," arouse, or stimulate a person to action, we are actually trying to change something about the environment in which a person does something, so that that particular thing will be more attractive, less repulsive, or less difficult.[3]

THEORIES AND MODELS OF MOTIVATION

Theories and models of motivation have emerged gradually over many years. In contrast to most accepted management theories, which were developed by observation of effective management practices, those related to motivation have been inferred from the behavior manifested by employees, as one cannot directly measure or observe what goes on in an individual's mind, but must infer the mental processes.[4] Some of the most popular theorists in the area of motivation are Abraham Maslow, David McClelland, Douglas McGregor, Rensis Likert, Chris Argyris and Frederick Herzberg. Their theories are the "content" theories of motivation. Another group of models and theories are the "process" theories of motivation: the expectancy theory, the equity theory and the Porter-Lawler model. These various theories and models will be examined to gain an understanding of each and to identify what they have in common; and guidelines will be established to assist managers in enhancing the motivation of individuals in the work environment.

The Content Theories and Models of Motivation: The content theories and models of motivation are based on psychological research. They focus primarily on identifying individuals' needs and leading people to act or make them *want* to work.

The first of these theorists is Maslow. He states that the needs of human beings are organized in a hierarchy and that a need at one level tends to come into operation as the needs at a lower level are satisfied.[5] At the bottom of the hierachy are the physiological needs, e.g., food, air, water, sleep, shelter, sex. At the next level are the safety and security needs, e.g., protection from physical harm, assurance of income. Above these are the social needs, e.g., belonging, acceptance, friendship, affection, love. At the next level are the esteem needs, e.g., a sense of self-respect, self-confidence, achievement, status, and recognition. At the top of the hierarchy is self-actualization, e.g., a sense of accomplishment and the development and utilization of one's potential capabilities. The implications of Maslow's hierarchy of needs for managers in recreation and leisure service agencies stems from the sociotechnological changes that have altered the character of American society. (For example, almost every household has a television and telephone, if not also a car and a VCR.) The vast majority of employees (as well as the consumers) of leisure services have been raised in relative affluence and tend to take it for granted. Their physiological and safety/security needs have been consistently satisfied; consequently, it is their social and esteem needs which are dominant. They want to be recognized as individuals and to be with pleasant people. They want opportunities to learn and grow and to exercise their talents and skills to the fullest. They want more control over the decisions in their work environment, especially as they affect their particular jobs; and they want the chance to accomplish something worthwhile.[6]

McClelland's model of motivation[7] stresses the higher-level needs. He classifies people in terms of three needs, namely, power, achievement, and affiliation. The need for power is expressed as the desire to influence others. It would be classified somewhere between esteem needs and self-actualization on Maslow's hierarchy. Individuals with need for power tend to exhibit behaviors such as forcefulness, outspokenness, willingness to engage in confrontation, and a tendency to maintain their original stance. They are not necessarily "power crazy," i.e., they do not operate in a dominant-submissive style, but in a more socialized form of influence. McClelland describes it as follows:

> The positive or socialized face of power is characterized by a concern for group goals, for finding those goals that will move men, for helping the group to formulate them, for taking some initiative in providing members with a means for achieving such goals, and for giving group members a feeling of strength and competency they need to work hard for such goals.[8]

McClelland's need for achievement also would be classified between Maslow's esteem needs and self-actualization. The essence of this need is the process of starting work and seeing it to successful completion. If managers want to motivate individuals operating on this need, they should assign them tasks that involve moderate risks, delegate sufficient authority so that they can take initiative and responsibility for completing the tasks, and give them specific feedback on their performance. McClelland states: "No matter how high a person's need to achieve may be, he cannot succeed if he has no opportunities, if the organization keeps him from taking initiative, or does not reward him if he does."[9] And, McClelland's third need, that of affiliation, is similar to Maslow's social needs. The individuals dominated by this need are attracted to work situations that provide considerable social interaction. They are interested in companionship, friendly relations, and a desire to assist others. Therefore, managers of such individuals should create environments that do not constrain interpersonal relations and should spend more time with these individuals.

McGregor[10] (in concurrence with Maslow and McClelland) pointed out that the assumptions underlying the traditional value system of managers are no longer applicable in present-day society with the new breed of workers. He labeled the assumptions of that system "Theory X." Managers operating under this system believe that people: (1) are fundamentally lazy and have to be pushed to work; (2) are basically sly and interested only in their own benefit; (3) respond best when disciplined and controlled; (4) take notice of punishment and work harder because of it; and (5) are essentially not interested in their jobs and work against their will.[11] In essence, McGregor stated that the carrot-and-stick approach has to be replaced. He proposed his "Theory Y." Managers operating under this system believe that people: (1) are fundamentally willing to work on meaningful tasks; (2) are basically honest and interested in the welfare of the group to which they belong; (3) respond when given responsibility and some freedom to make their own decisions; (4) take notice of honest praise and resent excessive punishment; and (5) are essentially interested in the quality of their professional and personal lives.[12]

Although no manager can exclusively operate under Theory Y (or for that matter under Theory X) McGregor's research demonstrates that those managers who tend to operate under the Theory Y assumptions are generally more successful in the following ways:

- Their departments have higher outputs.
- Their people show more motivation.
- They have fewer labor problems.
- They have lower labor turnover.
- They have less waste.
- They achieve greater profits.[13]

McGregor states that under Theory Y, as well as under Theory X, "Management is responsible for organizing the elements of productive enterprise—money, materials, equipment, people—in the interest of economic ends."[14] Under Theory Y, however, "the essential task of management is to arrange organization conditions and methods of operation so that people can achieve their own goals *best* by directing *their own* efforts toward organizational objectives."[15]

The shift from a Theory X approach to a Theory Y approach cannot and will not occur overnight. McGregor states: "It is worth noting that this difference is the difference between treating people as children and treating them as mature adults."[16] Employees, as well as managers, who work in a system which relies on the external control of human behavior cannot automatically adjust to one which relies on self-control and self-direction. Consequently, a sufficient amount of time and energy have to be invested in order to bring about change in a gradual manner.

Likert's concepts[17] are presented in four management systems which embody McGregor's concepts. Likert's systems are: System 1—Exploitative-Authoritative; System 2—Benevolent-Authoritative; System 3—

Consultative; and System 4—Participative. McGregor's Theory X is implicit in System 1, while the assumptions of Theory Y are the underpinnings for successful management under System 4. A discussion of the major characteristics of each system will make the point more apparent.

System 1: This system assumes that labor is largely a market commodity. The manager's job is characterized by decision, direction, and surveillance. He or she relies primarily on coercion as a motivating force, with little or no provision for the effects of human emotion and independence. Communication flows from the top downward, and it is frequently distorted. Top management sets the goals and makes the decisions, often based on inaccurate and inadequate information. Consequently, there is disparity between the interests and desires of the members and the goals of the organization. As a result, only top management feels any responsibility for the attainment of the goals. Dissatisfaction is prevalent, with the members having subservient attitudes toward supervisors, hostility toward peers, and contempt for subordinates.

System 2: This system assumes that labor is a market commodity, but an imperfect one. Consequently, it adds a fourth managerial duty to the three listed in System 1, namely, removing the annoying effect of subordinate members. The upper management still makes policies and basic decisions, but it sometimes provides opportunity for comment from subordinate supervisory levels. There are also some minor implementation decisions made at the lower levels; however, these have to be made within carefully prescribed limits set at the top. Again, only managerial personnel feel a responsibility for attaining the established goals. Attitudes toward supervisors are still subservient, and there is hostility toward peers; however, open contempt toward subordinates is absent.

System 3: This management system does not assume labor to be a commodity. Although the manager still reserves the tasks of decision and direction, he or she removes surveillance as a major function and there is little recourse to coercion. Instead, he or she uses consultation which provides some upward communication; consequently, communication is usually accurate. Although broad decisions are still made at the top, specific objectives to implement these are entrusted to lower managers for consultative decision-making. Therefore, a substantial proportion of the members feel responsible for attaining the established goals. Satisfaction is moderately high, with only some hostility expressed toward peers and some condescension toward subordinates.

System 4: This management system sees employees as essential parts of the organizational structure. It conceives of decision as a process, rather than the manager's prerogative; consequently, the manager does not decide by him/herself, but makes sure that the best possible decisions result. He or she focuses, therefore, on building a structure of highly motivated, cohesive, participative groups with overlapping memberships. Communication becomes adequate, rapid, and accurate. As all participate in establishing goals, and decisions are made with the participation of everyone affected, all members have the motivation to push in the direction of these objectives. Employees at all levels are highly satisfied, and there is reciprocal respect and trust.

In his research (primarily in industrial organizations, and in some government units) Likert has demonstrated conclusively that the nearer the management system is to System 4, the more productive the organization is. System 4 management also produces lower costs, higher earnings, better union relations, fewer strikes, fewer work stoppages, better worker attitudes, and high morale. Conversely, the nearer the management system is to System 1, the more it results in lower productivity, higher costs, poorer union relations, and lower worker morale.[18] Again, as discussed under McGregor's concepts, it may take several months to a year to provide the training in skills and knowledge that managers need to function in System 4 and to prove to all the people in the organization that the current system, whether it be 1, 2, or 3, is really changing to 4. The change, however, requires that the entire organization is convinced of the value of the change and invests the time and energy necessary to bring it about.

Argyris's theory[19] is that individuals are at a level of maturity that can be classified relatively on a continuum ranging from total immaturity to total maturity. And by recognizing individuals with respect to their maturity levels, the manager is in a position to create a motivating climate to meet the needs of individuals based on their respective maturity levels. In other words, the manager must recognize that every individual 1) is different; 2) responds differently based on his or her maturity level; and 3) must be treated differently—while maintaining fairness and consistency with the organization. Argyris pointed out that most organizations established strict hierarchal chains of commands and specializations of labor that kept workers at an "immature" level by limiting their individual initiative, stifling their creativity, and making them dependent on and passive toward their superiors. In Argyris's words: "These conditions inhibit self-actualization and provide expression of few, shallow, skin-surface abilities that do not provide the endless challenge desired by the healthy personality."[20]

In essence, Argyris's characterization of most organizations is similar to McGregor's Theory X. He indicated that when individuals join the workforce in the organizations, they are kept from maturing by the management practices which give them minimal control over their environment and encourage them to be passive, dependent, and subordinate. This results in their behaving immaturely and in low productivity. To combat this observed discrepancy between the needs of the mature personality and the needs of the organization, Argyris proposed the concept of "job enlargement." He advocated giving employees a greater number and variety of tasks so that they would have more opportunities to utilize their abilities, and simultaneously providing them with a greater sense of initiative, power, and responsibility in the work environment.

Herzberg's theory of motivation is most commonly known as the "motivation-hygiene" theory.[21] This theory is based on an understanding of the needs of individuals and their development level. Basing his work on that of Maslow and Argyris, Herzberg indicates that individuals are at different levels of maturity and that this must be recognized in relation to motivation in the work environment. He further states that most employees in this country are at the ego-need level as their lower-level needs have been met; therefore, if only lower-level needs are met in the work environment, then an individual will not be motivated. The individual may become dissatisfied with the job, but not motivated. The things that really motivate a person are the things that the individual is reaching for, and these are above the esteem level and at the self-actualizing level.

Only those activities which meet the needs that individuals are striving for and provide for job satisfaction, Herzberg labels as "motivators." And those activities which do not meet needs related to job context, i.e., "hygiene factors," provide only job dissatisfaction. These things do not motivate, they merely hold the potential of being dissatisfactions if they are not met. Herzberg's two-factor theory emanated from his analysis of workers' responses to the question: "Think of a time when you felt exceptionally good or exceptionally bad about your job. Tell me what happened."[22] Responses tended to fall into two categories: job satisfaction related to job content and job dissatisfaction related to job context. Specifically, those things that related to job satisfaction, the motivators, were: achievement; recognition for achievement; the work itself; responsibility; advancement; and possibility of growth. And the factors, which if not present or satisfactory can cause job dissatisfaction, the hygiene factors, are: supervision; company policy and administration; working conditions; interpersonal relations with peers, subordinates, and superiors; status; job security; and personal life.

The idea, advanced by Herzberg, is to create a job that is so exciting and enriching by loading it vertically, i.e., job enrichment. By expanding the complexity and completeness of the job, the individual is constantly encouraged to learn new things and reach for new achievements. Contrarily, horizontally loading the job, i.e., job enlargement (as advocated by Argyris), is not challenging or motivating to the worker; it just provides more of the same at the same level.

The Process Theories and Models of Motivation: The process theories and models of motivation also hold that needs motivate; however, they contend behavior is not solely a function of needs, it is also a function of an individual's perceptions and expectations about the situation and the possible outcome of a given behavior.[23]

The expectancy theory states that having an active need is not the only requisite for an individual to be motivated to channel behavior toward a certain goal. In addition, the individual must expect that behavior will lead to satisfaction or a desired outcome. In other words, expectancies are a person's estimate of the probability that a certain event will occur.[24] According to this theory, motivation is a function of effort-performance, performance-outcome expectancies and valence, i.e., value of outcome or reward. "Individuals are most highly motivated when they believe that their effort will definitely meet objectives and result in a highly valued reward. Motivation will decrease if the probability of attainment or the value of the reward is perceived as low."[25]

Equity theory holds that "people subjectively determine the ratio of reward to effort and compare it to what they perceive others receive for similar effort."[26] A comparison resulting in inequity causes psychological tension, and the individual will be motivated to reduce the tension and restore a state of equity. If the person feels underrewarded, effort will decrease; however, if the individual feels overrewarded, he or she will put forth greater effort.

The Porter-Lawler model includes elements of both the expectancy and equity theories.[27] It holds that motivation is a function of needs, perceived equity, and expectancies. "According to Porter and Lawler, performance is dependent on an individual's effort, abilities, traits, and the person's perceptions of his or her role. Effort varies with the perceived value of the reward and the expectation that a certain level of effort will in fact result in a certain reward. Moreover, the theory establishes a relationship between rewards and performance. Namely, an individual satisfies needs through rewards received because of performance."[28]

From these theories and models of motivation, certain conclusions can be drawn about the motivation of individuals and the role of the manager in the work environment. The manager can create a motivating environment if he or she:

1. Recognizes the needs of individuals and their maturity levels;
2. Understands which motivators and goals will meet the needs of various individuals;
3. Provides individuals with tasks that will enable them to achieve their goals and training to assist in meeting the goals;
4. Provides opportunities for individuals to meet their goals in their own ways;
5. Creates a positive expectancy (or rewards) if individuals reach toward achieving certain goals;
6. Reinforces positive performance with positive feedback;
7. Maintains a consistent and equitable environment with regard to workload and efforts rewarded; and,
8. Creates an environment that fosters creativity, communication and cooperation.

WHY DO MANAGERS FIND MOTIVATING EMPLOYEES DIFFICULT?

A statement by McGregor on motivation expresses the essence of the conclusions drawn from the theories and models as well as the responsibility of management. He states: "The motivation, the potential for development, the capacity for assuming responsibility, the readiness to direct behavior toward organization goals are all present in people. Management does not put them there. It is a responsibility of management to make it possible for people to recognize and develop these human characteristics for themselves."[29] If the ingredients are present, and managers have only to mix them and stir the pot, why do they find motivating employees difficult? The answer to this question lies in two main areas: one is within the manager him or herself, and the second is within the employee.

In the area of motivation, managers are artists as well as scientific managers; and great artists are fully engrossed in their art. Managers, who are effective at motivation, practice the art of motivation. They have deep concern or an obsession for motivating subordinates; and this requires that they concentrate on development of certain of their own human characteristics. Among these are:

- Knowledge of themselves, including their strengths and weaknesses in the art; and knowledge of others, both generally and specifically;
- Care for others, enough to assist others in growing and developing;
- A true sense of responsibility, i.e., a voluntary act, to respond to the needs of other persons;
- Respect for others, not fear or awe of them, but the ability to see other people as they are, to be aware of the uniqueness of individuals;
- Self-discipline, as required in the development of any art;
- Concentration on motivation as an essential management function, not on the manager's personal prestige or power; and,
- Patience with oneself and with others. Developing an art is a slow process which is subject to error, false starts, and slips.[30]

If managers do not learn and develop these human characteristics themselves, they will find motivating others an onerous, if not impossible, task. They must consciously develop and use themselves in the art of motivating subordinates.

The coin, however, has another side. Many times employees have found it difficult, if not impossible, to satisfy their needs in the workplace as they have worked in organizations that have operated on traditions and techniques that emphasized external control of their motivations. As mentioned previously, needs that are not satisfied produce tensions within the individual; and these unsatisfied needs motivate individuals to behavior that will relieve the tensions. However, if individuals cannot relieve or reduce the tensions, frustration occurs. Some individuals react to frustration with constructive behavior, while others react with defensive behavior. Healthy adjustment to frustration is part of the process of maturing. For example, an employee who cannot satisfy his need for recognition as a member of the staff in an community recreation center may volunteer in a therapeutic recreation program in a hospital and receive rewards and recognition in that capacity. Another employee of the same agency might volunteer in the public recreation agency of the township and work to get elected as a member of the recreation and park commission to satisfy his or her social and esteem needs. These are examples of constructive adaptive behavior which enables individuals to reduce frustrations at work and satisfy needs.

Serious or constant frustration may lead to maladjustment. When employees are unable to satisfy their needs with constructive behavior, they may evoke one or more defense mechanisms. These mechanisms, recognized and enumerated by Freud, are employed by all of us at one time or another; and they provide some protective function in helping us to cope with reality. Although they are not adequate for truly protecting us, they do not disadvantage us for the most part. But those adults over whom defense mechanisms have a commanding influence have trouble fulfilling their functions and responsibilities at work and their obligations to their colleagues in the work environment. Some of the common defense mechanisms are:

- Withdrawal—avoiding or withdrawing from those situations which are frustrating, e.g., excessive absences or lateness.
- Aggression—either a direct attack on the source of frustration, e.g., fighting a supervisor or colleague, or displaced aggression, e.g., inflicting pain or fighting another worker, spouse, or friend.
- Regression—reverting back to childlike behavior, thinking or attitudes to avoid the unpleasant situation, e.g., horseplay in the work environment.
- Projection—attributing one's feelings to someone else. For example, an employee may not like a task delegated by a supervisor, so he or she does not do it well. When questioned by a colleague, he or she is likely to respond, "The supervisor doesn't like this task, so he dumped it on me, and I am not going to do his dirty work well."
- Rationalization—the individual gives a reason for behavior which is a blow to his or her ego, e.g., poor construction of the performance appraisal system is blamed for his/her lack of receiving a high rating or a bonus.

In order for managers to reduce the need of employees to use defense mechanisms, they have to make decisions and arrange conditions which minimize employee frustrations. At the same time, they will be enhancing the likelihood of subordinates achieving organization goals and objectives while meeting their individual needs. A note of caution is appropriate at this time. Managers should not play psychotherapist in trying to determine why employees have particular needs or use specific defense mechanisms. This is not the job of managers. Managers must recognize that employees have individual needs which they are seeking to satisfy through particular behaviors. "The essential task of management is to arrange organizational objectives and methods of operations so that people can achieve their own goals best by directing their own efforts toward organization objectives. This is a process primarily of creating opportunities, releasing potential, removing obstacles, encouraging growth, and providing guidance."[31]

SUGGESTED GUIDELINES FOR MOTIVATING EMPLOYEES

Effective and successful managers are those who accomplish the goals and objectives of the organization which they were employed to achieve; and they do such by *managing*. Consequently, the vast majority of the actual work in any organization is performed by the employees who report to managers and for whom they are responsible. Therefore, managers are dependent on subordinates to be effective and successful; and subsequently, on the managers' abilities to release employees' work capacities. And, prerequisites to these abilities are an understanding of motivation and the development of strategies, approaches, and skills in creating a motivating environment. Some useful guidelines to assist managers in these tasks are:

1. Making a commitment to motivation as an essential management function.
2. Becoming aware of individual employee needs through observation and communication; learning their strengths and weaknesses; and allowing for differences.
3. Providing structured opportunities for individuals to communicate personal and career goals. Also, letting them know that they can comfortably approach their supervisors with problems or questions and that they will receive help.
4. Assisting employees in achieving personal goals by accomplishing organizational goals; acknowledging a job well done as soon as possible; making such reinforcement a consistent practice.
5. Establishing work objectives *with* individual employees, which achieved within a specific time frame are labeled "success," and incorporating these in position descriptions with standards of performance. In essence this is a management by objectives approach. And, acknowledging the importance of the employee and the employee's work and its significance to the organization and to its achieving its goals.
6. Scheduling formal, ongoing evaluation sessions in which employees and supervisors review work accomplishments, employee growth, employee performance assessment for future positions, and the creating of new objectives for interesting and challenging work.

7. Consulting with employees, their supervisors and colleagues when performance problems appear. Sometimes employees are hesitant to communicate directly with their managers when problems exist. Make it clear that the purpose of the inquiry is to assist in the resolution of the problem.

8. Providing opportunities to obtain vocational, leisure, or personal counseling to assist in making decisions and solving problems.

9. Removing roadblocks in the physical or administrative areas that may be demotivating; and providing amenities that will bring pleasure, e.g., coffee-maker, vending machine; or brighten the environment, e.g., artwork, plants, as well as employees' attitudes.

10. Providing human and technical resources to assist employees. If a sufficient budget does not exist to do all that should be done, let employees know that management is aware of the deficiencies and is working to improve them.

11. Providing opportunities for employees to obtain knowledge and skills through appropriate training when necessary to enhance task performance. And if necessary and possible, offering refresher courses or sessions.

12. Enhancing supervisory approaches and strategies if they are not adequate or if employees see them as inappropriate.

13. Providing opportunities which will enhance interpersonal relationships among colleagues, subordinates, and supervisors.

14. Providing payoffs or rewards that have meaning to the individual for successful performance. Included here are recognition, monetary rewards, additional challenges and responsibilities (including decision-making), promotions, and opportunities for personal growth.

15. Assessing strategies and approaches for creating a motivating environment on a continuous basis. As individuals grow and develop and thereby meet unsatisfied needs, additional unsatisfied needs emerge. Consequently, motivating strategies and approaches may need to be changed.

SUMMARY

This chapter was devoted to an exploration of motivation and its relevance in management. Motivation in the work environment was defined as "the process of moving oneself and others to work toward attainment of individual and organizational goals." The point was made that "Motivated behavior is internally activated, but it can be modified by external conditions in the individual environment."

In a productive work environment, satisfaction of individual needs and meeting organizational goals are harmonious. Therefore, managers attempt to create a motivating environment in which opportunities and appropriate goals are established to meet the needs of individual employees and are directed simultaneously at accomplishing or meeting organization goals.

An overview of selected theories and models of motivation was presented. These were the works of:

1. Abraham Maslow—associated mainly with his hierarchy-of-needs theory of motivation;
2. David McClelland—noted for his model of higher-level needs of motivation, i.e., power, achievement and affiliation;
3. Douglas McGregor—known for his Theory X and Theory Y assumptions about the nature of humans and their relation to their work;
4. Rensis Likert—the chief proponent of the participative group theory of organization;
5. Chris Argyris—an advocate of developing interpersonal competence to enhance individual maturity levels, stressing the need for integrating individual and organizations goals through job enlargement;
6. Frederick Herzberg—noted for his two-factor theory of motivation, i.e., the motivation-hygiene theory, and the need to create a job that is so exciting and enriching through job enrichment.

The difficulties managers have in motivating employees were explored through their belief in the carrot-and-stick strategy (with the carrot being the reward and the stick being fear); their not having a true commitment toward, a sense of responsibility for, and concentration on motivation as an essential management function. On the other side of the coin are employees who need to use defensive behavior in relieving frustrations resulting from their inability to satisfy needs in the work environment or to utilize constructive adapted behavior.

Fifteen suggested guidelines for motivating employees were presented. The guidelines were directed toward assisting managers and supervisors in creating a motivating environment. Such an environment is one in which employees are able to meet their personal goals while working productively to achieve the goals and objectives of the organization.

The chapter indicates that there are no simple solutions to motivating employees. It is hoped that the reader has a better appreciation of the complexities involved in motivating individuals in today's recreation and leisure service organizations.

NOTES AND REFERENCES

1. J.W. Robinson, Jr., R.A. Clifford, A.C. Wills, **Motivation in Community Groups.** (Urbana, Illinois: University of Illinois at Urbana-Champaign, 1975), p. 5.
2. M.H. Mescon, M. Albert, F. Khedouri, **Management** (3rd ed.). (New York: Harper & Row, Publishers, 1988). p. 305.
3. Robinson, et al., p. 5.
4. M.H. Mescon, M. Albert, F. Khedouri, **Management: Individual and Organizational Effectiveness.** (New York: Harper and Row, Publishers, 1981), p. 306.
5. Abraham H. Maslow, **Motivation and Personality.** (New York: Harper & Row, 1954).
6. Daniel Yankelovich, "The New Psychological Contracts at Work," and Patricia Enwich, Edward E. Lawler, and others, "What You Really Want from Your Job," **Psychology Today,** May, 1978, pp. 46–50 and pp. 53–65, 118.
7. David McClelland, "The Two Faces of Power," **Journal of International Affairs,** Vol 14, 1970, pp. 30–41.
8. Ibid., p. 30.
9. Ibid.
10. Douglas McGregor, **The Human Side of Enterprise.** (New York: McGraw-Hill Book Co., 1960).
11. David Francis and Mike Woodcock, **People at Work.** (La Jolla, California: University Associates, Inc., 1975), p. 76.
12. Ibid.
13. Ibid.
14. Douglas McGregor, "The Human Side of Enterprise," **Behavioral Science and the Manager's Role,** William B. Eddy and others, eds. (Los Angeles, California: NTL Institute for Applied Behavioral Science, 1969), p. 157 and p. 163.
15. Ibid.
16. Ibid., p. 164.
17. Rensis Likert, **The Human Organization: Its Management and Value.** (New York: McGraw-Hill Book Co., 1967).
18. William R. Van Dersal, **The Successful Supervisor: In Government and Business** (3rd ed.). (New York: Harper & Row, Publishers, 1974), p. 87.

19. Chris Argyris, **Personality and Organization.** (New York: Harper & Row, Publishers, 1957).
20. Ibid., p. 50.
21. F. Herzberg, B. Mausner, B. Snyderman, **The Motivation to Work.** (New York: John Wiley and Sons, 1959).
22. Ibid.
23. Mescon et al., 1988, p. 397.
24. Victor H. Vroom, **Work and Motivation.** (New York: John Wiley and Sons, 1964).
25. Mescon et al., 1988, p. 406.
26. Ibid., p. 407.
27. L.W. Porter and E.E. Lawler, **Managerial Attitudes and Performance.** (Homewood, IL: Richard D. Irwin, 1968).
28. Mescon, et al., 1988, p. 401.
29. McGregor, 1969, p. 163.
30. John Conway Associates, Inc. "Developing an Integrated Management System." New York: United Cerebral Palsy of New York City, Inc. Management Seminar, February 12–13, 1979, p. 58.
31. McGregor, 1969. p. 163.

The purpose of this chapter is to help the manager answer:

- Why are communications misunderstood so often?
- Why are clearly worded directions not followed as given?
- Why is it so difficult to communicate the intentions of communications and directions?
- Why don't employees respect the authority of the manager's position?
- Why don't employees fulfill their responsibilities?
- Why does the manager take home a briefcase full of work and the employees do not have enough work?
- How can work be delegated to employees in an effective manner?

Chapter 9

The Two-Way Streets of Communication, Authority, and Responsibility: Aspects of Delegation

Arnold H. Grossman

Managers of organizations, including recreation and leisure service agencies, recognize three essential tasks as central to their effective functioning as leaders: giving directions, exercising authority, and assigning responsibility. It is not surprising, therefore, when managers list complaints about their employees, the three items that usually appear on the list include: failure to follow directions, lack of respect for authority, and failure to fulfill their assigned responsibilities. What is surprising is the lack of knowledge and understanding possessed by managers to take the necessary action to ameliorate this discrepancy.

Most managers approach their positions with preconceived ideas about the management process. Among these ideas are:

- If I communicate a direction, it will be understood and followed;
- If I exercise authority, it will be accepted; and
- If I delegate a responsibility, it will be carried out.

Unfortunately, these traditional ideas are based on the faulty premise that the concepts of communication, authority, and responsibility are one-way streets.

This chapter is concerned with the development of the idea that the concepts of communication, authority, and responsibility are two-way streets. Then the process of delegation, which embodies these concepts, will be addressed.

Two-Way Streets

The idea of the two-way street indicates that traffic flows in two directions. In other words, in addition to the sender there has to be a receiver who understands (in the case of communication) and/or accepts (in the cases of authority and responsibility) what has been sent. If a manager communicates a message, authorizes an action, or assigns a responsibility, it cannot be considered communicated, authorized, or an assigned responsibility unless it is understood or accepted by the employee(s) to whom it is directed.

Communication: Communication is a complex phenomenon. No attempt is being made here to explore it in its various connected or interwoven parts. The purpose of this discussion is to emphasize that it is an essential managerial skill which is a two-way interaction. Communication involves not only active speaking (orally or in writing) and active listening (auditory and reading), it also involves understanding. In other words, communication not received is not really communication.

Some of the factors that inhibit effective communication in organizations are:[1]

- Seldom do two persons define a word in the same way;
- Words mean different things to people when used in various settings;
- Words conjure up different meanings to people based on their previous experiences;
- Words communicate one message, but emotional feelings communicate other messages;
- Words communicate one message, but actions communicate other messages;
- A person's position in an organization communicates something about the person, whether or not he or she intends to do so or not;
- Because of the constant bombardment of messages, people resist communication until they have had an opportunity to evaluate it;
- People lack listening skills—they tend to daydream or plan their rebuttal.
- People assume that their organizational positions provide influence and authority over employee listeners which will result in effective communication and gain compliance. (It is worthwhile

to remember two quotations in this regard: "He that complies against his will, is of his own opinion still."—Samuel Butler; "You have not converted a man because you have silenced him."— John Morley).

- The medium used for transmitting the message influences the content of the message. In fact, as Marshall McLuhan indicated, the medium often is the message.

The International City Management Association points out that three viewpoints are usually involved when a supervisor communicates work directions to an employee:[2]

- Those which the supervisor *thought* he gave.
- Those which the supervisor *actually* gave.
- Those which the employee *thought* the supervisor gave.

In order for managers (supervisors) to minimize the arc of distortion between what they intend to communicate and what they actually communicate (unintentionally), the following recommendations are presented:

1. Determine which employees should know about the information to be communicated, i.e., who will be affected by the information, who will have to make a decision and/or implement an action or decision.
2. Determine what part of the information various employees need to know. Extra information fogs the communication.
3. Determine the medium to be used in communicating, e.g., information affecting employee attitudes may be communicated more effectively in an oral manner, whereas information containing factual information in the form of data may be communicated more effectively in writing.
4. State the information in a clear, simple, and precise manner. Avoid the use of ambiguous, difficult-to-understand terms, and jargon. Scale the communication to the understanding and reading level of employees.
5. Make certain that the information to be communicated is accurate in terms of the subject matter. Check with the originator of the information, if possible. Communication passing through a number of people is vulnerable to change. (Remember the game "Telephone"?)
6. Make certain to include the "why" of the communication so it will make sense to the employees and so they can see its relationship to them, their jobs, and the agency.
7. If the task or project is to be delegated, get the employee to whom

it will be delegated in on the communication as soon as possible.

8. Provide a mechanism for feedback—one that requires more than a "yes" or "no" answer to the question "Do you understand?" Most employees will respond affirmatively to this question because they are embarrassed to say that they were not listening (in the case of oral communication) or that the manager's directions were not clear.

9. Acknowledge that employees' interests, desires, concerns, or job loads were taken into consideration. Employees should know that their positions are understood. They will be less likely to be unreasonable or defensive.

Authority: Managers tend to expect that the authority which accompanies their position will be respected; consequently, when it is exercised it will be accepted. This hierarchical view of authority is based on the "one-way street" idea. It recognizes the authority giver, but not the authority receiver.

Barnard's definition of authority, in the **Functions of the Executive,** describes authority as a two-part concept which involves both the authority giver and the authority receiver, i.e., one whose action is required to execute it. He states that it is "the character of a communication (order) in a formal organization by virtue of which it is accepted by a contributor to, or 'member' of, the organization as governing the action he contributes; that is, as governing or determining what he does or is not to do so far as the organization is concerned."[3]

Barnard suggests that a person can and will accept communication as authoritative *only when certain conditions simultaneously exist:* "(a) he can and does understand the communication; (b) *at the time of his decision* he believes it is not inconsistent with the purpose of the organization; (c) *at the time of his decision* he believes it to be compatible with his personal interests as a whole; and (d) he is able mentally and physically to comply with it."[4] Managers, therefore, have to be cognizant of the fact that employees receiving orders evaluate them and make decisions regarding the appropriateness of the manager's authority at the time of employees' decision-making. The ultimate decision is made by the authority receiver. If the employees refuse to carry out an order, they may be subject to punitive action; however, the fact remains that the order was not implemented and the authority, therefore, was not accepted.

Brown[6] points out that subordinates who do not desire to follow a requested course of action can usually find some way to do so without being directly disobedient. He notes that this is one of the reasons why insubordination is usually hard to prove. Some of the more common forms of gray area compliance which he lists are:

- The workers can revise the quality of what is asked.
- They can revise the quantity.
- They can revise the time schedule.
- They can revise the priority.
- They can revise the procedures they have been told to use.
- They can try to convince the boss that the job does not need to be done.
- They can claim they do not have the proper equipment (or manpower or ability).
- They can claim that they are too busy with other things.
- They can claim that it is contrary to existing policy, that it will not work, or that someone else should do it.
- They can make a scene or threaten to appeal to higher authority.
- They can become ill and remain at home.
- They can do something else and say that this covers what was wanted.
- They can assign (redelegate) the job to someone else.
- They can do a variety of other things that cancel the effect of what was wanted.

Brown sums up his discussion on authority with a quotation from a major character in Shakespeare's **Henry IV,** who announces, "I can call spirits from the briny deep." Another, doubting him, responds, "Ay, but when you call them, do they come?"

Responsibility: The point to be made with respect to responsibility has been suggested above in the discussion of authority. Managers can state that their employees will be responsible for executing a variety of tasks; however, if the employees fail to accept this responsibility, they are not *really* responsible. Responsibility is a personal trait voluntarily exercised by the employee(s). Employees respond in the needed manner only when each feels a responsibility for doing so.

Barnard suggests that "Formal authority is dependent on, and secondary to *acceptance* of responsibility."[8] Responsibility, which is a moral commitment comes first and authority comes second.

DELEGATION

As the title of the chapter indicates, communication, authority, and responsibility are aspects of delegation. In fact, the delegation process can be characterized by these three concepts. First, it is important to note that the word "process" is used. A process is a series of continuous actions that bring about a particular result. It is quite different from the word "dumping," which means to drop or throw down heavily or abruptly. On too many occasions, managers say, "I am dumping this in your lap." The latter is what the employees usually receive as the message with the result being anger, resistance, lower employee morale, and "What 'gray area' in terms of compliance can I employ?" (See above discussion of authority.)

In essence, the delegation process is:

1. Communicating orders or directions to employees which assign them to undertake certain tasks or implement certain actions.
2. Establishing authority which sanctions employees to make certain decisions and/or take the necessary actions to comply with the orders and/or directions.
3. Creating an obligation on the part of the employees to accept the responsibility for effective performance in achieving the desired result.

From the previous discussion of the concepts of communication, authority, and responsibility, it becomes apparent that delegation is indeed a process; and, it is a process that involves understanding and acceptance on the part of the employees. A task or a project is not delegated unless an employee understands the order or direction, accepts the authority of the manager at the time of his or her decision to comply, and accepts the responsibility for effective performance to achieve the desired outcome.

Delegation requires managers to relinquish some authority, and as the success of a delegated task or project depends on the acceptance of the employee(s), managers usually tend to underdelegate. This may be because: they lack the ability to direct; or they have an aversion to taking risks, based on the fear that employees may cause problems in doing the tasks or they will not do them; or the employees may find out more information than the manager wants them to know—a mechanism of power and control. The result is that managers who underdelegate do not have sufficient time to complete their routine work as well as the tasks delegated or dumped in their laps, while employees do not have a sufficient amount of challenging and interesting work to provide them with intrinsic rewards. As a result, managers usually lack the time or give less priority to meeting the human needs of employees or providing them with the necessary technical knowledge.

Managers have developed a series of rationalizations to support their tendency to underdelegate. Some of the common rationalizations are:

- None of the employees can complete the task as well as the manager.

- It is easier to do it than to explain it.
- It takes just as long to explain what has to be done to an employee as it will take to complete the task.
- The employees will gripe about the extra work. It is not worth the aggravation.
- The employees are too undependable or too untrustworthy to complete the task.
- The employees are too young or too old to undertake such an assignment.
- The employees lack the knowledge or experience to achieve the desired result. (This may be true. If it is, the manager has a training job to do.)

On the other side of the coin, some employees offer resistance to the delegation process. According to Newman,[9] subordinates avoid responsibility and block the delegation process for six major reasons:

1. The subordinate finds it easier to ask the boss what to do rather than figure out the problem.
2. The subordinate fears criticism for mistakes. Since greater responsibility increases the chances of making an error, the subordinate avoids it.
3. The subordinate lacks the information and resources needed to do the job successfully.
4. The subordinate already has, or believes he or she has, more work than he or she can do.
5. The subordinate lacks self-confidence.
6. The subordinate is not offered any positive incentives for assuming added responsibility.

Although not as great a cause for managerial failure as underdelegation, the tendency to delegate too much can also be a problem. The question that comes to mind is, what is too much? It is difficult to answer this question with a general statement. What is too much in one setting may not be too much in another. Factors such as levels of employee positions, knowledge and experience of employees, and length of service by employees have to be taken into consideration. A guiding principle, however, may be: Those decisions or tasks which are clearly the prerogative of the manager should not be delegated. Some examples of these decisions or tasks are: employee appraisal, employee promotion, disciplinary action, employee termination, employee grievances, overall policy-making, and such other areas that the manager's superior, e.g., executive director, board of directors, does not desire the manager to delegate.

Techniques of delegation: Bishop[10] identifies three techniques of delegation: direction, coordination, and control. *Direction* is the issuance of instructions by the manager to the employees. Instructions should be clear and complete, (no questions should be left in the mind of the employee); and compliance to the instruction should be reasonable. The manager has to obtain feedback from the employees in order to know that the instructions have been understood, and the manager has to follow up on an instruction to see that it is carried out.

Coordination is the mechanism by which the manager synchronizes the efforts of employees so that they are contributing to the attainment of the projected outcome. It involves planning, organizing, and scheduling of work, and clarifying the accountability of each employee for the achievement of definite goals. It is also incumbent on the manager to direct the interaction between the employees, and between the manager and the employees, to achieve a cooperative effort.

Control results from the feedback mechanisms established by the manager to monitor the assigned work. It involves follow-up with the employees on the progress of the work as well as the completed task or project.

STAFF MEETINGS

Most managers in recreation and leisure service agencies schedule and conduct staff meetings on a regular basis with employees for whom they are responsible. The purposes of staff meetings are primarily administrative in nature, i.e., concerned with how to get the work of the division, the department, or the agency as a whole done so as to accomplish the respective objectives. Consequently, it is primarily at staff meetings that the manager communicates, delegates and requests that employees accept responsibility for achieving agreed-upon end results. The manager accomplishes this by providing information, giving directions, coordinating the duties of the various employees, and establishing feedback mechanisms. Scheduling and conducting staff meetings is a most appropriate technique for achieving these aims. It gathers all of the employees under the manager's supervision in one place at one time. It provides opportunities for the manager to:

- Communicate to the employees and to ascertain immediately if the communication is received as it is intended.
- Give directions and determine if his or her authority is accepted.
- Enable employees to engage in planning, problem-solving, decision-making, and evaluation processes.

- Determine if responsibilities have been accepted.
- Coordinate the tasks of employees.
- Establish methods for maintaining control.

Although the primary purposes of the staff meetings are executive in relation to department, division, or agency, in-service and development training are valuable byproducts. The varied dialogue at staff meetings enables employees to contribute ideas, knowledge, and skills learned at conferences, workshops, professional meetings or in formal education courses at a college or university. In addition, opportunities arise for the discussion of professional concerns, issues, or ethics. A manager who is aware and alert can skillfully utilize the staff meeting as an informal and supplementary training vehicle.

SUMMARY

The chapter was devoted to an exploration of the concepts of communication, authority, and responsibility; and the process of delegation characterized by these three concepts was discussed.

Communication, authority, and responsibility are two-way concepts. They each require action on the part of a receiver as well as that of a giver. Communication is not communication unless what is communicated by the sender is understood by the receiver. Authority is not authority unless the receiver makes the decision to accept it from the sender. Responsibility assigned by the giver is not responsibility unless it is felt to be so by the receiver and thus accepted.

Delegation is a *process* characterized by communication, authority, and responsibility. It is not "dumping" by managers on employees. A delicate balance between underdelegating and overdelegating must be established. Some factors regarding the establishment of this balance were discussed. Then three techniques of delegation were addressed: direction, coordination, and control.

In order for managers of recreation and leisure service agencies to delegate in an effective manner, they must have confidence in themselves, must have the conceptual, human, and technical skills necessary for the job; must have confidence in the employees whom they are supervising; and each must have established a mature and constructive relationship with his or her superior. A manager responsible to a superior who displays trust and confidence in him or her and who perceives the manager as competent and self-reliant is more likely to delegate effectively than a manager who is responsible to a superior who frequently intervenes in the work, frets about details, and continually wants information about all aspects of the work.

The final section of this chapter was devoted to a discussion of the staff meeting as an effective technique for communicating, giving directions, delegating, and determining the acceptance of responsibilities. Although the staff meeting is primarily administrative in nature, the point was made that the aware and alert manager can use the opportunities which arise for informal and supplementary training of employees.

NOTES AND REFERENCES

1. Leslie E. This, "Personal Communication," **Looking Into Leadership Series: The Executive Library.** (Washington, D.C.: Leadership Resources, Inc., 1972), pp. 5–13.
2. International City Management Association, "Directing the Work," Bulletin 5 in a series on **Effective Supervisory Practices.** (Washington, D.C.: International City Management Association, 1965), p. 3.
3. David S. Brown, "Authority and Responsibility," **Looking Into Leadership Series: The Executive Library,** pp. 8–9.
4. Ibid., p. 9.
5. Ibid.
6. Ibid., pp. 11–12.
7. Ibid., p. 13.
8. Ibid.
9. William Newman, "Overcoming Obstacles to Effective Delegation," **Management Review,** January 1956, pp. 36–41.
10. Maxine H. Bishop, **Dynamic Supervision: Problems and Opportunities.** (New York: American Management Association, 1969), pp. 115–116.

The purpose of this chapter is to help the manager answer:

- Why stress management is important to recreation professionals?

- What are the specific components of the jobs of recreation professionals—in upper management, middle management (supervisor), and direct service delivery—that are reasons for dissatisfaction, stress, and burnout?

- What is normal stress and distress?

- What are some common sources of stress?

- Why is something stressful to one person and not to another?

- What is work-related stress?

- What is burnout?

- What is stress management?

- What are some guidelines I can follow as a manager to establish and implement a stress management program in my agency?

Chapter 10

Managing Work-Related Stress*

Arnold H. Grossman

Life in complex organizations can be a great source of stress for both managerial and subordinate staff. There is increasing evidence to demonstrate that workers are suffering extreme physiological and psychological symptoms from stress at work. This job-related stress often forces individuals to retire prematurely from active organizational life before they have had an opportunity to reach their potential or realize their ambitions. Cooper and Marshall indicate that these and other stress-related effects—tension, poor adjustment, impatience—also feed into family life, becoming potential sources of disturbance and thus pervade the individual's entire life experience.[1] On-the-job stress affects not only the individual, but the organization in which the person works. There is significant cost to the agency in terms of productivity, continuity, and retraining resulting from staff dissatisfaction with the work environment.

While recreation and leisure services traditionally has not been considered a high stress-profession, more practitioners are becoming less satisfied with their chosen career. At all job levels, from upper and middle management to face-to-face leadership in all facets of the profession, professionals are opting for other opportunities. One need only take stock at various professional conferences and workshops to see more new faces and fewer familiar ones. In the field, the situation appears to reflect not only the "up *or* out" proposition, but also an

*This chapter is based on an article written by Arnold H. Grossman and Lloyd A. Heywood, "Stress Management in Leisure Services," **Leisure Today:** "Coping With Stress Through Leisure," October 1982, pp. 7–8, 31.

"up *and* out" syndrome where advancement up the career ladder means greater exposure to stresses and strains. Bitterness, alienation, and low job performance often lead to dissatisfaction and eventual burnout. Why?

Despite popular opinion, persons employed in the field of recreation and leisure services are not paid for *playing* at work. On the contrary, they often work when others are playing—on evenings, weekends, holidays, and summer vacations. This situation combined with the idea that most people think one needs no special knowledge, skills, or training to work in recreation and leisure services (and feel free to say so) creates stress. Not only do most employees work in a low-status occupation when others have free time, but they usually also work under the constraint of tight budgets. Furthermore, they may experience many stress factors with which individuals in other occupations have to cope, e.g., competitiveness, hostility, meeting time restraints, non-productive meetings, as well as self-determined high expectations, standards, and personal demands.

Many recreation and leisure service professionals are becoming more concerned with their work environments and attendant job satisfaction. They question the negatives associated with placement in larger vs. smaller agencies, the public vs. the private sectors, various administrative levels within agencies, and even whether or not they should be in the leisure services field at all. The Institute for Social Research at the University of Michigan has identified stress-producing and organizational demands to which managers in the field should pay close attention. Size and structure of the agency, relations with co-workers and pressures to conform, opportunity for advancement, workload and variance in workload, travel, and responsibility for subordinates lead to such job-related effects as dissatisfaction, boredom, and pay inequities, and to general effects such as anxiety, depression, irritation, frustration, and lowered self-esteem. These in turn produce adverse personal and agency consequences.[2]

Fairly obvious reasons for dissatisfaction and distress can be seen in three job levels—upper management, middle management (supervisory), and direct service delivery. Upper management stresses may be generated by such factors as political stress, decision-making conflict, responsibility for actions of others, lack of autonomy, and frustration. Direct service workers are chagrined by work hours, job ambiguity, lack of job status, boredom, workload, salary inequities and being overqualified. It appears that the reasons for middle management's dissatisfaction, stress, strain, and burnout may be even greater. They encompass both those of upper management and of the direct service component due primarily to greater role ambiguity, as well as their own particular job-related concerns of workload, variance in workload, lack of autonomy, under-use, pay inequities, and unwanted overtime hours.[3]

Just as the cobbler often goes without shoes, managers in the leisure service occupation have not recognized the need to reduce the work-related stress of their employees. Working to provide recreation opportunities for others, including stress-relieving activities, they have assumed incorrectly that they themselves or their employees do not need these things. In fact, their need is probably greater!

When he was president of the Canadian Parks/Recreation Association, Harry Boothman laid much of the blame for job-related stress and turnover in recreation and leisure service on upper management's failure to recognize that the loyalties of many young career people were to their profession rather than to the organization, and they were addressing the wrong factors in trying to provide a meaningful and satisfying work environment for them.[4] Basically, he stated that self-esteem needs and not security needs have to be addressed in attracting and retaining staff. Today, we need to go beyond the self-esteem needs and find new answers to the retention problem. The stresses and strains exist, the burnout exists, the exodus exists, the costs of the exodus exist—and the problem for the profession exists. Recreation and leisure service managers must take action.

NORMAL STRESS AND DISTRESS

Stress itself is not the culprit. It is the quantity and intensity of stress that determines its potential effect on an individual. In fact, a certain amount of stress is needed for and is a positive factor in work as well as play. According to Selye, physician and author of several books on stress:

> No one can live without experiencing some degree of stress all the time. You may think that only serious disease or intensive physical or mental injury can cause stress. This is false. Crossing a busy intersection, exposure to a draft, or even sheer joy are enough to activate the body's stress-mechanism to some extent. Stress is not even necessarily bad for you; it is also the spice of life, for any emotion, any activity causes stress. But, of course, your system must be prepared to take it. The same stress which makes one person sick can be an invigorating experience to another.[5]

The incidents which cause stress are labeled "stressors" by Selye; and the physical reaction of the body to stress is basically the same, regardless of the stressor. Selye indicates that each individual has a finite and nonreplenishable amount of adaptation energy available to use in restoring equilibrium after a stressful incident.[6] In other words, "stress is the common denominator of all adaptive reactions in the body."[7] It is a physiological reaction, the general adaptation syndrome (or G.A.S.), to anything that threatens one's survival. Stress is not a stimulus. It is a reaction to a wide variety of stressors.[8]

Regardless of the source of stress, the nonspecific chain reactions in the body are the same. McQuade and Aikman enumerate five basic steps in the stress-response reaction which focus on the functioning of the autonomic nervous, gastrointestinal, and cardiovascular systems as well as the endocrine glands and their hormones.[9] For the sake of simplicity, Selye's less technical three-stage reaction will be presented here. Stage I is the *alarm reaction*. In this stage the body recognizes the stressor and prepares to fight or take flight. This is accomplished by the endocrine glands releasing hormones. The hormones cause an increase in the heartbeat and respiration, elevation of the sugar level in the blood, increase in perspiration, slowed digestion, and dilated pupils. The individual then decides whether to use this burst of energy to fight or take flight. Stage II is the *stage of resistance*. In this stage the body attempts to return to homeostasis. It replenishes the hormones and repairs any damage caused by the stress. If the stressor is not removed, the body cannot replenish and repair; consequently, it remains alert and enters Stage III, *the stage of exhaustion*. If this stage continues long enough, the body begins to run out of energy, and "diseases of stress" may develop, e.g., heart attacks, strokes, migraine headaches, hypertension, ulcers. Continued exposure may even cause bodily functions to stop.[10]

When the body cannot enter Stage II to replenish and repair itself, the individual experiences what Selye calls *distress:* damaging or unpleasant stress that causes one to constantly readjust and adapt.[11]

SOURCES OF STRESS

One is experiencing stressors no matter what one is doing. Whether a situation is pleasant or unpleasant, a demand is placed on the individual to readjust or adapt. A number of writers have attempted to classify the sources of stress. Adams uses a quadrant which classifies "Work Related" and "Nonwork Related" sources which can present either episodic or chronic stressors.[12] Levi writes about biological and emotional sources of stress.[13] And Gray classifies stress in three ways: 1) physiological stress, such as surgery, injury, or other threats to the physical well-being; 2) psychological stress, such as intensive competition and frustration; and 3) environmental stress, such as heat, cold, or noise.[14]

Robinson et al. list the following as the most frequent sources of stress in our daily lives: 1) *fear*—being afraid of some physical or psychological dangers, e.g., accidents, sickness, sarcasm, loss of love; 2) *an overload or underload situation*—having too many pressures, e.g., work and people pressure, noise, crowding, total lack of stimulation; 3) *life changes*—experiencing a major change in our way of life, e.g., loss of a loved person, change of jobs, getting married, outstanding achievement; and 4) *ambiguity*—being uncertain about a situation, our role or other people's expectations, e.g., a new job, going to another part of the country, or to another country.[15]

Neulinger extends the above approaches with a leisure perspective of stress. He notes that positive as well as negative events cause stress and quotes Kimmel giving examples of the positive ones, such as graduation, marriage, divorce, and retirement. Kimmel refers to these as "timing events—events that cause the person to modify the self." Neulinger conceptualizes these timing events as acts of separation and links them to *leisure lack,* the temporary or chronic absence of the experience of leisure. He states:

> Leisure, when viewed from a subjective, state-of-mind perspective is closely linked to meaning, through its essential conditions, namely *perceived freedom* and *intrinsic motivation.* These are variables, however, that are bound to be affected severely by acts of separation. Whenever such an event occurs, one is cut off from an important part of one's life and (particularly in the case of the elderly) feelings of loneliness and loss of identity are the most frequent consequences. Both of these syndromes relate intimately to the quest for meaning.[16]

INDIVIDUAL REACTIONS TO STRESS

What is stressful to one person is not necessarily stressful to another. In an interview, Lazarus stated: "Psychological stress resides neither in the situation nor the person; it depends on a transaction between the two. It arises from how the person appraises an event and adapts to it."[17] This view is consistent with Selye's concepts of internal and external conditioning.[18]

From a more behavioral point of view, Robinson et al. list three of the reasons for different stress reactions: perception, motivation, and stress tolerance.[19] In order for an individual to experience a situation as stressful, it has to be perceived as such. Whether or not one perceives any given situation as stressful depends on the resources the individual has to deal with the situation as well as the background and past experiences that affect the perception of that situation. The motivation level of the individual with regard to the particular incident also affects the stress reaction, as motivation is closely related to needs. If a strong need has been denied, a stress reaction is likely to result. Each of these is further affected by the individual's "stress tolerance." Individuals who have a high stress tolerance are able to respond to stress constructively rather than destructively. For example, such individuals would see a manager's criticism of a project which they just completed as a challenge to make it better rather than as disapproval and rejection leading to frustration and anger. Those who can tolerate high levels of stress are not easily discouraged by failure, disapproval, or adversity. On the contrary, "they actually seek stress, and then are continually challenged to improve their performance. Stress tolerance is a valuable trait, and it can be learned by acquiring sound adaptation skills."[20]

WORK-RELATED STRESS AND BURNOUT

There are at least three factors involved in the consideration of any individual's personal work performance—the task itself, the individual performing the task, and the environment in which the task is performed. These are common variables in the assessment of task performances; however, they can be considered in another way. When viewed in combination as possible causes of employee dissatisfaction, they begin to give some insight into work-related stress.

Workers in leisure service organizations share the occupational stressors of many other service disciplines because of the wide variety of settings in which they are employed. Those in municipal or community recreation services must deal with the demands of the public on a daily basis, while those working in psychiatric settings, prisons, institutions for the developmentally disabled, and hospitals work in different kinds of stressful situations—high patient-staff ratios, heavy caseloads, having to reach out to different departments to accomplish work objectives. In addition, workers in leisure service organizations traditionally have limited resources—usually the first to be cut at belt-tightening times; are expected to be "up" most of the time in facilitating leisure experiences for others; are expected to provide a service which people want and need and which simultaneously contradicts the predominant "work ethic" of society; and, traditionally, have been required to provide services with groups, attempting to meet the diverse needs of various individuals through a common recreation activity.

Notwithstanding the potential stressors unique to the leisure service occupations, these workers are subject to stressors which exist in most complex organizational structures. Examples of these are readily provided in the "Episodic, Work-Related Stress Evaluation" and the "Chronic, Work-Related Stress Evaluation" formulated by Adams.[21] The former lists such items as: "being transferred against my will to a new position or assignment;" "being shelved;" "being disciplined or seriously reprimanded by my supervisor;" and "encountering major or frequent changes in instructions, policies, or procedures" among events which have a high scale value in relation to the degree of disruption they cause in the average person's life. The "Chronic, Work-Related Stress Evaluation" lists day-to-day stressful conditions that often exist at work, and the individual indicates the relative frequency with which each is experienced. Some of the items listed on this scale are: "I am unclear about what is expected of me;" "the demands for my time are in conflict;" "I get feedback only when my performance is unsatisfactory;" "I feel overqualified for the work I actually do;" and, "I do not receive the right amount of supervision (too much or too little)."

The inability to handle continued stress on the job results in a state which Freudenberger has coined "Burnout." Burnout is defined as a wearing out, exhaustion, or failure resulting from excessive demands on energy, strength, or resources.[22]

The general burnout factor seems to be the greatest element in accounting for the professional's withdrawal from the field. Pit an individual against too much, for too long, with little or no results or rewards, and eventually ambition and productivity slacken and even disappear. The stresses and strains associated with burnout in agencies—large and small, urban and rural—can be drawn from a relatively small package of possibilities. Among those stated most often are role conflict, role ambiguity, conflict of purpose, under-use, workload dissatisfaction, work hours, pay inequities, boredom, lack of challenge, lack of self-esteem, frustration, and job future.

Burnout is manifested in a variety of ways, resulting from different coping mechanisms which individuals use to respond to job-related stress. It may be indicated by low worker morale, reduced efficiency and effectiveness (even though there is an increase in effort), high rate of absenteeism, minimized involvement with clients or consumers, petty bureaucracy, and high rate of employee turnover. In addition, a recent report by the national Centers for Disease Control said ". . . there are increasing data on the relationship between specific working conditions and psychological disorders."[23] It cited work conditions such as work overload, lack of control over one's job, nonsupportive bosses and colleagues, limited job opportunities, and undefined tasks, among others, as contributing to an employee's dissatisfaction at work. The report concluded that those factors can also cause psychological disorders including neuroses and depression, anxiety, irritability, drug abuse, sleeplessness, as well as physical complaints such as headaches and stomachache.[24]

STRESS MANAGEMENT

Both the leisure service profession and agencies have resources and strategies which might be employed to combat job-related stress. What is needed by both, however, is awareness that stress does exist. Perhaps the most important undertaking for the individual professional is the realization of personal susceptibility to stress and of stress-producing situations associated with work. Despite overwhelming evidence, recreation and leisure service professionals tend to ignore the fact they are under constant pressures. They fail to recognize that the insomnia, the depression, the irritability, the headaches that occur from time to time may be symptomatic of the stress generated by pressures in the workplace. The extra coffee, cigarettes, junk food, mood medication, "recreational" drugs, and alcohol consumption go unrecognized as stress-related behavioral outcomes that may themselves serve to compound the associated stress factors. Were leisure service professionals to become aware of these stress outcomes and feel that their behavior should be altered, they might consider adopting strategies similar to those that they advocate for others searching for stress avoidance and quality living. If recreation and leisure service professionals can tell others to vary routines, to search out satisfaction in nonwork activities, to separate their work lives and nonwork lives, to participate in physical exercise, to look inwardly at themselves to see what they want out of life, to learn relaxation techniques, to take on some consuming hobby, to seek lifestyle counseling, and to discuss problems openly with others, then surely they can take a little of their own advice.

"Developing, implementing, and evaluating a stress management program" should be a statement which is included in every leisure service manager's position description. It would be naive to assume that such a program would be implemented in an effective manner, simply because it is written; however, it is a starting point which creates an expectation. As with other managerial roles, a strong commitment by the manager is needed as a prerequisite to a successful program. In addition, the manager must learn techniques for self-management of stress and must recognize that these may or may not be effective for the employees. Stress management is not a once-a-month special event or seminar. It is an on-going process—a lifelong one at that. It should be implemented in small doses and results should not be expected immediately. Stress management involves changes in perception, attitudes, habits, motivation, and adaptation techniques, and with change comes resistance.

The leisure service manager can use the following guidelines in establishing a stress management program:

1. Provide educational opportunities for employees to understand stress, its sources and symptoms; potentially stressful situations; and stress management techniques.
2. Provide opportunities for employees to identify their work and nonwork levels of stress and self-management techniques for coping with stress.
3. Provide educational opportunities to assist individuals in coping with the pressures of the work situation more effectively, e.g., problem solving, decision making, time management.
4. Make role expectations clear through position descriptions, organizational policies, accurate instructions; reduce role ambiguity and conflict through improved organization, coordination, and communication.
5. Provide opportunities for employees to express their feelings and thoughts through participatory management and improved communication flow.
6. Establish programs to assist individuals in analyzing job suitability, assessing work stress for themselves and others, establishing career plans, helping others in managing stress, and obtaining help outside the organization.
7. Create support networks such as informal groups to discuss problems, brainstorm for potential solutions, or to take action on a particular project.
8. Provide opportunities for employees to explore the role of leisure in their lives (including the sense of "leisure lack," if appropriate) and opportunities for them to participate regularly in recreation and physical activities created especially to meet their interests.
9. Provide opportunities for individuals to learn "letting go" techniques, e.g., relaxation, meditation, as well as a "quiet spot" where employees can go for a break.
10. Monitor employee workload, relieving pressure in times of overload by demanding less, giving support and providing stimulation in times of underload through job enrichment, enlargement, or rotation.

11. Modify the work environment to reduce stressors, e.g., level of noise, extremes of heat or cold, unnecessary interruptions, crowding.
12. Implement annual comparative salary reviews for employees from various agencies in similar positions, and maintain competitive salaries in your agency.
13. Schedule vacations and encourage individuals to take them.
14. Help employees to learn that not all stress is bad, that inevitable stress may be used as a source of energy and creativity. If dealt with constructively, stress can lead to outstanding achievements and self-actualization.
15. Evaluate the stress management program periodically to determine if employees' responses to stress are becoming less destructive and more constructive.

Stress management is not a matter to be taken lightly, as the stakes are high. A survey of the statistics concerning what are commonly called "stress related diseases," drug prescriptions (especially tranquilizers), health and medical costs (including insurance) will reveal that these are staggering.[25] Although some individuals have a new level of consciousness in relation to stress management, most organizations—including those providing leisure services—have done little to acknowledge and deal with the problem. Stress is consuming the human resources of many of our organizations because of its cumulative rather than cause-specific effect. Although no manager has been held legally responsible for an on-the-job heart attack, can a manager—especially in a human service profession—who ignores the problem of stress, deny being a contributor?

SUMMARY

The role expectations of leisure service managers in reducing work-related stress was the focus of this chapter. The specific stressors related to the field of recreation and leisure services, e.g., working while others are playing and in a low status occupation, tight budgets, as well as the stressors which many working individuals experience, e.g., competitiveness, meeting time restraints, nonproductive meetings, were explored. And the various reasons for distress and dissatisfaction associated with job levels—upper management, middle management (supervisory), and direct service delivery were highlighted.

The point was made that stress itself is not the culprit, but that the quantity and intensity of stress determine its potential effect on a particular individual. In fact, a certain amount of stress is needed for and is a positive factor in work as well as play. Selye's three-stage reaction to stress was explained, i.e., alarm reaction, stage of resistance, stage of exhaustion.

Sources of stress have been classified by various individuals. Among these are Gray's physiological stress, psychological stress, and environmental stress. Robinson et al. categorize the common sources of stress as fear, overload or underload situation, life changes, and ambiguity. Individuals react differently to these sources of stress based on their perception, motivation, and stress tolerance.

Episodic and chronic work-related stressors were enumerated; and the burnout which results when an individual is pitted against too much stress for too long, with little or no results or rewards.

What is needed most is an awareness that stress does exist in the recreation and leisure service profession and that individuals must realize their personal susceptibility to it. "Developing, implementing, and evaluating a stress management program" should be a statement in every leisure service manager's position description. Stress management is an ongoing process and should be implemented in small doses. Fifteen guidelines which the leisure service manager can use in establishing a stress management program were presented.

NOTES AND REFERENCES

1. C.L. Cooper and J. Marshall, "Sources of Managerial and White Collar Stress," in **Stress At Work,** C.L. Cooper and R. Payne, eds. (Toronto: John Wiley & Sons, 1978), pp. 81–101.
2. J. Gaertner and J. Ruhe, "Job Related Stress in Public Accounting," **Journal of Accountancy,** June, 1981, pp. 68–74.
3. Ibid.
4. H. Boothman, "Whether Professionalism?" An address to the Canadian Parks/Recreation Association National Conference, Ottawa, 1972.
5. H. Selye, **The Stress of Life.** (New York: McGraw Hill Book Company, Inc., 1956), p. vii.
6. H. Selye, **Stress Without Distress,** England: Hodder & Stoughton, Ltd., 1977), p. 22.
7. Selye, 1956, p. 54.
8. Ibid., p. 64.
9. W. McQuade and A. Aikman, **Stress.** (New York: Bantam, 1975).
10. Selye, 1956, pp. 31–33, 38.
11. Selye, 1977, p. 16.

12. John D. Adams, **Understanding and Managing Stress.** (San Diego, California: University Associates, Inc., 1980), pp. 14–15.
13. L. Levi, **Stress: Sources, Management and Prevention.** New York City: Liveright, 1967).
14. J. Gray, **The Psychology of Fear and Stress.** (New York City: McGraw Hill, 1971).
15. J.W. Robinson Jr., R.A. Clifford, J. DeWalle, **Stress In Community Groups.** (Urbana, Illinois: University of Illinois at Urbana-Champaign, 1977), pp. 1–4.
16. Stephen Thayer and John Neulinger, "Stress and Leisure Lack," **Leisure Information Newsletter,** 8, 4 (Spring 1982), p. 6.
17. Richard S. Lazarus, "Positive Denial: The Case For Not Facing Reality," **Psychology Today,** (November 1979).
18. Selye, 1956, p. 98.
19. Robinson et al., p. 5.
20. Ibid, p. 7.
21. Adams, pp. 15–17, 19–21.
22. Herbert J. Freudenberger, "Burn-Out: Occupational Hazard of Child Care Worker," **Child Care Quarterly,** p. 90. 23. Gaertner and Ruhe, pp. 68–74.
23. "Stress on the Job Cited," **The New York Times,** October 23, 1986, p. C7.
24. Ibid.
25. Adams, pp. 2–3.

The purpose of this chapter is to help the manager answer:

- What is time management?
- What are the typical components of an effective time management program?
- What organizing decisions do managers have to make to conserve time?
- What are the major time wasters of managers?
- Why are "buffer time" and "downtime" important for managers?
- What are some strategies to cope with my own procrastination or that of my employees?
- Should I have an open-door policy?
- How do I handle uninvited visitors?
- What strategies can I develop to cope with the increasing amount of paperwork?
- What responsibility do I have to protect and conserve the time of subordinates?
- Are time management techniques useful in helping me meet my personal goals?
- What are effective time management techniques?

Chapter 11

Managing Time

Arnold H. Grossman

Peter Drucker, the dean of management consultants, says that until people know where their time is going, they cannot manage it; and until they can manage their time, they cannot manage anything else. "Time is the scarcest resource;" says Drucker, "and unless it is managed nothing else can be managed. The analysis of one's time, moreover, is the one easily accessible and yet systematic way to analyze one's work and to think through what really matters in it."[1] In other words, managing one's time is managing oneself. It calls for controlling those things that need to be controlled in order to reach the goals one has set for oneself.

Time is the scarcest resource; but it can neither be stored for future use, nor spent in advance. Furthermore it is irreplaceable, i.e., there is no substitute for it; and, if it is lost, it is totally irretrievable. Therefore, how one manages the 24 hours in a day, the 168 hours in a week, and the 8,736 hours in a year, and the years in one's life determines, in essence, how one has decided to live his or her life. To the extent that one permits others to waste one's time, he or she is letting others determine how one's life is lived.

TIME MANAGEMENT

Although the concept of time management usually refers to managing time at work, as the above paragraph indicates, it really applies to the way people live their lives. In other words, one should use the basic underlying concepts of time management in the *perspective of one's total life versus one's working life.* Time management can be useful in helping individuals to have more leisure experiences, with their concomitant joy and satisfaction. Lakein, author of *How to Get Control of Your Time and Your Life*, advises executives to get three-year, six-year and lifetime goals, which he suggests should be subdivided into categories "A," "B," and "C" in order of precedence. He suggests that individuals include personal as well as work-oriented goals. He recommends that individuals should identify their "internal prime time" (when they do their clearest thinking) and their "external prime time" (the best time for dealing with others). These prime times should then be used for pursuing "A" goals, i.e., A1, A2, A3.[2]

Time management is self-management. It is the management of the activities in which we engage during our time. It involves certain skills such as planning, organizing, implementing and controlling. "Time management means the *efficient use of our resources, including time, in such a way that we are effective in achieving important personal goals.* Efficiency has been defined as doing things right—effectiveness, as doing the *right* things right."[3] Ferner lists four major components of time management: 1) commitment (you must be committed to do something about it); 2) analysis (you must have data on where you spend your time, what the problems and causes are); 3) planning (effective management requires planning); and 4) follow-up and reanalysis (you must monitor results, detect problems, and modify the plan).[4]

The following are often listed as the typical components of an effective time management program:

- Analyze and monitor activities. Keep a time log as a systematic way of recording time use at regular activities during the day. This should be kept for approximately three weeks.
- Evaluate the log to eliminate "time wasters" from your schedule.
- Eliminate the "time wasters," and create blocks of time to accomplish higher priority tasks.
- Establish priorities, using the A-B-C method suggested by Lakein.
- Analyze existing habits and detect insignificant time wasting habits which when summed create significant time blocks, e.g., "slow starts," long telephone calls with more socializing than business, interruptions during peak work time, or fragmented approaches to activities.
- Create new effective time management habits, e.g., delegate tasks, limit meeting times, eliminate tasks that contribute little to outcomes, and learn to read faster.

Winston, in her book *Getting Organized*, suggests the following ideas for organizing work and life to be a more productive person:

- Understand one's biological clock. Determine the most productive time and tackle the most difficult tasks during this time.
- Organize one's day around three things: a day-to-day appointment calendar, a pocket-size spiral notebook for notes and reminders, and a daily "to do" list.
- Make the most of short bits of time, e.g., take along reading for layovers at the airport.
- Do not let perfectionism stand in the way of organization.
- Develop a filing system which one understands; and then use it.
- Believe in the organizing principle.[5]

Every individual has a unique means of coping with and organizing myriad data. For some, a simple spiral notebook and "in" and "out" boxes provide adequate control; for others index cards and manila folders do the organizing job; and for many, today's new time management computer software ensures more effective self-management. Each manager has to find his or her most effective organizing rhythm and make a judgment about what is and is not important in relating to the tools supporting this rhythm.

A major organizing decision relates to inflow, and the creation of a system for handling incoming mail. If a secretary or assistant opens and organizes the mail, it should be divided into two stacks: internal mail and external mail. A system should then be created for categorizing the two stacks of inflow. One example might be: (A) Action, for immediate follow-up; (F) File, required for doing business; (I) Information, useful, worth reading or scanning; and (D) Discard, dispensable (just slip into the wastebasket, as a piece may need to be recovered later in the day.)

Another organizing decision relates to organizing time. It is imperative to remember to include two types of time in one's daily schedule: "buffer time" and "downtime." A preplanned and tightly scheduled day does not permit time to react and respond to important situations as they arise. Buffer time permits individuals to handle matters as they arise rather than later, when one may have to refresh one's memory about the details of the situation and reschedule meetings with other people—both of which waste time. In addition, buffer time allows for interruption and devotion of time to an employee's exciting idea. Downtime refers to time alone, time to relieve pressure and get new energy with no phones ringing and no immediate demands. Some managers need a small amount of downtime, e.g., an hour, while others need two hours a day. It is the quality of the downtime rather than the amount of time which matters. Some individuals can use commuting time, lunch hour, exercise time or early morning and late night periods. It is important to do something one enjoys during this time.

TIME WASTERS

While many people are overworked, they are also underorganized. Time management consultants "have compiled a vast dictionary to describe these organizing ills. It includes terms such as 'Procrastination Quotients' (a high PQ indicates a tendency to dally on tough decisions), 'Stacked Desk syndrome' (enables an executive to say to him or herself: "Look how busy I am"), 'Open Door Myth' (invites interruptions), 'Fat Paper Philosophy' (induced by memoitis and spread by copy machines and magnetic-tape typewriters), 'Analysis Paralysis' (immobility caused by substituting study for courage), and 'Planning Paradox' (failure to plan because it takes time)."[6] Let us take a look at these organizing ills more closely, as they are frequently "time wasters" for managers as well for some of the subordinates whom they supervise. An understanding of them can certainly be valuable in assisting managers in enhancing their managerial effectiveness.

Procrastination: Procrastination or prolonged hesitation is putting things off until the last minute and then scampering to finish them and sometimes just not doing them. All of us have experienced such tendencies at one time or another. The situation becomes a problem when procrastination becomes more than a bad habit, but a way of life.

Before we continue with the subject of procrastination, we should distinguish between this phenomenon and "intelligent delay." Intelligent delay is: (a) putting off low-priority items (the "C" items) in hopes that there is a chance they will go away or subordinates will take care of them; or (b) the time is not right to do anything about the item; or (c) today's small problems are not as important as future long-range plans. Procrastination, on the other hand, causes us to suffer in the present while damaging the future. It is also counterproductive because it is time consuming and causes us to dwell on the "shoulds" while we do other things more slowly.[7]

Burka and Yuen indicate that procrastination is a complex phenomenon. They state, "While it may be tempting to label the procrastinator as lazy or disorganized or just plain ornery, what's often at the root of the behavior is fear. Delaying may be a strategy that protects a person from facing fears and anxieties, such as fear of failure or fear of success, fear of being controlled, fear of becoming too separate from others or fear of being too attached."[8] They make the following recommendations to procrastinators:

- Analyze one's procrastination history. What is the pattern? What was the motive(s)? When is it most likely to occur? What is the style of procrastination? (What is done instead of doing what is supposed to be done?)
- Set reasonable and reachable goals which are observable by the person and others.
- Reward oneself when one achieves a goal.
- Keep a daily schedule of activities. Include all the things one is committed to do. Do not overestimate the time one has available or underestimate the time it takes to complete a task. Include time for fun and relaxation.
- Use even little bits of time. (Often procrastinators never start a project because they insist on having the full amount of time it will take to complete it.) Consequently, learn to break down big jobs into manageable chunks and then do them one at a time.
- Enlist support from others. By telling others what one is going to do and when it will be completed, one is making a commitment for oneself.
- Reduce stress and do what can be done. Learn relaxation exercises.[9]

Other strategies for those who tend to procrastinate include: 1) start the job by doing something, even if it requires little thought and accomplishes very little; 2) once you start the job, let your momentum carry you, i.e., once you are into the job, keep it going; and, 3) end the job when it is finished, as something can always be improved and improved.

To employers of procrastinators, Burka and Yuen advise: "Procrastinators are people who are not utilizing their full potential. The challenge for you as a manager is to see how creative you can be in maximizing their hidden assets. You can help by setting clear limits and deadlines, clarifying concrete and specific goals, and rewarding progress along the way."[10]

Open-Door Policy: An open-door policy enhances informal communication between managers and subordinates. It assists managers in learning more about the organization's human resources; reduces workers' alienation; provides opportunities for managers to get direct feedback from employees; and provides opportunities to enhance workers' loyalty and cooperation. However, there are some negative aspects to an open-door policy, the biggest of which is "time wasting." There are the unscheduled interruptions in the manager's time with important as well as trivial items; and at the same time it wastes workers' time while they camp on the manager's doorstep. It also provides opportunities for employees to bypass their immediate supervisors, and it may entangle managers in employees' personal problems. Furthermore, managers may feel annoyed at times when they are interrupted by impromptu visits and may show it unintentionally or may be more critical than they intend. And, managers have to ascertain whether the open door is providing opportunities for employees to dump problems in the manager's lap which encroaches on the manager's time. Each manager has to balance the advantages and the risks and make certain that the open door does not become a trap door.

Uninvited Visitors: Although the open-door policy invites visitors, there are some bosses, colleagues, or subordinates who simply slip into a visitor's chair uninvited, whether the door is open or closed. Getting a long-winded visitor out of one's office without being rude is not easy to do. However, it becomes a necessary task if one does not want to permit the visitor to waste one's time. Some tried and true approaches include: breaking eye contact, failing to respond to the conversation, starting to act restless, mentioning work to be done or phone calls to be made, or starting to walk to the office door. If these do not work with some individuals, more assertive techniques have to be used, such as going to or scheduling meetings in the other person's office or in a neutral place. One can then get up and leave when one has to. Another method is to prearrange interruptions, e.g., have the secretary announce another appointment or have the secretary or another colleague telephone at a prearranged time. If all else fails, find another office or library to hide out to finish important work without interruptions.

Lack of Planning and Indecision: Through planning and decision-making we cause things to happen. Planning involves setting goals, finding ways to achieve those goals, deciding which is the best way, and scheduling specific steps to reach the goals. (The reader is referred to Chapter Four in which the planning process is discussed). The next step is taking action. Action is doing something, not just thinking about it. The best plans have little value unless we do something about them.

Managers often waste time due to lack of planning. They fail to see the benefit of planning, and they see themselves as action oriented. They must come to recognize that although planning takes time, it saves time in the end. In addition, they need to focus their thinking and planning so that results are emphasized, not activity.

In order to devote time to thinking, conceptualizing, and planning, managers should schedule time in their daily activities which can be devoted to the planning process. They should establish *short-range* and *long-range* plans; and they should integrate all programs or projects into these plans so that important outcomes are achieved. They should insist on efficient administration to execute plans and close coordination of all elements of a plan. If managers are not in the habit of planning, they should examine their weaknesses and decide what they are going to do about it and when they are going to do it.

Memoitis and Computeritis: Many managers drown in paperwork. It gets them so bogged down that it literally pulls them under. The knowledge explosion, memoitis, and computeritis have significantly increased the amount of paper which arrives on a manager's desk and on the desks of his or her subordinates. Therefore, one can easily create the "Stacked Desk Syndrome" by letting the paper pile up on one's desk, or one can limit the paper and forward to subordinates only that which is necessary. If one has the need to keep all the work to him or herself or keep others away, one can stack the desk so that people will feel guilty about adding another piece of paper (or reluctant because it may get lost in a stack and never found again). A more effective approach, however, is to learn to deal with the paperwork efficiently.

A manager should screen the paperwork which comes to his or her desk. In doing so the manager should remember the "Pareto principle" (named after the 19th century economist and sociologist Vilfredo Pareto). It states: the significant items in a given group normally constitute a relatively small portion of the total items in the group (usually interpreted that 20 percent will be high value; the other 80 percent will be low or medium value).[11] After screening that which needs to be read, a manager should learn to read selectively, reading only that information in the material which is imperative to accomplishing his or her goals and tasks. And, if the manager is not facile at reading quickly, he or she should enroll in a speed reading course. An alternative is to delegate reading which relates to subordinates' activities to them. Another effective approach, especially with regard to computer reports, is to "manage by exception," i.e., only significant deviations of actual from planned performance should be reported to the manager. This conserves the time, energy, and ability required in reading the total computer report.

Wasting Subordinates' Time: Managers have the responsibility of protecting and conserving the time of their subordinates so that they can accomplish those goals and tasks which are delegated to them through their positions (using job or positions descriptions) as well as those which are delegated on a daily or weekly basis. One important way to do such is to limit the memoranda and material which are sent to subordinates. Screening information sent to subordinates and keep-

memoranda limited to necessary information are effective approaches. In addition, managers should limit the committees they create and only involve subordinates who can make decisions regarding the committee's work. Parkinson noted that committees tend to spend more time on matters easily understood by all members than they do on highly complex issues. This is because many people are reluctant to demonstrate their ignorance by speaking on topics unfamiliar or controversial. Therefore committees tend to haggle ad nauseam on trivial matters (e.g., what to serve with coffee and tea) and make crucial decisions in a matter of minutes (e.g., a new computer record-keeping system). Parkinson calls this the law of triviality: "The time spent on any item of the agenda will be in inverse proportion to the sum involved."[12] A committee that wastes time on trivia should be disbanded.

Another way managers can conserve their time as well as that of subordinates is to limit the number of meetings scheduled. Managers who call many meetings usually do so because they fear the responsibility for decisions, are indecisive themselves, demostrate ineffective leadership, or have a desire to overcompensate. Such managers have to learn to convene only those meetings which are necessary and to use agendas and stick to the subjects on them. In addition, they have to learn to make decisions without meetings, even when some facts are missing.

Managers have a tendency to waste their time as well as that of subordinates by underdelegation. This causes the manager to do things which employees should be doing (not getting to his or her own work) as well as having subordinates waste time waiting for the manager to get to that which they need. Managers have to learn to delegate effectively. (The reader is referred to Chapter Nine in which the process and techniques of delegation are discussed.)

INTEGRATING PERSONAL LIFE GOALS WITH WORK GOALS

Someone once stated that they never heard a person on his or her death bed say that she or he regretted not having spent more time at the office. Consequently, it is important to identify and integrate one's personal life goals with one's career and work goals. Individuals in the field of recreation and leisure services should be most aware of this; however, as the cobbler often goes without shoes, persons in the field tend to neglect those goals that relate to leisure experiences, including intellectual, cultural, physical, recreation, social, and spiritual activities.

The personal life goals should be written down and carefully integrated with career, work, and professional activities. These should also be categorized and prioritized using the A, B, C method. And, as one organizes his or her weekly schedule, activities related to these goals should be included so as to create a balanced week, month, year, and the years in one's life.

MORE TIME MANAGEMENT TECHNIQUES: IN BRIEF[13]

Additional time management techniques which managers in recreation and leisure services will find helpful are discussed briefly—to save the readers' time!

Balanced scheduling. In reacting to cycles in the recreation and leisure services field, managers must make adjustments in their activities. For example, in the busy periods of summer and holidays managers would want to pay close attention to the myriad of trips, camping programs, and parties. In the relatively slow periods managers should schedule times for planning, budgeting, and cutting expenses. Managers have to change their emphases with the changing program cycle.

Eliminating routine administrative tasks. Managers who have completed a time analysis are usually amazed to find out how much time is tied up in routine activities such as approving expenditures, signing checks, making certain that work has been completed. These routine tasks should be delegated, and forms and reports should be countersigned where decisions have been made, i.e., at a subordinate level. Consequently, managerial approval should be reserved to exceptions to the routine and control over significant expenditures.

Use hand-written reports. Do not delay getting information and waste subordinates' time by requiring typewritten or word processing reports. Reports which contain columns of figures, e.g., budget requests, attendance figures, projected program enrollments, can be prepared in a fraction of the time normally required if subordinates have preprinted forms and simply fill in figures with a pen or pencil.

Substitute group meetings for individual sessions. Managers waste time repeating a discussion of general problems or guidelines in individual meetings. This is especially valuable when other people are involved, e.g., youth services, adult services, senior citizens, as a problem is likely to be solved faster or an effective guideline established when the coordinators affected can discuss the situation simultaneously.

Repeat decisions should be avoided. Managers waste time when they have to make the same decisions over and over again. If a problem is presented for a decision a second time, there is a need for a policy or guideline to be established.

Teach subordinates to make their own decisions and accept responsibility for them. Managers waste time making decisions which should be made at a lower level. A manager can save much time by teaching subordinates to make their own decisions and by stopping the buck-passing back to the manager.

Delegate routine correspondence to secretaries and subordinates. Division supervisors should be able to respond to routine mail about the programs in their divisions and secretaries should be able to respond to routine information about services, program schedules, fees and charges.

Respond to internal mail with a handwritten note on the original. Managers and their secretaries waste time dictating and typing formal replies when a handwritten note will accomplish the same purpose. A photocopy can be made if a record of the response is required.

Save telephone time. Use of the telephone can be a time saver as well as a time waster. A telephone call is quicker than dictating and writing a letter to communicate or receive information. However, the telephone can also be a time waster. Some guidelines to managing telephone time are: accept calls only at certain times; place calls according to others' best times to receive calls; limit long-winded callers using techniques similar to those for office visitors who refuse to leave; and use an intercom to get information which is needed during the call (as it wastes time to find out the necessary information and return the call).

SUMMARY

One of the most urgent problems facing managers is how to conserve their time, turn more of it to goals that really pay off, or simply cut down on excessive hours they are probably devoting to their work. "Managing your time," says Drucker, "is managing yourself. It's controlling all the things that need to be controlled to achieve the objectives you want to achieve."[14] That was the focus of this chapter.

Typical components of an effective time management program were enumerated as follows:

- Analyze and monitor activities in a time log.
- Evaluate the log to eliminate time wasters.
- Eliminate the time wasters, and create blocks of time to accomplish higher priority tasks.
- Use the A-B-C method to establish priorities.
- Analyze existing habits and detect time wasting habits.
- Create new effective time management habits.

It is imperative that managers identify their "internal prime time" (when they do their clearest thinking) and their "external prime time" (the best time for dealing with others). In addition, one must understand one's biological clock to determine the most productive time in which to tackle the most difficult tasks.

Ideas were then discussed for organizing work and life so as to help managers become more productive. Included in this discussion were: developing methods of organizing the myriad of data which comes across the manager's desk, and creating a system for handling incoming mail. Another organizing decision presented was the establishment of two types of time in one's daily schedule, i.e., buffer time (to respond to important situations as they arise) and downtime (time alone to relieve pressure and get new energy).

Time wasters for managers as well as for subordinates were presented. These are: procrastination; open-door policy; uninvited visitors; lack of planning and indecision; memoitis and computeritis; and, wasting subordinates' time.

The distinction was made between procrastination (i.e., prolonged hesitation in putting things off until the last minute and then scampering to finish them and sometimes just not doing them) and intelligent delay (i.e., putting off low priority items, or items on which the time is not right to act, or small daily problems which are not as important as future plans). In this area, we should all take a lesson from Scarlett O'Hara in *Gone With The Wind*. She comes back to her family's plantation and finds herself confronted by the wreckage left in Sherman's wake. Yet, she has to manage. So, she does what she can do and deals with what she cannot do by saying, "I'll think about it tomorrow."

The importance of integrating personal goals with work goals was established. Included among the personal goals were intellectual, cultural, physical, recreation, social, and personal activities that provide the opportunities for leisure experiences.

Additional time management techniques were discussed in brief. These included: balanced scheduling; eliminating routine administrative tasks; use of hand-written reports; substituting group meetings for individual sessions; avoiding repeated decisions; teaching subordinates to make their own decisions and accepting responsibility for them; delegating routine correspondence; responding to internal mail with a handwritten note on the original; and saving telephone time.

NOTES AND REFERENCES

1. Peter Drucker, **The Effective Executive.** (Great Britain: William Heinemann Ltd., 1967), p. 53.
2. Alan Lakein, **How to Get Control of Your Time and Your Life.** (New York: Peter H. Wyden, 1973).
3. Jack D. Ferner, **Successful Time Management: A Self Teaching Guide.** (New York: John Wiley and Sons, 1980), p. 12.
4. Ibid.
5. Stephanie Winston, **Getting Organized.** (New York: Warner Books, Inc., 1978).
6. Roy Rowan, "Executive Time Wasters," **Fortune,** 1978, p. 18.
7. Dick Samson, **How to Get Things Done: The Power of Purpose Through The Dynamic Par² System of Time Management.** (New York: National Institute of Business Management, 1987), p. 71.
8. "Procrastination," **The Voice** (New York State Recreation and Park Society), Spring 1987, pp. 6–8.
9. Ibid.
10. Ibid.
11. Ferner, 1980, p. 131.
12. C. Northcote Parkinson, **Parkinson's Law and Other Studies in Administration.** (Boston: Houghton-Mifflin, 1957).
13. Selected from "Executive Time Management," **Executive Skills Enrichment,** Frank Gruber, ed. (New York: The Research Institute of America, Inc., 1986), pp. 46–52.
14. Drucker, 1967, p. 52.

The purpose of this chapter is to help the manager answer:

- What is the Occupational Safety and Health Act?
- What are the obligations of the employer under OSHA?
- What are the rights and responsibilities of employees under OSHA?
- What causes employee accidents?
- How can employee accidents be prevented?
- What are the "hidden costs" of employee accidents?
- What are the principles of accident prevention?
- Which accidents must be recorded and which must be reported?
- What are the general provisions of workers' compensation laws?

Chapter 12

Employee Safety: Preservation of Human Resources

Arnold H. Grossman and Willoughby Ann Walshe

Safety runs like a thread through every recreation and leisure service manager's job. To a large degree, a manager has a moral obligation to maintain safe and healthful working conditions. At the same time, safe working conditions benefit an agency by contributing to overall staff efficiency. In the recreation and leisure services field, where the work area is also the service area, safety carries over to the client as well. Although the responsibilities for, and the advantages resulting from, effective employee safety practices are considerable, few agencies offer sufficient accident protection unless required to do so by law.

Health and safety has not been the subject of very many laws until recently. However, in the 91st Congress there were over a thousand bills introduce pertaining to the health and safety of the labor force. The Coal Mine Health and Safety Act was passed by Congress and signed into law December 30, 1969 by President Nixon. It provides compensation for victims of the coal miner's black lung disease. It also contains stricter safety standards which are designed to prevent coal mine disasters. Also signed into law in 1969 was the Construction Health and Safety Act. In 1970 the landmark Occupational Safety and Health Act (OSHA) was passed, for the first time putting real teeth into the enforcement of safety regulations at the national level.[1] Taking effect on April 28, 1971, OSHA ensured that all types of private business concerns would meet uniform standards and employees would have legal recourse in case of job-related accidents, diseases, or other undue occupational strains. But OSHA also requires all states to develop and maintain comprehensive health and safety programs for all employees. And Executive Order 12196, which became effective October 1, 1980, requires all federal agencies to comply with OSHA standards.

Safety and health laws are constantly being tested and revised; however, the language makes it increasingly clear that virtually any outfit which does business and has employees must comply with OSHA regulations. Thus, both nonprofit service organizations—such as some recreation and leisure service agencies—and commercial firms are covered under OSHA.[2]

The hierarchy of responsibility for employee health and safety starts with the recreation or leisure service manager, who is in the best position to ensure that protective measures are taken to avoid hazards. Watchdogging these procedures is the Occupational Safety and Health Administration, (under the jurisdiction of the Department of Labor), which is assigned the task of setting standards and enforcing them.

The procedures for implementing an accident-free environment involve common-sense principles and constant application. This chapter looks at why accidents are caused and how safety measures can be implemented in the recreation or leisure service agency to prevent casualties. Finally, it briefly discusses general OSHA requirements and workers' compensation laws.

CAUSES OF ACCIDENTS

Accidents do not just happen, but are the natural result of a chain of circumstances. Management can usually control the direction these circumstances take because accidents are caused either by exposure to unsafe conditions or by performing an unsafe act. While it is true that forces completely outside the control of management sometimes cause accidents, they are generally the result of a manager's or employee's negligence.

Unsafe conditions: If the physical work environment is not safe, accidents are likely to happen. Employees may bump into protruding objects, fall off unguarded landings, slip on newly waxed floors, and mistake unmarked, dangerous chemicals for look-alike safe ones. Improperly stored objects can fall or create fire hazards. Thus, poorly maintained buildings are potentially dangerous.

When unsafe conditions are found to exist, they should be eliminated wherever possible. Failing elimination, management (which has the final control over the buildings, equipment, tools, and materials with which employees work), should provide safeguards against these harmful hazards. In addition, the employees should be protected from possible accidents.

Agencies maintaining swimming pool facilities, for example, are required to introduce concentrated chemicals into the water periodically. There is no way the chemicals can be eliminated; however, they can be placed in a locked storeroom. Employees can further be required to wear gloves and protective garments when working with the chemicals.

Unsafe acts: Surprisingly, even though working conditions may be dangerous, they are not the major cause of on-the-job accidents. It has been estimated that as many as 90 percent of all work-related injuries result either directly or indirectly from some personal act. Thus, while managers must take responsibility for seeing that working conditions under their control are safe and lawful, their major duty is to ensure that workers perform their tasks safely and take all necessary precautions against accidental injury.

Generally, unsafe acts are caused by negative attitudes, unskilled employees, and overtired people. Of course, there are many management techniques for dealing with these problems. Negative attitudes can be turned around through supervisory conferences, group meetings, counseling, and personal examples. Recruitment and hiring methods can be examined and revised to select qualified personnel who know how to handle equipment properly. Interviews can be held with chronically overtired employees to determine the reasons for their conditions and resulting negligence, and plans can be formulated to transform their lackadaisical attitudes into alertness.

Adverse employee accident experience will produce debit ratings or other penalties that will greatly increase insurance costs. These are visible costs and do not reflect true costs, which include the incidental or hidden costs not covered by the workers' compensation insurance policy. These include:

- Cost of lost time by persons, other than the injured employee, who stop work out of curiosity, sympathy, or desire to assist— or who lose time for other related reasons.
- Cost of time spent by administrators and supervisors to assist, investigate, arrange for replacement of an injured employee, train a new employee, prepare accident reports, and attend Workers' Compensation Board hearings.

- Cost of first aid and medical treatment if provided by the agency, which is not normally paid for by the insurance company.
- Cost of damaged equipment or property due to the accident.
- Cost due to interference with operations and schedules, including necessity to utilize outside agents, per-diem help and overtime payments.
- Cost of waiting period wages, supplementary wages, and employee fringe benefits not reimbursed by the insurance company.
- Loss in value when employee returns to limited work.
- Possible idle equipment and curtailed service if replacement cannot be found.
- Weakened employee morale.[3]

Although most accidents are caused by unsafe acts rather than by exposure to unsafe conditions, the latter should be attacked first in order that the good housekeeping standards can encourage the employees to develop appropriate habits. The result is generally one of responding to the clean, safe, working conditions with a heads-up attitude and a feeling of pride in the work accomplished.

PRINCIPLES OF ACCIDENT PREVENTION

Planning for safety saves a recreation or leisure service agency time and aggravation in the long run. Its management, therefore, must be aware of the hazards in the work environment and take steps to prevent accidents. Once the agency's premises are clean and orderly (in compliance with OSHA regulations), it is necessary to further become aware of the hazards in the work environment and take steps to prevent accidents from occurring.

Following are a dozen ways to create and maintain an accident-free environment:

1. Make certain the employees in the agency are knowledgeable in depth about the OSHA Act and are kept up to date on new developments. It is advisable that the agency manager become well acquainted with the regulations applying to his or her type of organization. Technical or legal advice may be required in some cases to determine whether or not certain regulations apply.

When familiar with the OSHA regulations, it is incumbent upon the manager to do whatever is necessary to bring the agency into compliance in order to prevent accidents. This will also avoid inspections imposed on,[4] and fines levied against violators. At the same time, because employees are guaranteed a number of rights under OSHA,[5] the manager must be careful not to violate those rights while attempting to enforce safety regulations.

2. Keep a close watch on all potential hazards. Correct dangerous conditions as they are brought to attention. This can be accomplished by critically examining existing safety and health conditions at the agency's facilities. Evaluate all aspects of the job, identify all possible hazards and attempt to correct them. Previous accident experience should be reviewed completely. If help is needed, don't hesitate to obtain it.[6]

Some agencies involved in recreation or leisure services prepare a check list for employees working in administrative, activities, and sports areas. Items that can be surveyed include:

- Are filing cabinets bolted together and anchored to the floor or wall to prevent tipping?
- Is the electrical wiring intact, with no loose connections?
- Do the employees know the locations of fire extinguishers and how to use them?
- Are cords from telephones, typewriters, or other business machines located out of the aisles?
- Are ladders provided for reaching high places and are they in good condition?
- Do stairs have handrails and are employees told to *walk* up and down?
- Are there sharp, protruding objects from the tables, walls, doors, and shelves in the activity centers or nails protruding from benches, fences, and bleachers on the playing fields?
- Is the gym or swimming pool floor slippery?
- Are pointed pieces of equipment, such as fencing foils and billiard cues, stored in a safe place?
- What hazard does a ceramic kiln present to the employees who fire it?
- Is there broken glass lying on the playing fields, floors, or playgrounds?

Naturally, the list could be infinite and beyond the ability of a single manager to ascertain.[7] Therefore, it is wise to solicit the employees' help. Ask them for suggestions on how to improve the facility's safety conditions. Do this by talking with them individually and in groups.

Incident recall interviews is a method used by a number of firms. The interviews are conducted on company time once a week in a private room. An employee is picked at random and asked to recall one near-miss accident in which there were no injuries or damage to equipment or material. After the interview, the personnel manager analyzes the incident, takes immediate remedial action and alerts higher management. Once the employee is interviewed, he or she is dropped from the list until the personnel manager has spoken to all employees. Tightening up on safety in this way can bring a steady decrease in accidents.

3. Clean things up right away. When tackling this housekeeping chore, remove the trash, dirt, debris, and other junk that have accumulated in the offices, halls, activity rooms, grounds, and parking areas. Arrange all equipment where it can be quickly accessible. Put activity materials on shelves and in cabinets. Store any equipment or machinery not being used in a location (preferably locked), where it is inaccessible to employees and clients.

Having efficient conditions and fewer accidents will improve employees' morale and productivity. In addition to making the work safer, it will give them more room to work. After the working area has been cleaned and unsafe conditions have been eliminated, keep it that way. All equipment and tools related to the work operation should be arranged in an orderly way and marked for others to find easily.

4. Analyze and strengthen, where necessary, the agency's safety and health program. After the potential hazards have been located, plan ways for controlling them. It is also important to select the right methods and the right people for the job.

Once a plan of action has been developed, it should be put to work. Make specific work assignments and give instructions. Check to see that each person understands what is expected of him or her and that it is done. Remove, or protect against, hazards and insist on safe practices.

The primary organizational difference between large and small recreation and leisure service agencies, as far as safety administration is concerned, is the presence of staff assistance in a large organization. Where the agency has a full-time safety officer, it is his or her job to provide assistance to the departments and help them carry out their safety programs.

Lack of such assistance can be compensated for in smaller agencies. Outside help can be tapped for technical assistance when needed. The insurance company or state agency handling workers' compensation insurance can be helpful in providing posters, accident report forms, films, and safety training materials, as well as safety engineering.

Many local, state, and federal health departments have developed a great deal of material on the subject of health, which can be used. State experts are also available for mechanical and electrical engineering jobs. By getting in touch with the state department concerned with employee safety, this expert knowledge usually can be tapped to solve the agency's safety problems.

The city fire and police departments are also valuable sources for informing people about safety. Where the agency operates vehicles and maintains a parking area, for example, local police departments and state police agencies can provide traffic safety tips. In addition, the city's safety engineer or traffic engineer can lend technical assistance in establishing effective traffic regulations and procedures, or in solving traffic problems.

    5. Purchase equipment and materials with regard to applicable federal safety standards and obtain all recommended safety guards or devices with each purchase.

Many government agencies have been formed to conduct surveys of consumer goods, investigate complaints from public sources, and establish standards for product manufacture and use. Some of the federal agencies that provide information on building, equipment and materials safety are: National Bureau of Standards, Office of Consumer Affairs, National Business Council for Consumer Affairs, Federal Trade Commission, General Services Administration, and the Government Printing Office.

    6. Enforce safety regulations by encouraging employees to wear appropriate clothing for the job. Just as each sport and activity has its protective gear, so should social agency employees be alerted to dressing appropriately for the work being performed.

This can be accomplished by providing and requiring each employee to use regulation clothing, shoes, and equipment for the activities in which they are involved. The agency should provide aprons and tools for arts and crafts classes, issue or ensure the use of proper clothing and footwear for sports activities, and make available lockers for the storage of the clothing and equipment. Furthermore, employees should be encouraged to keep their footwear and clothing clean and in good repair. The leisure service agency manager might insist that they wear leather shoes instead of sneakers or sandals when working on building projects or on campsites. In addition, good quality work gloves should be worn when handling rough, splintered, or sharp materials. All employees who wear eye glasses should wear safety guards when engaged in such activities as softball and basketball. Eye safety guards should also be worn by all employees, as well as clients, engaged in woodworking or craft programs utilizing machines such as lathes, skill saws, and drill presses, or using spray paints.

7. Identify hazards and hazardous materials by labels, signs, and instruction sheets. These serve as warnings to new employees and reminders to employees of long standing. Of course, the labels should be marked in bold, black letters; signs should be posted in conspicuous locations; and instructions should be clearly and concisely stated.

Potentially hazardous materials and areas in recreation or leisure service agencies may include inflammable and toxic chemicals, steep stairs, slippery floors, and blind or swinging doors. Labels for chemicals, for example, should contain antidotal instructions as well as the cautionary language. Signs in the dangerous areas should both advise and warn.

"Walk don't run, slippery floors." "Open slowly, door enters stairwell." "Hold hand rail, stairs are steep." "Dark corridor, turn on light switch before entering." These are examples of signs that give explicit directions and caution against the impending danger. Naturally, places where inflammable materials are used should be designated "no smoking" areas, and the inflammable materials should be stored under lock and key.

8. Make certain the agency has an effective internal safety training program for employees. The new employee must be well trained in all phases of his or her job. It is the manager's duty and obligation to see that employees have the appropriate attitude toward the prevention of accidents. This can be accomplished through supervisory meetings. Hold a group discussion (rather than a safety lecture), on accidents which have occurred in the work group. The employees should be encouraged to express their ideas. A group conclusion as to how the accident could have been prevented should be reached.

Another type of safety meeting is one in which the supervisor presents a problem which has developed because of new work or new equipment. The employees should be invited to express their ideas towards a solution to the problem.

A third type of safety meeting presents actual demonstrations and allows the group members to practice safety measures. For example, proper methods of tree trimming and cutting could be demonstrated.

Then the employees hired for that job could go through the motions.

Above all, the meetings should be interesting. The subject should be timely and thought out in advance. Some supervisors let the employees rotate as leaders of the safety meetings. Other use films and other visual aids available on safety subjects. (A list of these films can be obtained from the National Safety Council.)

9. Identify accident-prone employees and provide special counseling for them. A few employees take the attitude that it is the employer's sole responsibility to provide them with a safe work place. While legal responsibility for employee health and safety are growing daily for the employer, this is not a one-way street. The employee has a greater responsibility than ever before to comply with safety regulations.

Before any treatment or education can get to a person, he or she has to realize there is a problem, i.e., working habits. Safety personnel are finding that a near miss of a disastrous accident often converts the safety scoffer to a safety observer. When a person suffers a painful injury, that's a good time to give a gentle reminder that safety has been ignored. The victim should be led to realize there is a problem and to decide that no more chances will be taken.

Another method of treating accident-prone employees is to teach them the right way to do each job. Working safely is as much a part of on-the-job training as the actual work operations. Hold regular safety meetings using slides and discussion guides. Encourage employees to get training in first aid, cardiopulmonary resusitation, and the Heimlich maneuver through local Red Cross chapters. Alternatively, the agency can sponsor an employee for the Red Cross instructor course and he or she can offer training for the employees as well as for clients.

Knowing what employees can and cannot do and their attitudes toward their jobs provides important clues to their safety behavior. Once attitudes have been ascertained, a manager may want to reassign jobs to employees who are able to perform them without an accident.

10. Be active in professional associations with regard to safety and health standards. Make use of community resources to set health and safety standards. This can be done in the following ways:

- Apply for accreditation with professional organizations, if such exist in the areas of service provided by the agency, e.g., American Camping Association's accreditation of day and resident camping sites and programs.

- Suggest and encourage educational sessions and discussions to be led by safety experts or public health and safety officials at professional conferences or conventions.
- Advocate for the enactment of legislation establishing health and safety standards which would protect employees as well as the consumers of services.
- Be active in the community, working with other recreation and leisure service agencies to plan strategies for safety in the community. Topics such as vandalism in the parks and schools, safety in the streets, traffic routes and speed limits, the refurbishing of recreation and park facilities and the enforcement of health and safety rules and regulations affect employees as well as consumers.

11. Cover safety and health in agency publications and at administrative meetings. No stone should be left unturned to remind employees of their responsibilities in observing safety procedures. Dissemination of safety information can be accomplished by:

- Starting a regular safety column in the agency's newsletter to employees.
- Presenting new employees with a safety booklet. Some of the topics that could be covered include the location of fire alarms and fire extinguishers; procedures for fire drills; use of tools and specialized equipment; first aid for accidents, (including the location of first-aid supplies); repair of damaged or broken equipment; maintenance repair in the facilities; travel in agency vehicles or on public transportation with groups; procedures to be followed if caught in a lightning storm; rules and regulations regarding the use of elevators; rules and regulations with regard to the swimming pool, woodworking shop, and physical fitness apparatus; housekeeping and cleanliness in the agency's facilities.
- Issuing weekly safety tip leaflets to all employees.
- Posting safety prevention ideas on the bulletin boards.

12. Investigate accidents thoroughly. Determine causative factors and necessary corrective action. Keep a permanent file for each employee.

The manager needs to know the causes of accidents and how to prevent them. Whenever an accident or near-accident occurs in a work group, it should be investigated. The thing to remember is that all the facts must be obtained about the accident. This forms the basis for action that will prevent the accident from happening again.

Many different factors must be looked for in a complete investigation, including: unsafe condition (e.g., faulty wiring), type of accident (e.g., collision through swinging doors), unsafe act (e.g., not watching where one walks), unsafe personal factor (e.g., improper attitude, lack of skill), and part of the body involved (e.g., head, leg, arm).

These factors give an idea of some key points to consider when investigating accidents. Every accident is different and each one should be investigated and judged separately. The most important factor is to determine how to prevent a similar accident from happening again. After having carefully considered all the facts, it is easy to decide what action is best to take.

OCCUPATIONAL SAFETY AND HEALTH ACT

The Occupational Safety and Health Act requires that preventive measures be taken to avoid accidents, (such as posting notices furnished by OSHA), and also that accurate records be kept and timely reports be made to OSHA's area director. Violations are subject to fines.

Posting of notices: Notices furnished by the Occupational Safety and Health Administration must be posted in a prominent place to acquaint employees with the protections and obligations of the law.

Recording: OSHA forms are available to agencies for accurately recording every injury and illness resulting from occupational hazards. The person in charge of employee safety is required to list each injury and illness within 48 hours after receiving information that such a case has occurred.

Recordable injuries or illnesses fall into three categories:

- Fatalities. Deaths must be recorded regardless of the time elapsing between the injury or onslaught of illness and the death.
- Lost work days. When the employee is prevented from performing his or her normal assignment during any work days following the accident, this time must be logged.
- Other cases. Nonfatal, nonlost work days, which result in transfer to another job, termination of employment, medical treatment (other than first aid), lost consciousness, or restriction of work activity, including any diagnosed occupational illnesses which are reported to the employer but are not classified as fatalities or lost work day cases, must also be recorded.

Records must be maintained on a calendar basis. They are to be made available for inspection and copying by OSHA's compliance officers or representatives of the Bureau of Labor Statistics; Secretary of Health and Human Services; state agencies; or states accorded jurisdiction for inspection or statistical compilations. It is recommended that the agency executive who maintains the safety regulations should decide who will accompany the OSHA compliance officer on the safety inspection.

Reporting and Violations: Within 48 hours of a serious accident, (i.e., one that is fatal to two or more employees or requires the hospitalization of five or more employees), the agency must report the details by telephone or telegraph to OSHA's area director.

In order to enlist employee cooperation in observing safety rules, reporting hazardous conditions, and on-the-job injuries, safety rules and regulations such as in the sample in Figure 12.1, should be conspicuously posted where employees commonly congregate.

There are plenty of teeth in the OSHA law. Violations are subject to fines and inspections can be instigated by employees.

WORKERS' COMPENSATION LAWS

This chapter would not be complete if state workers' compensation laws were not included. Such laws are in existence in each of the fifty states, and they preceded OSHA. Although they vary from state to state, workers' compensation laws have the general purpose of protecting employees from economic hardships arising out of work-related injuries or illnesses. Generally, they provide compensation relative to the injury or illness, including rehabilitation services. And they usually award death benefits to survivors. It is incumbent on the managers of recreation and leisure service agencies to investigate the law in their specific states to determine if the law requires mandatory participation by all employers, who is covered by law, and what work-related injuries are covered.

Although state workers' compensation laws do not require health and safety policies, education, and training, they support such through economic incentives. The premium that an employer pays for workers' compensation is determined by the annual number of employee accidents; consequently, the fewer number of accidents, the smaller the premium.

Generally, workers' compensation laws have been expanding as to whom is covered under the law. In many states temporary and seasonal employees are covered; and in certain states "volunteers" who

---

SHAWNEE RECREATION CENTER

RULES AND REGULATIONS

SAFETY AND ACCIDENTS

1. SAFETY
   A. POLICY
      Employees are required to observe all safety rules and to exercise care and reasonable caution in the performance of their duties to prevent injuries to themselves, to other employees, or to clients.
   B. PROCEDURE
      Employees are required to report to their supervisors any hazardous condition they observe in their work area which could result in an accident or injury.

2. ACCIDENTS
   A. EMPLOYEES
      Employees are required to give a full report of any on-the-job injury they sustain. This report will be given to their supervisor. If the injury results in absence from work, employees are required to notify the personnel office.
   B. CLIENTS
      Employees who witness a client accident are required to notify their supervisor immediately and to give a full account of their observations to the person authorized to fill out the accident report form. Expressing opinions about the accident to the client or any other employees is expressly forbidden.

Figure 12.1 Sample of rules and regulations regarding safety and accidents to be posted for employees.

receive such items as meals, expenses, uniforms, or equipment to help them fulfill their job assignments are also covered.[8]

SUMMARY

Taking a professional approach to safety eliminates many problems. When working conditions are safe and employees are alert to safety factors, the recreation and leisure service agency's clients are also less susceptible to injury. The big side benefit of this, of course, is the lessening of the chances that accidents resulting in liability suits, (which are not only extremely expensive but generally result in unfavorable publicity, as well), will occur.

Managers should become familiar with the mandates of the Occupational Safety and Health Act and the workers' compensation law in their particular state. In general, a good safety record requires managers to pay careful attention to: 1) establishment of safety and health policies; 2) safety engineering in equipment, layout, and work routines; 3) adequate safety gear and equipment; 4) staff training; 5) general safety education; 6) safety enforcement; 7) analysis and recording of accidents with appropriate correction after such; 8) first-aid and medical support. These require management and employees to work together as a team. Management should take the lead in minimizing risks and hazards, but it falls to first-level supervisors and workers to see that safe practices are followed.

NOTES AND REFERENCES

1. J. D. Dunn and Elvis C. Stephens, **Management of Personnel: Manpower Management and Organizational Behavior.** (New York: McGraw Hill, Inc., 1972), p. 138.
2. There are some exemptions for self-employed persons and family-type businesses with no paid employees. Organizations which provide comparable protection under different regulatory agencies are also exempt.
3. It is estimated that for every dollar paid out by insurance companies for actual compensation medical, wage, and award payments, four or more additional dollars are spent or lost in incidental or hidden costs.
4. According to the U.S. Supreme Court decision on May 23, 1978, employers have a constitutional right to bar federal job safety inspectors from their work places unless they have search warrants.
5. For example, employees have the right to file anonymous complaints with OSHA against their employers, requesting on-site inspections. An employee may accompany the OSHA officer on any inspection of the place of work and employees have the right to meet and talk privately with the inspector before and after the walk-around inspection. The act prohibits employers from punishing or discriminating against employees who exercise these rights.
6. In most cities, safety consultants, (who conduct OSHA surveys, reconstruct accidents, prepare technical reports, and provide professional testimony), are listed in the Yellow Pages.

7. A check list for facility planners, which includes safety considerations and which can be used as the basis of an evaluation form, is contained in **Planning Facilities for Athletics, Physical Education and Recreation** published by the American Alliance for Health, Physical Education, Recreation, and Dance (Reston, Virginia: 1985).
8. A. Frakt and J. Rankin, **The Law of Parks, Recreation Resources, and Leisure Services.** (Salt Lake City, Utah: Brighton Publishing Company, 1982), p. 244.

The purpose of this chapter is to help the manager answer:

- What is employee appraisal?
- What is employee assessment?
- What is an evaluation program for personnel?
- Why is evaluation important?
- What are the purposes of an evaluation program?
- How is an evaluation program developed and implemented?
- What are personnel rating scales?
- What are the strengths and weaknesses of rating scales?
- How are rating scales developed?
- How does employee appraisal utilizing management by objectives and results (MOR) differ from appraisal utilizing management by objectives (MBO)?
- What methods can be used to assess employee potential?
- What is the personnel assessment center and what are the steps necessary for its establishment?
- What is participative performance-oriented evaluation?
- What are the purposes of an appraisal interview?
- How does the manager prepare for and conduct an appraisal interview?

Chapter 13

Evaluating Professional Personnel

Doris L. Berryman

One of the major responsibilities of the manager in a recreation and leisure service agency is determining the extent to which and how well staff members are performing their assigned tasks and how much potential they have for other jobs in the future. This responsibility cannot be taken lightly since the manager uses information on employee performance to make important decisions that will affect the lives of and the functioning of the program and the agency. This chapter will define evaluation, discuss its importance in overall agency management, describe some methods and techniques of appraising personnel performance, and explain ways in which the results of appraisals may be used.

DEFINITION OF EVALUATION

Evaluation can be defined as the process of systematically obtaining information in order to make informed judgments, which in turn are used to make decisions. Judgments concerning personnel performance will play a part in virtually every decision a manager makes regardless of whether the decisions are concerned with budgeting, programming, planning, fund raising, or various aspects of personnel management.

Judgments are estimates of a present condition or status or predictions of future performance. In order to form judgments, the manager must have the necessary and appropriate information. *Information,* the essential ingredient of evaluation, provides the data base for making judgments and takes many forms. It can be quantitative or qualitative, general or specific, and it can be about people, materials, programs, or processes. In this chapter, the concern is with obtaining information about people.

Information about people is obtained by some form of performance appraisal or behavior assessment. The usefulness of the information obtained depends on:

- how carefully the judgments and decisions to be made have been specified;
- how accurately the information needed has been described; and
- the appropriateness of the procedures and content of the assessment or appraisal instruments used.

Performance appraisal of personnel can be defined as: "A systematic review of an individual employee's job performance to evaluate the effectiveness or adequacy of his or her work. . . ."[1] *Assessment* of personnel is carried out to obtain information concerning how much potential an individual has for other jobs in the future.

A well designed evaluation program enables managers, executives, and policy-making bodies to:

- determine if objectives of the agency are being achieved;
- insure the flexibility essential for continuous reorientation of programs to meet changing needs of the clients served;
- provide the public with a sense of social accountability and responsibility;
- obtain the data needed for interpreting to the community the validity of the agency and its social function; and
- provide an effective stimulus to the growth of the professional and other workers and volunteers who participate in the evaluation process.

In addition to the above, Pecora and Austin[2] point out that "Sound performance evaluations help supervisors and managers to distinguish agency-related problems that should be corrected through some form of organizational change from worker-related performance difficulties that may be corrected by in-service training or formal staff development." Another important outcome of a sound performance appraisal system is the assistance it provides agencies in meeting the requirements of equal opportunity laws in the areas of promotion and discipline.

Importance of Evaluation

Evaluating personnel performance is important for several reasons. One is ". . . that employees need and deserve feedback on their performance. They need to know what they are doing well and what they are doing poorly. They need to be told this frequently so that they can take advantage of their own abilities to improve without getting too entrenched in bad habits, and so they get the right amount of reinforcement when they do something well."[3]

A second reason for evaluating personnel is that managers need a current and accurate appraisal of each employee's performance to determine if program goals and objectives are being met—as well as to assess their own effectiveness as supervisors. Managers also need this information to get a reasonably accurate picture of whether or not the talents, skills, and abilities of the staff members are being used most effectively in light of program and agency objectives. Performance appraisal provides a better basis than off-the-cuff judgments for making decisions regarding promotion, demotion, transfer, and salary increases.

A third reason for personnel evaluation is that assessment of employee potential assists the manager in identifying those employees who have the best potential for success in particular positions and specific training the employees might need in relation to prospective positions.

If properly conceived and designed, the evaluation program defines standards of performance for each job, measures employee performance in relation to the standards, establishes procedures for taking corrective action to improve employee performance, and provides for assessing employee potential.

Development of an Evaluation Program

In planning an evaluation program, one of the first considerations is to establish and specify the purposes for which the evaluation program will be used. According to Yoder and Heneman,[4] various studies have shown that there are at least 15 different purposes that organizations have listed for their personnel evaluation programs. These are:

- To give employees an idea of how they are doing;
- To identify promotable employees or those who should be demoted;
- For salary administration (to determine individual salary treatment);

- To provide a basis for supervisor-employee communications;
- To help supervisors know their workers better;
- To identify training needs;
- To identify employees for layoff or recall;
- To assist in placement;
- To validate the selection process and evaluate other personnel activities, such as training programs and psychological tests;
- To improve departmental employee effectiveness;
- To determine special talents;
- To determine the need for disciplinary action;
- To determine progress at the end of probationary periods;
- To furnish inputs to other personnel programs, such as manpower and succession planning; and,
- To supply information for use in grievance interviews.

It is, of course, essential that the purposes decided upon be congruent with the organization's philosophy and objectives and have the support of the top management.

It is not uncommon for organizations to incorporate 3, 4, or more of the 15 purposes listed above into one program. This can result in confusion on the part of the people who must use the program. Two of the most common purposes for using performance appraisal, improvement of performance and as a basis for personnel action, can create conflicts in the mind of the manager who tries to use the program for both purposes. For example, a manager would likely rate employees conservatively when performance-improvement is the purpose, but would want to rate them higher when wage adjustment is the purpose in order not to place them at a disadvantage in relation to employees being rated by other managers. In planning the evaluation program, it is important to acknowledge that such conflicts can occur, particularly in relation to the purposes of the performance appraisal aspect, and to design appropriate procedures to minimize these conflicts.

The preponderance of literature in the area of personnel management indicates general agreement that formal personnel evaluation programs are needed. Both performance appraisal and assessment of potential, however, do take time, and the payoff for the time required is often difficult to see. In addition to the problem of time and questionable results, managers often raise other objections: "We don't like to sit in judgment"; "It's too difficult to get consistent ratings"; "It just opens the door to unnecessary questions." But even managers who agree on the necessity for evaluation programs can prevent them from being effective by carrying out the various procedures, including the appraisal interview, in such a perfunctory manner that the programs have little or no value. Some reasons for this resistance, cited by Yoder and Heneman, are:

- A normal dislike of criticizing a subordinate (and perhaps having to argue about it);
- Lack of interviewing skills;
- Dislike of new procedures with accompanying changes in ways of operating; and,
- Mistrust of the validity of the appraisal instrument.[5]

These authors point out that such resistance is often justified, especially if the program is developed independently by a staff unit and imposed from above. Thus, a critical factor for success of an evaluation program is involvement of the users in the various planning, designing, and implementation processes. As Drucker pointed out long ago, "Workers must be provided with opportunities for participation that will give them a managerial view."[6]

Other important aspects of planning and designing an evaluation program are:

- determining and specifying the way in which personnel evaluation information will become a part of management's total information system in order to assist the organization in achieving its goals;
- testing the evaluation program with a sample of supervisors and subordinates; and,
- communicating the program to the remainder of the people in the organization in such a way that they know that top management is behind the program, thinks it is important, and believes it is needed in the organization; and the "whens," "hows," and "whys" should be explained fully and clearly to all who will be participants.

IMPLEMENTING THE PROGRAM

Implementing a new personnel evaluation program, regardless of whether it is an initial attempt on the part of an organization or a revision of an existing program, requires careful attention to three activities: training supervisors, orienting subordinates, and deciding what approach to use in initiating the program.

An effective training program for supervisors would include both cognitive and experiential training and include such elements as planning, writing job descriptions—based on task analysis, interviewing, role playing, coaching, and group dynamics. The basic objectives of the training program should be to make supervisors more aware of their roles and responsibilities in an evaluation program and to train them to execute their functions more effectively. Use of audio or video taping of role playing or feedback practice sessions during training is invaluable in increasing supervisors' skills in the area of providing feedback to subordinates. By improving supervisors' perceptions of how they come across to their subordinates, their skills in conducting appraisal interviews can often be improved considerably in a very short period of time and they will feel more at ease in participating in the process. An evaluator's manual containing information concerning the philosophy, objectives, and administration of the program should be developed as part of the training program.

There are several approaches which can be used to orient subordinates to the evaluation program. In a small organization, it might be best to hold a meeting or series of meetings in which top management explains the goals and mechanics of the program to all those involved. In a larger organization, representatives from the personnel department could help department heads present the concepts of the program in a series of meetings. Another approach would be to have the supervisors, after they have completed the training program, explain the evaluation program to their subordinates individually or in groups. Whichever of these approaches is used, time should be allocated for questions and answers. Another, but probably less effective approach, is merely to send a letter from the top manager explaining the program to those involved.

How an organization initiates an evaluation program will, to a large extent, depend upon the size of the organization and the number of areas, units, or departments that are to be involved in the program. The approach which Yoder and Heneman[7] feel has the greatest chance for success is to start at the top. This emphasizes top management's backing and involvement in the program and allows people at all levels of management to experience first the role of subordinate and then that of supervisor in the program. Another approach, particularly useful in a large organization, is to institute the program in a single department or geographical location. This approach has the advantage of making it easier to coordinate and control the effort; and by dealing with a small and homogeneous group, valuable experience may be gained before the program is extended to the remainder of the organization.

No matter which approach is used, an organization should not try to do too much too fast or to expect results overnight. If the program is an initial attempt or a radical departure from the manner in which evaluation has been conducted in the past, people will need time to adjust to it. Even if the program is simply an updating of an existing one, it is best to proceed slowly so that people can become comfortable with the new program.

After the evaluation program has been implemented, efforts must be directed toward maintaining it. Consequently, systematic procedures must be established for monitoring and revising the program on a continuing basis. An orderly approach to monitoring and controlling the flow of forms to and from those involved in the program can be accomplished by establishing procedures keyed to one or more of the following: birthdates, employment anniversary dates, promotion anniversary dates, by month for alphabetical groupings, or by month for a department or division. Effective use of appraisals and assessments can be checked by asking such questions as: What is the turnover rate? Are people being promoted from within or does the organization have to go outside to obtain qualified people to fill vacancies? How do personnel involved in the program feel about it? Do they feel that it is meeting their needs and needs of the organization? Is the program being revised to meet changing organizational goals? Revisions should be made based on the responses to these questions at periodic intervals.

Effective maintenance of the program requires the training and involving of new supervisors in the evaluation program. It is important for a new supervisor, whether promoted from within or hired from outside the organization, to receive proper training in the philosophy, mechanics, and objectives of the organization's evaluation program.

Methods of Evaluating Performance

There is general agreement in the literature that, to be successful, a personnel evaluation program must be based on the following premises:

1. Performance appraisal is concerned only with appraising the behaviors of employees on the job for which they have been trained, i.e., measuring discernible actions against specific standards that are known to both the supervisor and the subordinate.
2. Techniques for assessing potential are an integral part of the program.
3. Personnel evaluation is an ongoing process which includes both periodic and annual reviews.

Personnel Ratings: Personnel ratings are typically accomplished by having a manager complete some type of rating form for each subordinate supervised. The purpose of the form is to record judgments or observations related to employees' past, present, or future behavior or performance in a work setting. Generally, ratings are used to evaluate or appraise employees as individuals and to make comparisons among individual employees within some specific work group. "In either situation, the evaluation may be diagnostic and directed toward specific aspects or attributes of behavior in the work setting, such as quantity or quality of performance; or comparative and directed toward some comprehensive combination of attributes, such as overall performance or potential."[8]

Dunnette'[9] suggests that the following factors must be kept in mind when designing a rating scale:

- Only those aspects of job performance or behavior which are relevant to getting the job done properly should be used;
- Items should be carefully identified by extensive sampling and interviewing of employees and supervisors, and they should reflect stable aspects of job behavior; and,
- It is essential to involve both those who are affected by and those who must administer the ratings. (If involvement of both groups does not occur, increased resistance to the program, misunderstanding, and reduced effectiveness are likely results.

It is important to be certain that the entire range of behavior essential to performing the job is covered in the scale. Ratings will be deficient to the extent that the various behavior domains required for performing the job are sketchily or incompletely defined. Ratings will be contaminated to the extent that job elements or behaviors not directly related to proper performance are included in the scale. Many performance evaluations tend to focus too much on subjective personality traits or on the peripheral aspects of the worker's performance, e.g., attitude, punctuality, and orientation to manager.

Thorndike and Hagen[10] suggest that there are two types of factors which influence the obtaining of valid appraisals through ratings. First, there are the "factors that limit the rater's *willingness* to rate honestly and conscientiously, in accordance with the instruction given to him."[11] The rater may be unwilling to take the necessary pains to give careful and thoughtful ratings. Also, the rater may identify with the person, positively or negatively, to such an extent that objectivity in rating is not possible.

Second are the factors that limit managers' abilities to rate consistently and correctly, even when presumably well motivated and doing their best to provide valid judgements. These center around the lack of opportunity to observe the individual being rated, the covertness of the trait being rated (e.g., insecurity, self-sufficiency), ambiguity of meaning of the dimension being rated (e.g., initiative, personality, adaptability), lack of uniform standard of reference (e.g., outstanding, above average, average, below average, unsatisfactory), and specific rater biases and idiosyncracies.

The effects of the two types of factors, i.e., those limiting the raters' willingness to rate conscientiously and those limiting one's ability to rate accurately, can be seen in such distortions of ratings as: the "halo" and "horns" effects; in relatively low reliabilities; and in the doubt raised as to the basic validity of rating procedures. Negative factors may be controlled, however, by refinements in designing the rating instruments and in planning and conducting rating procedures.

Refinements in rating instruments. The simplest and most conventional forms of rating instruments consist of a series of trait names with numerical or adjectival response options. The example below illustrates three versions of these types of instruments for the trait dependability.

INSTRUCTIONS: Indicate by a checkmark (   ) where this employee would fall in regard to the following factor:

Dependability—Capacity to stick to the job in spite of difficulties.

a. /_____/_____/_____/_____/_____/_____/

      Low   Average   High

b. /_____/_____/_____/_____/_____/

   1   2   3   4   5   6

c. /_____/_____/_____/_____/_____/

| Gives up quickly | Often needs a push to complete assign- ments | Does the routine work. Lets hard jobs slip | Not easily discour- aged. Sel- dom gives up | Never gives up. Each job a chal- lenge |

Formats such as these examples appear to encourage most of the shortcomings discussed above. As a result, many variations and refinements of format have been tried in the attempt to overcome or at least minimize these shortcomings.

Users of ratings have tried to get greater uniformity of meaning in the traits to be rated and have attempted to base the ratings more closely upon observable behaviors. According to Thorndike and Hagen,[12] these attempts have modified the stimulus aspect of rating instruments in three ways: (1) trait names have been defined, (2) trait names have been replaced by several more limited and concrete descriptive phrases, and (3) each trait name has been replaced with a number of descriptions of specific behavior. The example below illustrates the latter refinement.

WILLINGNESS TO ASSUME RESPONSIBILITY

Consider whether s/he has shown willingness to take on additional and more responsible duties.

On the basis of his/her actual performance, indicate which of the following statements is most accurate:

☐ 1. Generally accepts and discharges responsibilities willingly and follows through to conclusion;

☐ 2. Seeks additional responsibility and authority. Carries out projects to satisfactory conclusion;

☐ 3. Unwilling to assume responsibility;

☐ 4. Reluctant to accept responsibility for any but easy projects.

Briefly state instances which have occurred during the past twelve months which illustrate the extent of his/her willingness to assume responsibility. Alternatively, give general comments supporting your rating.

_____

_____

_____

_____

Personality-based and generalized description systems (such as the examples above), though widely used in human service agencies, have serious limitations. "In contrast, recent research indicates that the results-centered (e.g., MBO) and behavioral description systems (e.g., BARS) provide more job related and valid measures of performance and withstand litigation well."[13]

Management by objectives (MBO) requires that individual performance objectives and their standards be mutually developed by workers and their supervisors. In order to accomplish this, both workers and supervisors must have a clear idea of what specific job tasks must be accomplished. The typical MBO approach to performance appraisal involves the following steps:

1. Identify the key results areas of the job and the corresponding skills and actions.
2. Assess worker knowledge/skill in each performance area.
3. Set objectives for key results areas consistent with the above assessment.
4. Rank objectives by priority.
5. Develop acceptable performance standards for each area stated in terms of measurable outcome criteria where possible.
6. Develop action plans for objective attainment, with target dates assigned.
7. Modify or reorder objectives prior to implementation as indicated through supervision/consultation.
8. Implement objectives and monitor performance/progressions.
9. Final review.[14]

A refinement of MBO, management by objectives and results (MOR), emphasizes key results areas, performance indicators, and standards. A major advantage of the MOR approach is its flexibility and ability to incorporate performance targets for both job output and personal development. One modification of MOR described by Morrisey[15] uses three different types of objectives. The first type, *regular and routine,* refers to everyday tasks that are governed and described by a standard of performance (e.g., activity evaluation reports must be submitted within 24 hours after the activity was held). The second level refers to *problem-solving objectives* that are concerned with "correcting problems that arise in connection with the regular and routine objectives."[16] For example, if the recreation worker fails to submit his or her activity evaluation reports on time, then a problem-solving objective might be established to determine possible causes and necessary corrective actions. The third and highest level, *innovative objectives,* relates to involvement in such innovations as developing new programs, redesigning services or interventions, or expanding agency resources and technical capability. The MOR process is composed of the following six steps:

1. *Defining roles and missions.* A common understanding, by both workers and supervisors, of the central purposes, goals, functions, and philosophy of the organization serves as a foundation for both worker commitment and clarity of job tasks to be performed.
2. *Selecting key results areas.* The five to ten job tasks or major activities of greatest importance in terms of the worker's time, energy, and talent are selected for the appraisal plan.

3. *Identifying indicators.* Indicators are those measurement factors or criteria that can be used to assess worker performance. Only what will be measured is identified, not how much or in what direction.

4. *Developing performance objectives.* The worker and supervisor collaborate to develop statements of the measurable results to be achieved for each key results area.

5. *Listing of action plans.* Action plans state the specific worker behaviors that must be carried out in order to achieve the objective. Pecora and Austin suggest that "The level of detail may vary from general statements listing what major steps must be taken to detailed plans listing who will do what, when, how, and at what cost. The critical function of action plans is mapping out what needs to happen to achieve the objective in sufficient detail in order to establish accountability for completing each of the substeps and to establish a basis for supervisory monitoring."[17]

6. *Establishing controls.* These are the methods for keeping the supervisor or manager informed of the progress made in relation to the objectives.

In reference to successful implementation of MOR, Morrisy states that "Communication is the catalyst that ties the whole process together. MOR is not a mechanical system, it is a human one. The process must serve as a communication vehicle among the people affected. As people become involved in the decisions that affect them they become committed to carrying them out. That is where the real payoff comes."[18]

Another method for developing performance appraisal instruments which has become popular is the behaviorally anchored rating scales (BARS). This method is a behaviorally based approach and has the advantage of concentrating on effective work behaviors. The emphasis of the BARS method is on the work behaviors necessary to achieve program objectives and not primarily on the results or the objectives themselves as found in the MBO and MOR approaches.

According to Thorndike and Hagen,[19] this technique calls upon the supervisors who will use the rating scales to participate in their development and requires three work stages for developing a scale. During the first stage, a group of managers who will be future raters, after several discussions, agrees upon dimensions that can be identified as aspects of performance of a job, e.g., knowledge and judgement, skill in human relations, observational ability, and skill in leading groups. The potential users, during the second stage, generate a pool of critical incidents of actual observed behavior which illustrate superior, average, and inferior performance in each of the identified dimensions. A new group of raters is then called upon to assign each critical incident to the dimension to which it applies.

The third stage requires that each person in a new group of judges indicate where on a scale of excellence (e.g., 1 unacceptable to 7 excellent) each critical incident statement falls. A subset of items is retained in which each item shows good agreement among judges and for which the complete set shows a wide range of average scale values. The following illustration provided by Thorndike and Hagen shows three items ". . . drawn from the scale entitled *Interpersonal Relations with Students* on an instrument for college faculty (Harari and Zedek, 1973). The scale has a possible range from 1 (low) to 7 (high).

Scale Value   Statement

6.8   When a class doesn't understand a certain concept or feels "lost," this professor could be expected to sense it and act to correct the situation.

3.9   During lectures, this professor could often be expected to tell students with questions to see him during his office hours.

1.3   This professor could be expected to embarrass or humiliate students who disagreed with him.

In application, the set of statements for each dimension is provided, and the rater indicates which statement comes closest to describing the person being rated. Users have reported (Campbell et al., 1973) that this procedure "yielded less method variance, less halo error, and less leniency error" than more conventional rating procedures.[20]

While behaviorally anchored scales are an improvement in both development procedures and format of performance-appraisal systems, they do have the following disadvantages suggested by Yoder and Heneman:

• "They require considerable time and commitment of manpower for their preparation.

• "Separate forms must be developed for specific jobs. By their very nature, behaviorally based scales rule out the development of an omnibus form appropriate for a broad spectrum of jobs across an organization.

• "Preparation of behaviorally based rating scales requires statistical analysis during the development stage. These are not scales which can be developed off the top of one's head in a headquarters ivory tower."[21]

Pecora and Austin state that a number of authors "feel that the BARS approach is more appropriate for the jobs where the responsibilities and work procedures are clearly defined and involve less discretion or professional judgment."[22]

ASSESSING EMPLOYEE POTENTIAL

Programs for assessing employee potential address two types of questions. One type of question relates to the development of individual employees, such as, "What potential does this individual have for advanced leadership or management positions in our organization?" Another type of question relates to management, such as, "How do we select the best person for promotion?" or "How do we select the best candidate for a new position?" To a large extent, answers to the latter type of questions hinge on how well the first question is answered.

Methods for assessing employee potential include:

- Establishing a profile of employee's existing strengths and weaknesses based on information gathered as part of the appraisal process;
- Identifying the next logical position to which an employee might progress, matching the employee's abilities to the position's requirements, and identifying the training needs to be met;
- Allowing employees to demonstrate skills not required in their present positions through special assignments, (e.g., if a manager wants to know how well an employee might organize a job, the manager could give the employee a special assignment which requires organizing skills and observe the employee's performance); and,
- Delegating various tasks usually done by the manager to identify specific skills and abilities.

A tool for assessing employee potential which is being increasingly used in business and industry is the "Personnel Assessment Center" concept. The Assessment Center is a method of group assessment which grew out of the experiences of the U.S. Office of Strategic Services during World War II. Such centers are really a process, not a place, and their object is to determine how candidates will handle themselves in new situations.

The process involves having a number of candidates, usually from six to ten, observed intensively by a number of trained assessors. The behaviors observed occur in a series of simulation exercises and games related to management situations which are designed to elicit observable behaviors, such as problem solving, leadership, oral and written communication, planning and organizing, energy, and motivation.

The assessors look for examples of these behaviors and of other pre-determined requirements for management-level performance in a particular organization. The assessment center may be conducted for a one-, two-, or even three-day period. "After participating in the various exercises, the candidates are dismissed and the assessors refine their observations and prepare final evaluations of each participant outlining their impressions of potential and defining the development actions appropriate for both the organization and the individual participants."[23]

Brademas states that "the use of simulation exercises minimizes prediction error because the performance observed is very similar to the performance actually required of a manager. . . . In addition, the assessment center method is particularly appealing to many organizations because studies have shown that it is equally fair for any race or sex."[24]

Byham outlines the following steps in establishing an assessment center:

1. Determine objectives of program.
2. Define dimensions to be assessed.
3. Select exercises that will bring out the dimensions.
4. Design assessor training and assessment center program.
5. Announce program, inform participants and assessors, handle administrative detail.
6. Train assessors.
7. Conduct center.
8. Write summary reports on participants.
9. Feed back to participants a summary of performance at center and development actions.
10. Evaluate center.
11. Set up procedures to validate center against a criterion of job success.[25]

Assessors are generally selected from management ranks one or more levels above the candidates being assessed, and they are rigorously trained in the assessment process, in the mechanics of the exercises they will be observing, and also in the techniques of observation and reporting.

Yoder and Heneman suggest that candidates for assessment center participation may be identified in several ways:

- Nominations by supervisors; e.g., employees whose current performance is minimally satisfactory and who appear to have potential for advancement.

- Allowing employees to nominate themselves. This can overcome some of the biases inherent in processes which rely solely on supervisory judgment.
- Making assessment center participation automatic for employees who reach a specified job level.[26]

PARTICIPATIVE PERFORMANCE-ORIENTED EVALUATION

Participative performance-oriented evaluation programs represent a promising marriage of current behavioral science research and theory with practical management objectives. Such programs should be viewed as a system which: (1) establishes a process that ensures participative involvement of both manager and employee in planning the work and establishing criteria for effective performance; (2) provides a nonthreatening environment in which the employees can be motivated to change their behaviors and their attitudes; and, (3) provides a tangible record of both performance and potential related to the organization's need for information in making personnel decisions, planning its manpower, and providing training and development services.

Yoder and Heneman have identified seven principles which underlie a participative performance-oriented evaluation system.

1. The appraisal of subordinates' job performance is part of the normal, day-to-day responsibility of every supervisor and relates directly to his or her responsibility for planning and assigning work.
2. Criteria of job performance should be related to the job itself. Sufficient flexibility should be maintained so that achievement measures can be set to reflect accurately and realistically the unique requirements of different positions, levels of assignment, and operating conditions.
3. While personal qualities such as honesty, loyalty, integrity, and conscientiousness are presumed to be prerequisites for any job, they need not be enumerated. Discussions of personality characteristics should be oriented to their effect on job performance, not on the employee as a person.
4. Improvement in job performance can be accomplished most effectively if employees participate directly in establishing the achievement measures for their jobs. To do a better job, they should know what is expected of them, how they are doing on the job, and how and where they can get assistance when they need it.

5. Employees are inclined to accept suggestions for improving or maintaining their performance when they are offered feedback in a less concentrated form than is the case with an annual discussion. Studies of the learning process indicate that feedback is less effective the more time is allowed to elapse between performance and feedback (reinforcement).

6. The supervisor's prime responsibility is as a coach and collaborator in individual development, not as a judge. Two major forces in an employee's development must be given full consideration to achieve maximum results:

   (a) The employee must recognize the understanding and concerns of his or her immediate supervisor as those of an active partner in helping him.

   (b) The supervisor must recognize and be concerned with the employee's personal aspirations, motivation, and growth needs.

7. The primary purpose of conducting a formal performance appraisal is to further develop the productive skills of an employee. Forms and procedures are only tools.[27]

The participative performance-appraisal program is based on two major procedures: (1) a continuing work planning and progress review process between managers and their individual employees and (2) the preparation of an annual performance review form which the supervisor and employee discuss in detail during the annual appraisal interview.

Work planning and progress reviews: The work planning phase consists of two interrelated activities involving supervisor-employee participation and agreement in the following:

1. Using the objectives listed in the "Effect on End Results" section of the position description (see Figure 2.4), the major job requirements, duties, and goals are outlined.

2. Achievement criteria or measures are established to determine the level of performance and end result of the job. These should be specific criteria for determining whether or not the goals identified have been accomplished. Figure 13.1 is an example of a work planning worksheet.

Progress reviews are follow-up sessions held periodically to enable both the manager and the subordinate to determine the extent to which job requirements and goals are being or have been met, by comparing them against actual performance on the part of the employee. The exact timing of these sessions will vary with the nature of the job

ABC RECREATION AGENCY
PERSONNEL EVALUATION PROGRAM
WORK PLAN FORM

Employee Pat Leisure	Manager L. Player	Date
Job requirements (projects, goals, specific tasks to be accomplished)	Achievement Measures (Due Dates, etc.)	Priorities
Administration		
Maintains membership and participation records (DUTY)		
Prepares and administers budget for youth program (DUTY)		
Submit future participation and expenditure reports on time (GOAL)	All monthly program participation and expenditure reports will be submitted no more than 24 hours late for the next quarter.	
Promotes membership enrollments (DUTY)		
Promotes day and resident camp enrollments (DUTY)		
Develop and implement new procedures to promote early enrollments for day and resident camps (GOAL)	With key camp staff design new recruitment procedures within the next three months	

Program Supervision Plans and organizes, with appropriate co-workers, a well balanced activity program which meets community need and agency priorities & objectives (DUTY) Develop new program model to meet needs and interests of increasing number of teen-aged girls attending center (GOAL) *Community Relations* Maintains facilitating relationships with other community youth workers and youth serving agencies (DUTY)	Survey 14- to 17-year old girls to identify interests and with assistance of staff and committee of girls, draft new program plan within the next three months.

Figure 13.1 Work Planning Worksheet

and the participants, but they should be held often enough to ensure that both manager and employee recognize results or a lack thereof on a timely basis. Figure 13.2 is an example of a progress review worksheet.

Annual performance review form and interview: The annual performance review form is a formal statement of accomplishments during the past year, and describes job requirements or principal duties, achievement measures, and results achieved. In essence, it is a summary of what occurred during the work planning and progress review process. (See Figure 13.3-A). Since it serves as the basis for the annual appraisal interview, the form should also make provision for adding additional information regarding such concerns as training and development and potential for increased responsibilities. (See Figure 13.3-B.)

Yoder and Heneman state:

Participative performance-oriented appraisals offer a number of advantages over more traditional performance-appraisal programs.

1. They provide a structure for a continuing management-by-objectives supervisory style.
2. Their orientation to each subordinate's job provides a practical vehicle for introducing new employees to their work and the job environment.
3. They provide a basis for ensuring the continuity of individual job functions as personnel and supervisory changes occur within the work group.
4. They produce evaluations related specifically to each employee's day-to-day performance on his job.
5. They afford a practical basis for guiding and encouraging the development of individual employees.[28]

THE APPRAISAL INTERVIEW

Regardless of the methods and procedures used for appraising performance and assessing potential of employees, most recreation and leisure service organizations require managers to carry out an annual appraisal interview with each of their employees. Even a poorly conceived performance-appraisal system can be an effective control if skillful appraisal interviewing is practiced. It is equally true, however, that a well-conceived system can have its effectiveness diminished considerably if managers view the annual interview as time to find fault and criticize poor performance or bad attitudes.

Essentially, the manager should seek to accomplish two things in the appraisal interview. The first is to motivate the employee to improve

ABC RECREATION AGENCY
PERSONNEL EVALUATION PROGRAM

PROGRESS REVIEW FORM

Employee Pat Leisure	Manager L. Player	Date
Progress to Date	Problems	Suggested action
Membership participation records were submitted three or four days late each month this quarter.	Group leaders for two units were late with their membership reports each month.	Pat should find out why leaders are late and provide necessary assistance or motivation to make sure they are prompt this next quarter.
Draft of new procedures for recruitment of day and resident campers has been submitted.		
Survey of 14- to 17-year old girls completed; has met with committee to begin drafting new program plan.	Survey took longer than expected; many girls late returning their forms.	Continue work with committee; try to complete draft of plan in the next 30 days.
Has attended monthly meetings of the community council of youth and recreation agencies; agreed to serve on committee to plan city-wide youth play and fitness festival day.	Will need extra release time to attend committee meetings.	Submit request for release time at least two weeks in advance of each meeting.

Figure 13.2 Progress-Review Worksheet

ABC RECREATION AGENCY

PERSONNEL EVALUATION PROGRAM

ANNUAL PERFORMANCE REVIEW FORM   Employee: Pat Leisure   Supervisor: L. Player

Period Under Review: July 1, 1987–June 30, 1988

I. Review of Accomplishments

Job Requirements—Describe the major responsibilities or goals of this job	Achievement Measures—Indicate specific results or objectives you and employee expected to be accomplished during the period under review	Results Achieved—Describe the extent to which the employee has met the Achievement Measures for each of the requirements listed
1. *Administration* (JOB REQUIREMENT) DUTIES: Maintain membership and participation records; prepare and administer budget for youth program; promote membership enrollments.	Establish better method of obtaining monthly membership, participation, and expenditure reports from group leaders & other staff so that Youth Division reports to management will be on time.	With the help of staff in-put at several meetings, Pat designed new report forms and changed assigned job functions and responsibilities so that by March all reports were coming in on time.
GOALS: Submit participation and expenditure reports on time; develop and implement new procedures to	Have new procedures for earlier camp enrollments ready for implementation by February 15.	The new procedures developed by Pat and Youth Division staff were implemented on time. They worked

		very well for the most part, but some revision will need to be made for next year.
promote early enrollments for day & resident camps.		
2. *Program Supervision* (JOB REQUIREMENT) DUTIES: Plan & organize, with appropriate co-workers, a well balanced activity program which meets community need and agency priorities & objectives. GOALS: Develop new program model to meet needs and interests of increasing number of teen-aged girls attending center.	New program plan for teen-aged girls to be implemented by April.	Survey to identify interests of 14- to 17-year old girls took longer than expected; also, the staff/member planning committee had trouble initially in communicating. Plan not actually completed until early June. Some activities will be implemented during summer. Both staff and girls seem pleased with plan.

II. Overall Evaluation of Performance:

Figure 13.3-A Annual Performance Review Form

ANNUAL PERFORMANCE REVIEW FORM
(Continued)

III. Highlights of Performance:

    A. What are the employee's most outstanding qualifications?

    B. How does the employee need to improve within the present job?

IV. Training and Development Plans:

    To what training or educational activities should this employee be exposed during the coming year to assist him or her in improving individual performance?

V. Potential:

    What is the employee's capacity to handle increased responsibilities within the next two years within present type or sphere of work? Specify:

    Outside present type or sphere of work? Specify:

VI. Discussion of Review:

    A. Employee's Reaction to this performance review:

    B. Employee's Acknowledgement: The contents of this form have been reviewed with me.

    Employee's Signature _____ Date _____

    C. Reviewer's Signature _____ Date _____

VII. Second Level Supervisor's Comments:

    Signature_____ Date _____
    (Attach separate sheet if additional space is required)

Figure 13.3-B Annual Performance Review Form

job performance or engage in self-development activities, or both. The second is to create a deeper understanding between the manager and the employee. In order to accomplish these goals, the manager should: prepare for the interview, encourage the employee to prepare for the interview, arrange for uninterrupted privacy during the interview, discuss both strengths and weaknesses of the employee, encourage the employee to talk, identify new goals with the employee, and decide upon the time for accomplishing the things planned.

Preparing for the appraisal interview involves two factors. The first is the appraisal information. If the information required is based on previously stated goals with specified performance criteria, it is likely to be rated objectively by the manager, although it is a good idea for the manager to jot down examples of specific behaviors which demonstrate points that the manager thinks should be discussed. Where an organization's appraisal system calls for trait evaluation, e.g., loyalty, dependability, initiative, and creativity, the manager should be prepared to provide illustrative incidents or examples to substantiate the rating the employee has been given. The second preparation factor is the interview *per se*. The manager should determine beforehand the specific objectives of the interview and give some thought to the personality of the employee to be interviewed. The manager should consider such questions as: How would I react if I were in this employee's shoes? How can I put the appraisal so the employee will react positively? If there is little chance of a positive response, can the manager at least make the employee understand without a display of emotion? As Boyd points out, "A person who is on the defensive can't see any viewpoint other than his or her own, and this applies to employees and supervisors equally."[29]

If the manager's objective of creating a better understanding with subordinates is to be realized, the employees should also be thinking about the appraisal interview. In organizations where employees participate in identifying their work goals and objectives and specify the criteria against which achievement will be assessed, the employees are probably not only well prepared for the interview, but look forward to it. Where this type of system is not in place, the manager can help employees to feel that they are active partners in the process by speaking with them a few days prior to the interview and asking them to write and bring with them a listing of what they consider to be (1) the most important aspects of their jobs, (2) examples of good performance, (3) problems or conditions which hinder their job performance, and (4) any ideas on solving the problems or removing the negative conditions.

A good approach to conducting the interview is to take one job responsibility or task at a time and discuss it, with both the manager and the employee giving their views on the strengths and weaknesses of the factor being appraised. When talking about performance and describing a strength or weakness, the manager should always give an example, and as recent a one as possible. It is of little help to the employee simply to say, "You need some improvement in leading the current events discussion group," or "You do a fine job of getting along with teenagers." The managers need to be able to say, "You need to work on your skills in leading discussion groups. I observed the other day, when one of the group members wanted to change the discussion topic, you became very resistant and refused his request," or "You really have developed your skills in working with teenagers. The way you handled that situation in the gym the other day was a good example of your human relations skills with this group. As I saw it, what you did very well was. . . ." By giving specific examples, the manager is able to reinforce the strong points in the employee's performance and to illustrate the areas in which the employee needs to improve.

As the interview progresses, the manager can tell quickly whether or not the employee is getting uptight about the way things are going, or if the employee is accepting the things being said. People can accept the positive things better than the negative things. This fact gives all the more reason to mix them together, rather than discuss all the positive points first and then all the negative ones. If the interview is not going well, it is almost always the manager's fault. Somehow, the discussion has not been maintained on an adult level. The manager, for example, may have used the incorrect tone in pointing out a weakness or trying to prove a point. Once the manager senses that the interview is not going well, Broadwell suggests that there are a couple of things managers can do:

> One is that we can ease off, and be sure our voice is on a very even keel. A quiet voice is essential in keeping things calm. Then we can let the employee do more of the talking. Not arguing, just talking, letting out feelings perhaps, saying things that we don't have to react to, taking over the conversation for awhile . . . . We nod or say "I see," and let the employee keep on talking. We use reflective techniques such as . . . "You feel you have grown in this area, then . . ." Or we can use open questions—questions that can't be answered yes or no—like, "What training do you think you need?" rather than, "You think you need some training?"[30]

Using techniques such as these will usually get the discussion back on the proper footing and it can proceed normally. It is essential that the employees leave the appraisal interview with a clear understanding of what they are doing well; what they are doing poorly and what the plans are for correcting any weaknesses; what the goals are for the period between this interview and the next scheduled meeting with the manager; and what performance standards will be used to assess achievement of the goals.

During the course of the interview, a manager may very well have made suggestions or offered help that should not be forgotten. Boyd warns that the "effectiveness of the entire performance-appraisal system can be threatened by a failure to follow up on promises made during the interview. . . . If the interview resulted in planning for improved performance or in trying to correct a performance deficiency, the supervisor will certainly want to check progress with the employee periodically rather than wait until the next appraisal interview. It's in these follow-up actions that the supervisor demonstrates sincerity in trying to make the appraisal an effective control."[31]

The appraisal interview, if skillfully handled, is of great benefit to the employee, the manager, and the organization. Employees gain a sense of direction and participation in the development of their careers and they feel that they have a voice in managing their own jobs. Managers feel that they are directing and controlling their departments by correcting, adjusting, and upgrading employee performance.

SUMMARY

An evaluation program for professional personnel is concerned with appraising personnel performance on the job in relation to specified behavioral objectives and expectations and assessing personnel to obtain information concerning how much potential an individual has for other jobs in the future.

A well designed program defines the standards of performance for each job, measures employee performance in relation to the standards, establishes procedures for taking corrective action to improve employee performance, and provides for assessing employee potential.

Critical factors for the success of an evaluation program are: specifying the purposes for which the evaluation program will be used: involvement of the users in the various planning, designing, and implementation processes; and communicating clearly to all staff in the agency the "when's," "how's," and "why's," of the program and assuring them that top management believes in and supports the program.

It is generally agreed that rating scales should appraise only those aspects of job performance or behavior relevant to meeting specified standards and objectives known to both the manager and the subordinate. Items incorporated in the scale should sample the entire range of behavior essential to effective job performance and reflect stable aspects of job behavior. Two types of factors affecting the obtaining of valid appraisals were discussed, i.e., those that limit the rater's willingness to rate honestly and conscientiously, and those that limit the rater's ability to rate consistently and correctly even when motivated to provide valid judgments.

Methods for refining rating instruments and improving rating procedures were discussed and scale development utilizing management by objectives, management by objectives and results, and behaviorally-anchored rating scales were discussed.

Basic questions underlying the concept of assessing employee potential were identified and some methods of assessment outlined. One tool for assessing potential, the Personnel Assessment Center, which employs group assessment techniques, was described in some detail.

The participative performance-oriented evaluation system, which has received increasing support in recent years, was presented. This system (1) insures that both manager and employee are involved in planning the work and establishing criteria for effective performance, (2) provides a nonthreatening environment in which employees can be motivated to change both their behaviors and their attitudes, and (3) provides the agency with a tangible record of employee performance and potential.

The chapter concluded with a discussion of the importance of the appraisal interview in the evaluation process. Techniques for planning and conducting the interview were described and the point was made that the skillfully handled appraisal interview is of great benefit to the employee, the manager, and the organization.

NOTES AND REFERENCES

1. H. S. Roberts, **Dictionary of Industrial Relations.** (Washington, D.C.: The Bureau of National Affairs, 1971), p. 401.
2. Peter J. Pecora and Michael J. Austin, **Managing Human Services Personnel** (Newbury Park, CA: Sage Publications, 1987), p. 56.
3. Dale Yoder and Herbert G. Heneman, Jr., eds., **ASPA Handbook of Personnel and Industrial Relations, Volume I, Staffing Policies and Strategies.** (Washington, D.C.: The Bureau of National Affairs, 1974), pp. 4-162–4-163.
4. Ibid., p. 4-163.

5. Ibid.
6. Peter Drucker, **The Practice of Management.** (New York: Harper and Row, 1954), p. 303.
7. Yoder and Heneman, p. 4-166.
8. Yoder and Heneman, p. 4-175.
9. M. D. Dunnette, **Observing and Recording Job Behavior.** (Belmont, CA: Wadsworth Publishing Co., 1966), p. 86.
10. R. L. Thorndike and E. Hagen, **Measurement and Evaluation in Psychology and Education.** (New York: John Wiley and Sons, 1977), pp. 451–458.
11. Ibid., p. 451.
12. Ibid., pp. 463–464.
13. Pecora and Austin, p. 64.
14. D. K. Granvold, "Supervision by Objectives," **Administration in Social Work,** 2 (2), 1978, pp. 199–209.
15. G. L. Morrisey, **Performance Appraisals for Business and Industry.** (Reading, MA: Addison-Wesley, 1983), pp. 42–45.
16. Ibid., p. 43.
17. Pecora and Austin, p. 75.
18. G. L. Morrisey, p. 28.
19. Thorndike and Hagen, pp. 472–473.
20. Ibid., p. 473.
21. Yoder and Heneman, pp. 4-190, 4-191.
22. Pecora and Austin, p. 82.
23. Yoder and Heneman, p. 4-198.
24. D. James Brademas, "The Personnel Assessment Center," **Management Strategy,** 2 (Fall 1978), p. 6.
25. W. C. Byham, "The Assessment Center as an Aid in Management Development," **Training and Development Journal,** 25 (No. 12, 1971), pp. 10–21.
26. Yoder and Heneman, p. 4-172.
27. Ibid., pp. 4-171, 4-172.
28. Ibid., p. 4-175.
29. Bradford B. Boyd, **Management-Minded Supervision,** (2nd. ed.). (New York: McGraw-Hill Book Company, 1976), p. 311.
30. Martin M. Broadwell, **The Practice of Supervising: Making Experience Pay.** (Reading, MA: Addison-Wesley Publishing Company, 1977), p. 145.
31. Bradford B. Boyd, p. 312.

PART FOUR
Managing Volunteer Personnel

The purpose of this chapter is to help the manager answer:

- Why do people volunteer?
- What kinds of services can volunteers provide?
- What must be taken into consideration in assigning a volunteer to a service?
- How does one start a volunteer program?
- Where and how does one recruit volunteers?
- How does one select dependable and effective volunteers?
- What type of training do volunteers need?
- How does one train volunteers?
- How does one supervise volunteers?
- How does one provide recognition for volunteers?

Chapter 14

Volunteers for Recreation and Leisure Services

Edith L. Ball

Volunteers are not new in community life. From earliest recorded time people have helped each other when they needed assistance in solving problems. During the settlement of this country, there were barn raisings at which the whole community came together to help one person put up a barn, for this was a task too great for one to do alone. The barn raising also became a social occasion. When the barn was completed, a feast was laid out in it, and following the feast there was a barn dance.

Today, in our complex society, this informal kind of helping is rarely possible, particularly in the enormous urban centers where people scarcely know their neighbors and have much less knowledge of their needs. In early civilizations, churches took the lead in ascertaining those who were in need, and helped them in solving their problems. In doing this, they enlisted the help of church members, particularly women, to assist the clergy. Sometimes this aid was in the form of caring for children or for the sick. At other times, food to feed a family was needed. From these beginnings there has grown the myriad of social service agencies that exist today. They are organized to care for a variety of needs related to poverty, education, health, leisure, child care, and others too numerous to mention.

Just as the early churches could not employ professional people to care for other than the spiritual needs of people and were required to turn to the laity for help in carrying out certain services, so the social

agencies today find it necessary to call upon lay people to help with
the provision of the services that are the reason for the existence of
the agency. Without the voluntary work performed by these lay people, the churches, hospitals, schools, leisure services, correctional
institutions, and services to the handicapped and the aged could not
operate. A corollary to this is that the agencies supported by the tax
or donated dollar could in no way pay people for the amount of
volunteer service provided.

Although volunteer services are sorely needed by agencies, it must
be recognized that the people who volunteer also benefit from the
services that they give. People volunteer for a variety of reasons:

- They have time with nothing to do;
- They need to be needed;
- To use their talents or special skills to develop similar interests
  and skills in others;
- To promote a cause, e.g., "protect the environment";
- To develop the skills necessary to become a professional worker;
- To have the opportunity to meet people;
- To develop feelings of self worth;
- To give service rather than money to their community.

Whatever reasons volunteers may have for volunteering, they must
be assigned to services in relation to their particular competencies and
also to services that will satisfy the need that made them apply for
volunteer work. Volunteers who freely state that they would like to
be in a situation where they can meet people would be unhappy and
probably useless if placed in a room alone and asked to file a pile of
reports or similar situations. The job and the volunteer must match.

SERVICES THAT VOLUNTEERS CAN GIVE TO AGENCIES

There are many services that volunteers can give to agencies. Just
what service will depend on three things:

1. What service is needed by the agency?
2. What are the capabilities of the volunteer?
3. What does the volunteer expect to receive from volunteer service?

Each of these questions must be answered if the maximum benefits
to the individual, the agency and the community are to be realized.
Some of the major categories of service that volunteers perform in
agencies are discussed on the following pages.

Board and commission members:

1. Policy making and interpreting the agency to the public.
2. Service on Agency Committees. The committees necessary in an agency are many and varied, and the organization of committees are just as diverse. Some committees will be completely composed of board members, while others will have a board member as chairperson with the remainder drawn from the total membership. Sometimes the committee will represent the community at large. The types of committees that are needed in agencies are:

- Finance, including fund raising and collection of donated material;
- Survey committee to determine needs in the community to be met through the services of the agency;
- Personnel management, including both paid and volunteer workers;
- Public relations, including the formation of speakers' bureaus, to provide speakers for community meetings to interpret the agency's services.

Leaders of groups: As the people in a community find that they have increased free time, there is a demand for increased leisure services. Unfortunately, the financial capacities of communities do not keep pace with the demand for services. This means that an agency or department is unable to provide adequate numbers of paid leaders to supply the services that are requested. This necessitates a curtailment of services unless volunteers can be recruited for group leadership services.

It is possible to carry on an extensive program with volunteers and a single paid staff member. The paid staff member will assume the responsibility for continuity of services, program supervision, and the necessary administrative tasks. Agencies such as the Boy Scouts, Camp Fire Girls, hospitals, and settlement houses, to name a few, have operated many programs using this organizational structure. Some of the activities that can be conducted by volunteers are:

- Sports clubs or leagues;
- Dance activities;
- Music groups;
- Drama groups;
- Trips and outings, including camping;
- Arts and crafts activities;
- Discussion groups;
- Games, such as bingo;

- Card clubs;
- Aquatic activities;
- Social clubs for varying age groups;
- Playground activities;
- Library activities; and,
- Photography.

There are many other activities that could be led successfully by volunteers, but these are representative of the variety that is possible. If an individual has a certain talent or skill, likes to help others to enjoy that activity and has time to give service in an agency, that person has the potential for becoming a valuable volunteer and an asset to the agency. It is the responsibility of the agency to use that potential in a way that will benefit the agency and satisfy the volunteer.

Transportation of agency clientele: Many agencies that provide recreation and leisure services have members or potential members who would use the agency frequently if they could get to it. Persons in this category include the many types of disabled people. This group alone represents a vast number of people, ranging from the elderly poor, who do not have money for transportation, to the physically handicapped, who may not be able to use public transportation and have no one to drive them to a facility.

Volunteers are needed in several capacities to help people get to programs at an agency. They are:

1. Drivers
   - For agency cars;
   - Private cars to be used in a car pool or to pick up people at home to bring them to the agency;
   - For agency buses to be used in daily transportation or for trips;
   - For meals-on-wheels programs for the homebound.
2. Personal assistants. These people are needed on buses or in agency cars to assist with children or disabled individuals. They help people onto buses or into private cars and take care of them on the trip.

Administrative tasks: Volunteers for administrative service can make the difference between inadequate service and exceptional service. The services that are included are:

- Receptionist;
- Secretary or typist;
- Telephone switchboard operators;
- Bookkeeper;
- Accountant;

- File clerk or business machine operator;
- Word processor.

Agencies frequently can manage to staff programs with paid or volunteer staff, but can find no one to perform the supportive services that make it possible for an agency to operate efficiently and effectively.

Maintenance tasks: In the maintenance area, it is possible to involve the skilled trades people in the community, particularly those who are retired and are looking for something to do. A great variety of skills of this kind can be found in the membership of almost any agency. The only problem is that the work that is done must be of a kind for which the agency would not hire union labor. For example, a volunteer might be used to assist the cook in a nursery school or to maintain a flower garden in the front of the building, but not to put new electric wiring in the building.

Speakers' bureau: Volunteers for a speakers' bureau need some experience in public speaking. They also need to understand thoroughly the services provided by the agency so as to be able to interpret those services to the public and to answer questions about them.

Whatever type of service is given by a volunteer, that person must feel that the work is valuable for carrying out the purposes of the agency. In addition, the volunteer must gain a sense of self-worth from the service and must find satisfaction in the tasks that are being performed. If this is to be achieved, each job must be matched to the skills and personality of the volunteer. This requires careful selection and screening and sufficient orientation and training.

SOME SUGGESTIONS FOR VOLUNTEERS AND AGENCIES USING VOLUNTEERS

A recreation or leisure service agency that plans to use volunteers should expect that the volunteer will:

- Like people;
- Accept the participants in the agency's program and treat them with respect as individuals, rather than to maximize their shortcomings;
- Be dependable, sincere, thoughtful, and cooperative;
- Have a strong sense of responsibility;
- Be able to take direction;
- Be creative;
- Be able to take initiative within the limits of the assigned responsibility;

- Be appropriately dressed for the work to be performed;
- Enjoy the work assignment in the agency;
- Be able to stimulate participation;
- Be physically, mentally, and socially fit to perform the assigned work.

The volunteer should expect the agency to:

- Give all directions for conducting an activity well in advance so that the volunteer can plan effectively;
- Define the time, place and length of activity; the group or groups to be expected and the number in each; any special considerations that are needed in conducting the activity; the supplies, the equipment, and facilities that are to be used; and the money, if any, that is available for activity expenditures.

RECRUITING VOLUNTEERS

Agencies that plan to use volunteers to augment the services of the paid staff, must recognize that if the volunteers are to be used effectively there must be careful planning and organization of the volunteer program. Agencies will differ in their organization plan, but there must be a plan.

Steps to be taken in starting a volunteer program

1. The first step to be taken in developing a volunteer program is to determine the needs in the community or in the agency for volunteers. A committee should be appointed to survey the entire community or an agency's needs for volunteer services. In an agency, depending upon its size and type, the committee will include representatives of the various segments of the agency. In a private agency, such as a Boy's Club, the committee might involve board and staff members. In a public department, the committee would probably include the director and all major section heads within the department.

The purpose of the committee would be to define unmet needs for goods and services within the agency. In defining these needs, there should be an indication of materials or services that are required. As an example, one section might indicate that it had been unable to offer a given program because of the lack of a competent leader. Another section might say that a program that had been started had so many participants that assistants are needed to help the leader to function more effectively. Each of these services requires a different type of volunteer.

The responsibility of the committee will be to draw up a list of needs by sections to determine the kinds of volunteers needed by the department. For each of the services that are to be performed by volunteers, a position description must be written. This is essential if a good recruiting program is to be developed. Two types of position descriptions should be written. The first is a detailed outline of the tasks to be performed. This will be used by the agency when it assigns volunteers to a given service. The second position description is a short summary that may be used in newspapers or spot announcements on local TV or radio stations or for notices to be sent to colleges or industries for their bulletin boards. (See Figures 14.1 to 14.4 for sample position descriptions.)

If the volunteer program is a community-wide effort, the committee to define needs must look at the needs of all of the agencies in the community. Then a list of the needs in each agency by categories should be compiled. The committee membership in this case should include representatives from every type of agency in the community, governmental units providing group work or recreation service, educational institutions, and industry. When committee works begins, the committee can be broken down into subgroups to study the needs of specific categories of agencies. In this way, a total community-wide survey can be made. When the reports from the various subcommittees are completed, a report can be assembled to show the volunteer needs throughout the entire community. (See Figure 14.5 for a sample form which can be used to request volunteers and which provides the basic information for a report.) At regular intervals, this survey will need to be updated, for the needs of the agencies will change as community needs change.

2. The second step to be taken in developing a volunteer program is to survey the community to determine possible sources of volunteers. Each community will have different methods of seeking out volunteers. Some communities, over the years, have developed central volunteer bureaus. These centers correlate the agency volunteer departments and publicize the kinds of volunteers that are needed through the mass media or other resources. The person wishing to volunteer contacts the central bureau and it, in turn, refers the person to an agency that needs the capabilities of a given individual. The central bureau has many advantages:

- It knows the sources of volunteers, e.g., schools, industry, churches, senior citizens' clubs;

POSITION DESCRIPTIONS

VOLUNTEER GROUP LEADER (detailed description)

Under the general supervision of the unit supervisor, to lead a group of people who are elderly at a recreation center in needlecraft activities, including sewing, knitting, and crocheting.

Specific Tasks:
1. Determine the types of needlecraft each person wants to do.
2. Assemble the materials necessary to carry out the activities.
3. Make models of a variety of projects that people might make.
4. Give each person the materials necessary for the project.
5. Divide the group into sub-groups of those working on the same project.
6. Instruct each group in starting the project, in a step-by-step procedure.
7. Instruct each group on how to complete the project.
8. Write a report on the work of the group each day.
9. Participate in conferences with supervisor.
10. Participate in staff meetings when possible.

Qualifications:
1. Ability to instruct in the skills of knitting, sewing, and crocheting. This includes both the basic stitches and advanced stitches.
2. Ability to make models of projects.
3. Ability to complete a simple report.

Where to Apply:

Recreation Center, 1200 Smith Street. Telephone number: 123-876. Any time between 9 a.m. and 5 p.m., weekdays.

When Service Is Needed:

Wednesday from 1 to 3 p.m., for 12 weeks starting March 1.

VOLUNTEER GROUP LEADER (description for mass media)

Help a group of people who are elderly enjoy sewing, knitting, or crocheting, or all three. Some are beginners and some are advanced. They not only want to do needlecraft but also to socialize. Call 123-876 for more information or drop into the Recreation Center, 1200 Smith Street, between 9 a.m. and 5 p.m. any weekday.

Figure 14.1 Sample position descriptions for volunteer group leader.

POSITION DESCRIPTIONS

VOLUNTEER MAINTENANCE MAN (detailed description)
Under the supervision of the maintenance supervisor to assist with a variety of maintenance tasks.

Specific Tasks:
1. Do simple cleaning of building and grounds.
2. Empty trash cans.
3. Weed and water flower beds.
4. Assist in repairing plumbing and heating.

Qualifications:
Some knowledge of simple maintenance skills and the ability to follow instructions.

Where to Apply:
Come to the Recreation Center at 1200 Smith Street between 9 a.m. and 5 p.m. any weekday or call 123-876 for more information.

Hours of Work:
Any time between 9 a.m. and 9 p.m., seven days a week, for a period of three or four hours.

VOLUNTEER MAINTENANCE MAN (description for mass media)
The Recreation Center at 1200 Smith Street needs a person to help keep the building and grounds clean and attractive so that people will like to come to it. Hours of work are completely flexible. Call 123-876 between 9 a.m. and 5 p.m. any weekday or drop in to talk with us.

Figure 14.2 Sample position descriptions for volunteer maintenance man.

- It has contacts with the mass media, where the needs for volunteers can be publicized;
- If a person who wishes to volunteer does not seem to fit in one agency, he or she can be referred to another.

Some agencies, however, prefer to find their own sources of volunteers. They feel that in this way the needs of the agency can be interpreted best. They also feel that a special rapport with the volunteer can be developed from the outset.

POSITION DESCRIPTIONS

VOLUNTEER CLERK (detailed description)
   Under general supervision of the agency secretary to perform general office work.

Specific Tasks:
1. Operate agency switchboard.
2. File correspondence.
3. Maintain membership file.
4. Greet people who come to the agency and direct them to the person or group whom they are seeking.
5. Type reports.

Qualifications:
   Ability to do simple filing, type, greet people, and operate a switchboard.

Where to Apply:
   Recreation Center, 1200 Smith Street, any weekday from 9 a.m. to 5 p.m. or call 123-876 for more information.

Hours of Work:
   Any day, seven days a week, between 9 a.m. and 9 p.m. for periods of two to four hours.

VOLUNTEER CLERK (description for mass media)
   The Recreation Agency at 1200 Smith Street serves people who want to participate in leisure activities, but can't do it as well as they might if they had someone to help with filing, answering the telephone, typing, and greeting people who come to the agency. Can you help? Help is needed every day, seven days a week, from 9 a.m. to 9 p.m. The hours of work are flexible. Call us at 123-876 or drop in for more information.

Figure 14.3 Sample position descriptions for volunteer clerk.

Sources for Volunteers: There are certain sources for volunteers that are available in most communities. The sources that have proven to be productive through the years are:

POSITION DESCRIPTIONS

VOLUNTEER SUPERVISOR FOR A BOWLING LEAGUE (detailed description)

Under the supervision of the Athletics Director, to organize and conduct a bowling league for senior citizens from all of the recreation centers in the city.

Specific Tasks:
1. Compile a list of teams from each center with average scores of each player.
2. Assign handicaps to teams as needed.
3. Arrange for the use of bowling alleys at given times.
4. Draw up the schedule of play for teams for each week during a 12-week period.
5. Keep records of scores of teams.
6. Arrange for trophies for winning teams.
7. Collect entry fees and deposit them with department finance officer.
8. Attend league sessions each week.

Qualifications:

Knowledge of bowling and experience in running a bowling league.

Where to Apply:

Call the Athletics Director at 123-456 or come to the Department's main office at 100 Center Street any time on Monday or Wednesday from 10 a.m. to 1 p.m.

Hours of Work:

League sessions each week and additional time to complete necessary league reports.

VOLUNTEER SUPERVISOR FOR BOWLING LEAGUE (description for mass media)

There are about 50 older persons from the Recreation Centers in the city who would like to bowl in a league, but need someone to organize the league for them. Can you do this? If so, call John Downs at 123-456 for an appointment to talk it over. Call between 10 a.m. and 1 p.m., on Monday or Wednesday, February 1 or 3.

Figure 14.4 Sample position descriptions for volunteer supervisor of bowling league.

REQUEST FOR VOLUNTEERS

Name of Agency   Date

Address   Telephone Number

Person to Contact

Volunteers that are needed:

1. Brief job description

2. General qualifications

3. Number of volunteers needed in this category

4. Time required each week:
   number of days
   hours each day

5. Length of time service is needed (please check)
   1 month   2 months   3 months
   6 months   one year or more

6. Special qualifications

Figure 14.5 Request for volunteers form. This form should be completed by an agency to be sent to a central volunteer bureau or by a section of a department to be sent to the department's volunteer office. A separate form should be completed for each type of volunteer needed.

- *Church groups.* From earliest times, members of churches have assisted the clergy to help people in need or to help the church carry on its work.
- *Women's groups.* Women, traditionally, have given the greatest amount of volunteer service. The various women's clubs today

can be rich source for volunteers to serve agencies in a great variety of ways. They can serve in the agency or they can go out into the community to solicit funds or materials needed to carry on the work of the agency.

- *Service clubs.* There are many clubs which have service to the community as a major purpose. They may define a special group to be served, such as the Shriner's Hospitals for Children, or they may indicate that they will give service as needed.
- *High school clubs or courses.* In many high schools today, service to the community is considered part of the total educational process. Some clubs are organized for this purpose. In other schools, this service is considered part of the curriculum and students receive credit in a specific course for the service that they give.
- *Professional men and women.* Many professional men and women are willing to give volunteer service to people in the community who need their service but cannot afford to pay for it, e.g., the doctor or dentist who gives volunteer service in a clinic one afternoon a week.
- *Retired people.* As people retire at continually earlier ages, more and more look for some kind of meaningful activity. These people have had years of experience in one or more fields and can bring their expertise to volunteer service. The possibilities in this group are almost unlimited.
- *Parent groups.* Parent groups in schools or agencies can give a variety of services ranging from leadership of a group to providing repair service for televisions.
- *Commercial and industrial organizations.* Many organizations of this type have employee clubs. One type of club that is popular is the service club. This kind of group may give regular service to an agency or simply provide one service such as gifts at Christmas.
- *Colleges.* In more and more college programs, some type of preservice training on the job is required as part of the curriculum. These students can supply valuable services, even though they will require close supervision and the agency will need to assure the college that it is providing an educational experience, not simply receiving free service.
- *Indigenous leaders.* Many clubs or groups of older teenagers or adults prefer to have a leader from the group. A volunteer leader of this kind understands the purpose of the group and is respected by the group members and chosen by them.

Some newer sources of volunteers have evolved in recent years. These include:

- Children and teenagers;
- Senior citizens clubs, retired senior volunteer program (RSVP), foster grandparents.
- Professional sports groups, e.g., the Harlem Globe Trotters, National Basketball Association;
- Disabled people;
- Environmental protection groups;
- Banks and other industries. (A number of these institutions have begun to give their employees leaves of absence, during which time the employees work as volunteers in agencies and their salaries are paid at the usual rate by the bank or industry.)

Methods of recruiting: When potential sources of volunteers have been determined, the committee responsible for recruiting must plan a volunteer recruitment campaign. Whether recruitment is done by a central bureau or a single agency, there are certain steps that must be taken. They are:

1. Organize a recruitment committee to formulate a specific plan. On this committee should be a representative from the various organizations in the community where there are potential volunteers.
2. The first responsibility of the committee will be to define the methods that will be used to tell the public of the needs of the agency or agencies for volunteers. Methods that have proven productive are:
   - Mass media advertising, e.g., newspapers, radio, TV, bus cards, sound trucks in various neighborhoods.
   - Billboard posters on streets and highways.
   - Personal contacts
     (1) Organize a group of volunteers to make telephone calls to people whom they know and whom they think might be good volunteers.
     (2) Organize a group of volunteers to write letters to their friends asking them to help.
   - Interviews and dramatic presentations for the mass media.
   - Store window displays.
   - Exhibits in a park or public building of work done by the agency.
   - Films or videotapes of agency work given at public meetings.
   - Fliers given to people at neighborhood markets, bus stops, or posted on bulletin boards.
   - Speakers at meetings.
   - Letters to college field work coordinators.

3. At the same time that the committee is planning the campaign to publicize the need for volunteers, it must also plan how the people are to apply and how those who apply will be screened. If the volunteer recruitment is community-wide, a central location needs to be found where people can apply and where interviews can be held for all applicants. This means that a core of volunteers must be recruited to man the central application center for receiving applicants, interviewing, and referral to an agency. This is a large undertaking and must be organized to the last detail if it is to be effective. The problems to be solved include:

- What central location can be found that will be donated by its owner for the purpose? And who will furnish the equipment which is needed?
- Who will donate telephone service?
- Can the agencies in the community recommend people who will man the center?
- Do the agencies have any personnel whom they could send to the center to do the interviewing and referral?
- Should the committee plan a training course for volunteer interviewers? If so, what shall be included in the course, and who will give it? In any community there will probably be enough trained professionals, either currently employed or retired, who would be willing to participate in such a training course.
- What will be the procedure when a referral to an agency is made and the agency rejects the volunteer whom they feel does not meet their needs?

In some communities there will no doubt be other problems, but these are some of the basic ones that must be considered.

If volunteer recruitment is being done by a single agency, the procedures are similar, but they are somewhat more simplified. Some of the above problems are automatically solved. The agency will have the basic space and equipment requirement that will be needed for the volunteer recruitment campaign. Beyond these, the volunteer recruitment committee in the agency will need to consider all the other problems listed above for the community-wide recruitment committee. This means that they must consider the methods to be used, how applicants will be processed, including distribution of application blanks, interviewing and referral of applicants to specific sections of the agency, and what will be done if a given section rejects a specific volunteer. (See Figure 14.6 for sample application form and Figure 14.7 for sample referral form.)

VOLUNTEER APPLICATION FORM

Name _____ Telephone Number _____

Address _____ U.S. Citizen: Yes _____ , No _____

What hours can you work? (please check)
Morning _____ , Afternoon _____ , Evening _____

How many hours can you work each week? _____

How many days can you work each week, and which days?

_____

Do you own a car?   Yes _____ , No _____

Do you have a driver's license?   Yes _____ , No _____

Do you have a chauffeur's license?   Yes _____ , No _____

Health

Indicate how you would rate your health.
Excellent _____ , Good _____ , Fair _____ , Poor _____

Describe any health handicaps or disabilities that you have that may limit your activities. _____

_____

_____

Education

Circle the number of years of education that you have had.

1 2 3 4 5 6 7 8 9 10 11 12 13 14 15 16 17 more

Describe any kind of special education that you have had, such as computer programming or ceramics.

_____

What kind of work do you do? Include housework in your own home.

_____

How many years have you worked? _____

Have you ever done volunteer work before? _____

Activities

On the following list check the activities for which you would like to volunteer your services.

Office work   _____
Maintenance work   _____

Leadership of groups in:

Art   _____
Children's play group   _____
Crafts   _____
Dance   _____
Gymnastics   _____
Music   _____
Outdoor activities   _____
Individual sports   _____
Dual sports   _____
Team sports   _____
Social activities   _____
(parties, picnics)
Water activities   _____
Winter sports   _____
Supervisor of a sports league   _____
Lead activities for disabled   _____
   people (blind, deaf,
   physically handicapped)
Lead activities for elderly   _____
   people
Other _____

_____

_____

Figure 14.6 Sample volunteer application form.

VOLUNTEER REFERRAL FORM

The volunteer office has interviewed (Mr./Ms./Mrs.)

We find that _____ is interested in _____

and would particularly like to work with _____
                                              (type of people)

in a _____ program, on _____
                                              (days)

from _____ to _____ .
       (hours)   (hours)

   Please indicate below whether you can use this volunteer.

Check one:

I can use _____ .

I cannot use _____ at this time, but have arranged

with him or her to come into the agency on _____ .
                                                   (date)

I have assigned _____ to be a _____

for _____ . He/she will continue in this assign-
       (type of group or work)

ment for the next _____ months.

Figure 14.7 Sample volunteer referral form.

---

   4. If the decision is reached to use volunteers as interviewers, it is
      necessary to plan a training program for these interviewers. The
      training program should include the following major topics:

How to start an interview.
- Establish rapport with the applicant. Find a topic in which there is
  a common interest, e.g., an event in the community, a hobby, or a
  recreation pursuit.
- Make the applicant comfortable, e.g., find a hanger for his/her coat,
  pull a chair in position for him/her, offer a cup of tea or a cool drink.
- Arrange the furniture so that there are no barriers between the
  interviewer and the applicant.

Training hint: Have the volunteer interviewer practice starting an interview.

The purpose of the interview

The major purpose is to discover further information about the applicant that cannot be learned from the application blank. The interviewer needs to ascertain how the applicant feels about various types of service, e.g., although the person has indicted that he or she can both lead beginning swimming and teach modern dance, which does the applicant really prefer, and why? With this kind of information the interviewer can make a better referral for service. To gain this information, the interviewer must learn to ask questions. One basic principle in interviewing is: Never ask questions that can be answered with "yes" or "no." What you are seeking in an interview is insight into the capabilities of the applicant. Questions should be phrased to gain this, or leading statements should be made. A leading statement might be: "Tell me about your work with disabled children." It should not be: "Did you like your work with disabled children?" Another way to gain this information would be: "Why did you like working with disabled children?"

Training hint: Have your volunteer interviewers write three leading statements and three questions. Then have the group critique them to decide how much information can be gained from them.

Closing the interview.

When the interviewer has gained as much information as he or she deems possible, the interview should be closed. Several methods for closing the interview are possible. The situation will determine which one is to be used.

(1) Refer the applicant to an agency or section of a department where the need for this type of service has been indicated.

(2) Give the applicant the opportunity to choose from among two or three agencies, the one to which he or she would like to be referred.

(3) Refer to a volunteer training class. Many agencies and communities that use volunteer services have preferred to refer all applicants to training classes. In some cases, these training classes have been short, one-to-two-hour sessions that merely serve to present an overview of the responsibilities of a volunteer. The major points that are usually covered in a short course of this kind are:

- The need for dependability;
- How promptness affects the program;

- The volunteer should not overload his/her schedule;
- Simple tasks that are "well done" are as important as big tasks;
- Each person brings special skills or talents to a program;
- Each job is important—none more, none less.
- The volunteer benefits from his or her service and will receive both extrinsic and intrinsic rewards.
- Volunteer service should be for a stated period of time, after which the volunteer may renew his or her service or terminate it.
- Every volunteer is on probation, at least for his or her first month of service.

In addition to this type of short course, referral to courses of longer duration may be made. These longer courses give basic skills in specific types of service, e.g., a course to train leaders to work with senior citizens might include responsibilities of the volunteer (goals, limitations), needs of the elderly (physical, mental, social), how to motivate older people, and skills and techniques of activities for older people in areas such as music, drama, or crafts. This kind of course might be only four or five two-hour sessions in length. For volunteer services with the handicapped, longer training courses that also include fieldwork in a medical setting, have been developed. These usually are about 15 two-hour sessions in length. (See the next section for a sample of courses.)

(4) If the applicant seems unfit for volunteer service, the interviewer should specifically state this and indicate that his or her capacities do not seem to qualify for volunteer service.

Training hint: Have interviewers practice closing an interview. Give each interviewer one of the four ways of closing an interview and have the group assess how effectively it was done.

Assessing the attitude of the applicant toward volunteer service.

This is probably the most difficult area to evaluate. Some of the key areas that will assist the interviewer to make this evaluation are: appearance, speech patterns, indications of biases, indication of beliefs and values, and excesses such as in smoking, clasping and unclasping hands.

Each of the four major areas regarding interviewing should be given at least a two-hour session. The session should be divided into three parts: lecture, discussion and practice. If it is possible, each interviewer should have the opportunity to interview an applicant with the trainer observing the interview. A discussion should then be held by the trainer to discuss with the interviewer the strengths and weaknesses of the interview. Suggestions should then be given to the interviewer for improving his or her interviewing techniques.

Trainers for the interviewers' training classes can be found in an agency or in the community from among supervisors or administrators in the agencies who have training and experience in interviewing. Each will approach the task somewhat differently. The training course outlined above is merely a suggestion of important topics to be covered.

Whoever does the interviewing and whatever method is used for selection, it must be recognized that, although many volunteers are needed, those selected must have the qualifications that will enhance the agencies' services. There is no test or scale that completely will insure the aptitude of the individual to provide effective service in recreation and leisure service. There are many characteristics that make for successful volunteer service, but it is the distribution and sum total of these characteristics in each individual that will produce the best job performance.

ORIENTATION AND TRAINING

In recreation and leisure agencies there are a multiplicity of tasks that are performed by volunteers. For this reason, educating a volunteer for service in an agency takes a variety of approaches. There are four major parts to the education of a volunteer for service in an agency. They are:

1. Pre-service training;
2. Orientation to the agency in which he or she is placed;
3. Continuous in-service training through supervisory conferences, staff meetings, and some type of in-service training course or workshop;
4. Development training courses for more advanced knowledge or skills or new techniques.

Pre-service training: The trend is for agencies to require that volunteers not only have an orientation to the agency, but also, at least a brief pre-service training program. Frequently, agencies prefer to recruit volunteers for a pre-service course, given either by the agency or conducted by a group of agencies that use similar types of volunteers. For example, the recreation and leisure service committee of a council of social agencies may offer a pre-service course at frequent intervals. The course is given at various times of the day and night to be convenient for the schedules of volunteers who wish to give service in the morning, afternoon, or evening. This type of pre-service course necessarily must be rather general and relate to the responsibilities of volunteers that are common to all recreation and leisure service agencies. A pre-service course given by an agency may include orientation to the agency and more specific training for the tasks to be performed in the agency.

The areas that should be included in a pre-service training course for a group of agencies are:

1. A brief exploration of the history and philosophy of the fields of group work, recreation, and leisure services.
2. The meaning of leisure and what leisure experiences can bring to people.
3. General characteristics of people who come to recreation and leisure service agencies.
4. The kinds of agencies that offer leisure services and how public and private agencies relate to each other. In addition, it should be indicated how different purposes within the field are achieved by these two types of agencies. There also should be some discussion of the ways in which private and commercial agencies help to meet the leisure needs of people, even though volunteers are seldom used in these agencies.
5. Skill workshops to give volunteers an exposure to the several types of skills that are used in these agencies. The skills that should be included are: arts and crafts; how to lead a discussion; simple music, drama, and dance activities; games for varying age groups; and social activities.
6. The responsibilities and limitations of volunteers. These include:

   a. The function of the volunteer office in an agency.
   b. Volunteer ethics, including the need for confidentiality of all participant records and staff discussions.
   c. How to work with participants, including all of the do's and don't's related to service in the agency.
   d. Relationship between paid and volunteer staff. The volunteer is part of the staff, just as the paid worker is.
   e. General rules and regulations found in agencies, such as those relating to appropriate dress, smoking, use of alcoholic beverages.
   f. Dependability and punctuality. Stress needs to be put on these. A volunteer must be responsible for telephoning if he or she is unable to report or, if the agency is so organized, to find a substitute back-up person for a given day.

   g. Health requirements in agencies. Many agencies require a physical examination before a volunteer begins to work. This is particularly true in agencies serving the disabled, in nursing homes, hospitals, and other medically-oriented settings.

   h. Safety precautions needed in agencies and particularly those to be used in work with the disabled or aged.

   i. The volunteer's responsibilities relating to agency public relations.

   j. Volunteer expenses, and how they may be financed under certain circumstances, e.g., through federal, regional, or local funding.

   k. Kinds of activities that agencies conduct for those who volunteer.

   l. Awards that are given for volunteer service.

A pre-service course of this type will cover essentially the same material regardless of the agency giving it, but it will relate specifically to the particular agency in which it is given.

This kind of training program should be no less than six two-hour sessions in length. A program of this kind will serve two purposes. First, it will help to give volunteers confidence that they can perform assigned tasks in an agency. Secondly, it may give volunteers insight into the fact that this is *not* the kind of service that they want.

Orientation: Orientation must be related to a specific agency and frequently to a specific service. For example, in a hospital, the volunteer office will give a brief orientation program for all hospital volunteers. Included in the program will be the volunteer's responsibility to the volunteer office, hospital rules and regulations, how to relate to patients, and do's and don't's regarding confidentiality. Also included will be volunteer uniforms, probationary periods for volunteers, the importance of dependability and punctuality, and how volunteer expenses will be met. Volunteers will also be shown how to complete records and reports to be filed in the volunteer office.

At the completion of this short orientation to the hospital, the volunteer will have an orientation given by the service to which he or she is assigned. When a volunteer is placed in a therapeutic recreation service in the hospital, that service conducts the orientation to that department. This will include observation of activities, where supplies and equipment are kept, the organization plan of the department, the person to whom the volunteer will report, the records and reports he or she will need to complete for the department, and the general characteristics of the patients with whom a specific volunteer will work.

In a community center type of agency, orientation must be not only to the agency, but also to the neighborhood in which the agency is located. Orientation to this kind of an agency must include: an observation survey of the neighborhood, (a walk around the neighborhood with an agency staff person is one way that this can be done, with the staff member pointing out salient features); the need for dependability and punctuality; the volunteer's responsibility to his or her group; agency rules and regulations; appropriate dress for work with specific groups (such as shorts or slacks for slimnastics and a smock for crafts); how expenses of the volunteer will be met; and the need for impartiality in working with participants. Furthermore, a given agency may have certain specific procedures that are peculiar to that agency and to which the volunteer must be alerted. In addition to face-to-face orientation, the volunteer should be given a manual that outlines all of the operating procedures in the agency.

In general, it could be said that the purpose of orientation is to make the volunteer feel comfortable in the agency.

Supervisory conferences and staff meetings: A volunteer is a member of the total staff of the agency. As such, a volunteer should have regular conferences with his or her supervisor. Because a volunteer comes to an agency only at specified times, the supervisor should arrange for a short conference either directly before or after the volunteer's period of work. The supervisory conference should be planned for, and considered as, a time for on-going training. It will be oriented more to specific problems that the volunteer may be encountering, but it can also be a time for brief exploration of new methods that a volunteer may learn, or be an opportunity to learn a new skill that can be used with a group. It might also be a time when a supervisor shows the volunteer how to use a new piece of equipment or some new supplies. Whatever the focus, the conference should be viewed as part of a learning experience, an experience that the supervisor and the volunteer share. It is the supervisor's responsibility to set aside the time for each volunteer conference at regular intervals. These should be at least once a month, and preferably more frequently, especially when the volunteer begins his or her service in the agency.

In addition to regular individual conferences with volunteers, the supervisor should try to arrange for volunteers to attend staff meetings—at least occasionally. Attendance at these meetings can be considered part of the training program, at which the volunteer learns more about the functioning of the entire agency.

In-service training and development courses: When volunteers have been working in an agency for a period of time, it is well to consider recommending that they attend a workshop or some type of course where they can acquire new skills which they might want to use with their groups. Workshops or a longer course may be offered by the agency or through a community educational institution, such as an adult education program of a public high school or of a local college.

The workshop is usually a one-day program built around a specific topic. For instance, for craft leaders, there might be a workshop on latch-hook rug making. All volunteers working in crafts would be invited to attend. This type of workshop is usually sponsored by the agency or department and held in the craft room of the agency. It might be open to all agency personnel in the community or may be only for the personnel, both paid and volunteer, in a given agency. The instructor is usually a department member who is expert in the activity to be learned.

Development training courses are generally longer in duration than a workshop, and frequently are given in a community educational institution. Volunteers should be recommended to them in accordance with their interests and the need of the agency for persons with the advanced knowledge, skills, or techniques that are to be learned.

Developing volunteer training courses: There are several basic concerns that an agency contemplating giving a volunteer training course must consider. They can be summed in the words: who?, what?, when?, and how?

Who? When looking at who the volunteers are, it is necessary to consider their general characteristics. Are they housewives, business-women from offices, factory workers, or skilled artisans? Each of these people will bring a different background to volunteer service. If there are some of each type in the group, the volunteer instructor will need to assess their common characteristics, consider their differences and gear the training program to both. On the other hand, if the volunteers are all high school students taking a course in community services, it can be assumed that their general characteristics will be somewhat similar, even if they are individually different.

What? The content of a basic course, as indicated above, must be general, for it is impossible to go into depth in a course of only four or five sessions. The basic course must include the behavior charac-teristics of the people to be served, the kinds of activities that they are seeking in the agency, some skills that might be used with groups and the responsibilities of volunteers in agencies. Refresher courses or workshops will include indepth information on a given topic.

When? The training program must be scheduled at a time and place that is convenient for the volunteers. Because volunteers work in agencies at different times of the day and night, it will be necessary to schedule classes in the mornings, afternoons, and evenings to correspond to the time when volunteers will be in the agency.

How? or, Methods of conducting training courses: As indicated in the section on recruitment, it is commonly thought desirable to recruit for a training course to be given on a community-wide basis for volunteers who will work in a variety of agencies. However, agencies often prefer to conduct a combined orientation and basic training program in their own agency. This kind of program may be just a single session or it may be a number of sessions.

Those who are responsible for training volunteers must approach their task with a clear understanding of why people volunteer. They also must have had teaching experience with people of varying ages, backgrounds, and levels of capacity. Since the majority of volunteers are adults, it is an asset for the volunteer trainer to have had experience in teaching adults. The trainer must understand how to organize the training program and conduct it in such a way that it will bring satisfaction to the potential volunteer. A volunteer may not have worked in a leisure service or recreation program before, but he or she has certain capacities. The trainer must know how to activate those capacities without making the volunteer feel inferior in any way. The joy and adventure of learning something new should be the approach of the trainer. In addition, the trainer should take a step-by-step approach to learning so as to give the volunteer an illustration of how one can work successfully with participants in the programs that one will conduct.

In conducting the volunteer training program, the trainer needs to involve the volunteers through participation in discussions, skill learning, and doing activities, whether it is leading songs or filing reports. In general, lecturing to a group of volunteers is a poor approach. Involve them in doing and help them decide what methods are most effective. Films and other visual aids should be used. The best approach is to try to have the learner use all five senses in order to remember what he or she has learned. The extent to which all the senses are used will indicate the potential for remembering. So, show, tell, touch, smell, and taste literally or figuratively, to the extent that it is possible, if you expect the volunteer to absorb what has been taught.

PLACEMENT, SUPERVISION AND EVALUATION

Careful selection and training will be a wasted effort unless volunteers are placed so that their capabilities are utilized, supervision is given to help them with their problems, and evaluation of their performance is made.

Placement: The placement of volunteers should be made in accordance with the needs of the agency *and* the needs and competencies of the volunteers. If volunteers are placed after a pre-service training program, they should be placed, immediately, in an agency program. Placement must be a real work situation, not busy work. Busy work would only be an admissable assignment when an emergency in the agency requires it to meet a program need, such as addressing letters to participants to tell them about a change in the program. In placing the volunteers in a program, two purposes are achieved: first, to provide assistance with the program, and secondly, through the volunteers to inform the public about the program. Volunteers will talk to their friends and neighbors about the program and, in so doing, become direct public relations agents for the agency. If they like what they are doing and they consider the work that the agency is doing important to the community, the volunteers will transmit these beliefs to people, and the agency and its purposes will be seen as a valuable part of community living.

General procedures in placing volunteers. The following procedures have proven to be effective in the placement of volunteers:

1. Place volunteers in real jobs, directly following an interview, or after pre-service training.
2. Discuss the placement that is planned with the volunteers to ascertain that it is satisfactory to them. In the discussion indicate that the placement is for a probationary period, at which time the volunteers or the agency will be able to make a change if such seems desirable.
3. Specify exactly the hours and days that the volunteers will work.
4. Orient the volunteers to their placement.
   a. Tell them the procedures to follow when reporting for work, including where and how to sign in, changing to a uniform if such is required, where to hang coats and put purses, and how early they are to report for work before their regularly scheduled time. (Adequate locker or other space should be provided where volunteers may lock up coats, purses, briefcases, and other personal articles.)
   b. Take volunteers to areas in which they are to work and show them exactly where all supplies and equipment that they will use are located.
   c. Introduce them to all personnel with whom they will be working.
   d. With the volunteers, observe the programs in which they will be working. After the observation, the volunteers will then

be in a position to ask pertinent questions about the program.

5. When the volunteers report to work the first time, introduce them to the participant groups with whom they will be working as an assistant, leader, or in whatever capacity they will serve.

6. Arrange with the volunteers for supervisory conferences, indicating the person with whom they will be having them and the time and place of the conference.

7. Give the volunteers detailed job descriptions showing the tasks that they will be expected to perform, the persons to whom they are to report, and the kind of dress or uniform that they are expected to wear.

Supervisors or leaders who accept volunteers for help with the program for which they are responsible must recognize that the volunteers' work must be well planned. Volunteers will have certain skills or expertise that they bring to the agency, but agency personnel must plan how to use those skills to a maximum extent, so that the agency will benefit from them.

Before placing a volunteer:

- Review the agency's need for the skills of the volunteer;
- Plan how these skills will be utilized;
- Supervise the volunteer to ascertain that he or she has necessary support to give the agency the benefit of those skills; and
- Recognize the service given by the volunteer through some type of award other than the satisfaction that the volunteer receives from the service given.

Supervision: Supervision of volunteers entails the same procedures as those used in supervising paid personnel. Supervision should be viewed as a shared experience between the supervisor and the person supervised. Its purpose is to bring about better job performance which, in turn, will bring better services to participants. It is primarily a helping process. Although critical analysis is part of the process, the aim of the analysis should be positive and the criticism constructive, *not* destructive. The approach should be, "Try this," not, "don't do that."

Supervisors in a recreation or leisure service agency must bring to the supervisory process the same kind of helping purposes that are the foundation of the agency. They must eliminate the attitude of the factory supervisor who frequently only looks for what is wrong with a worker rather than what is right. The wrong or wrongs in that situation then form the basis for termination. Too often the things that are right are overlooked until they build into a big pile, at which time the worker is reluctantly recommended for promotion. In any supervisory position, supervisors may feel that good workers threaten their positions. Supervisors, consequently, must examine their own attitudes and constantly guard against unwarranted criticism of workers, whether they are paid or volunteer.

Motivating volunteers. An important function of a supervisor of volunteers is to motivate them to high levels of job performance. Persons who volunteer do so because they believe that work as a volunteer will make their lives more satisfying. Some of the benefits that they think they will derive from this service might be:

- Their beliefs, concepts, and values are compatible with those of the agency and so will be acceptable to the agency;
- Through their skills they can help other people to acquire similar skills and the satisfaction in doing them;
- They can use their creativity, initiative, and intellect to promote a better climate for living for themselves and others;
- They can use their capacities to help solve problems and thus help the agency to achieve its objectives;
- Through volunteering they will gain status with their peers; and
- Through volunteering they will be able to help others and so gain a better feeling of adequacy.

As supervisors work with volunteers, they must recognize these human needs of the volunteers. They can then help the volunteers to meet them at the same time that they are helping the volunteers to enhance their services in the agency.

Problems in supervising volunteers. Although the process of supervising volunteers is similar to that used with paid workers, some problems are evident that do not exist or are minimized with paid workers. These problems include, but are not necessarily limited to:

1. Dependability. This is one of the biggest problems related to volunteer service. Because they receive no monetary remuneration for the service that they give, many volunteers feel no responsibility for reporting to work regularly. Definite rules regarding regularity of service must be established and carried out. Volunteers must recognize that when they sign up to serve it means they will report on time every day when they are scheduled to be there, unless an emergency occurs.

2. Liability. The agency must establish legal responsibility for the volunteers in the agency. This involves:

   - Responsibility of the agency when a participant under the supervision of a volunteer is injured;
   - Responsibility of the agency when a volunteer is injured.

The injury in either case could be to either the person or his/her property.

3. Getting to the job. One of the problems in agencies is finding means for volunteers to reach the agency. This is particularly a problem in suburban areas, and is a special problem for agencies which use high school boys and girls as volunteers, particularly for work in evening programs. Sometimes it is possible to use an agency car to pick up volunteers at given locations. Another solution would be to form car pools among the volunteers to drive all who need transportation on a given day. Parents of high school students may also be recruited to drive a group to the agency.

4. Group behavior problems. It is frequently necessary for the supervisor to help group leaders understand behavior problems of groups and how to cope with them. Supervisors often find it necessary to deal with these problems at individual conferences because of the impossibility of assembling a group of volunteers who work different hours. If a group can be brought together, however, this might be the most effective way in which to discuss these kinds of problems.

5. Maintaining an *esprit de corps* among volunteers. Because volunteers work at varying times of the day or night, it is difficult to find a way in which they can gain a feeling of belonging to a larger whole. Generally, agencies have used the technique of an activity *for* volunteers. This might be a picnic, a luncheon or dinner, or it might be a one-day or evening workshop. At the time of this event, only basic activities of the agency are scheduled; all others are suspended so that the full staff may concentrate on the activity for the volunteers.

Some Do's and Don'ts for Supervisors

The Do's	The Don'ts
Do be an inspiration for improvement.	Do not oversupervise.
Do be supportive as necessary.	Do not limit initiative.
Do be a guide and teacher.	Do not fail to recognize differences.
Do be an outlet for the expression of hostilities, difficulties, or failures.	Do not be authoritarian.
Do be a model of what is best.	Do not keep people dependent.
Do uphold the policies of the worker.	Do not be critical rather than understanding.

Organizing volunteers. There are many ways in which volunteers in recreation and leisure service agencies may be organized. The organization patterns range from almost no organization to the very formal.

In some agencies there is simply a person who is responsible for recruiting and placing volunteers. Once the volunteer is placed, it becomes the responsibility of the section in which he or she is placed to supervise the volunteer and give the volunteer the recognition that is used to show appreciation for his or her service.

Other agencies, mostly the larger ones, have more formal organizations. These frequently follow the pattern of the auxiliary in hospitals and other medically-oriented settings, such as residential schools for the retarded or emotionally disturbed or nursing homes. The purposes of the auxiliary are many. It may engage in fund raising to supplement the regular funding of the agency. Sometimes an auxiliary will fund the salary of a volunteer office, which office, in turn, assumes the responsibility for all volunteers in the agency. The organization of an auxiliary is that of a private group with a constitution and by-laws, and officers elected in accordance with the constitution. This type of auxiliary, related to tax-supported public agencies, may also incorporate under the laws of the state as a separate entity so that it may engage in fund raising which the tax-supported agency may not. Auxiliaries for other than tax-supported agencies may carry on fund raising as well as service activities without the need to incorporate. In these agencies, the auxiliary must simply comply with the policies of the agency as approved by its board of directors.

Evaluation: The supervisor must evaluate the work of the volunteers, just as they evaluate other members of the staff. Partly, this is done at each supervisory conference through the assessment with the volunteer of the effectiveness of the service that he or she is giving; however, at intervals, there should be a more formal evaluation. This should include a discussion of:

- Strengths and weaknesses as seen both by the supervisor and the volunteer;
- The benefits that the agency is receiving from the volunteer's service;
- The benefit that the volunteer is receiving from the service that he or she is giving;
- The desire of the volunteer to remain in the same placement or change to a different kind of service; and
- Specific problems that the volunteer is having in his or her placement, including relationships with staff or participants; insuffi-

ciency of facilities, equipment or supplies; or personal problems of the volunteer that may make continued service difficult or impossible.

RECOGNITION OF VOLUNTEERS

People who volunteer for service in an agency should receive some recognition for this service. Paid staff members receive salaries for their work and are recognized by their peers, thus gaining certain status. Volunteers receive nothing but the satisfaction they derive from service unless the agency makes a specific effort to provide some kind of recognition for volunteer service.

There are many ways of doing this. A very simple way is to put an article in the local newspaper listing the names of all the people who have given volunteer service to the agency. This accomplishes two purposes: It indicates to the volunteers that their service is appreciated, and it gives the volunteers status in the community, showing their friends and neighbors what they have done.

When volunteers complete any type of training course, they should receive certificates indicating the work that they have completed. These are usually presented at a ceremony by the head of the agency or his or her representative. The certificates should be printed so that they have the appearance of an official document and should be signed by the appropriate agency officials.

In some cases, the participants want to show their appreciation of the service of the volunteers. They will do this by staging some kind of activity, taking full responsibility for it, asking the staff to help only when it is absolutely necessary.

The volunteers' hours of work in the agency should be recognized at regular intervals. Through the years, agencies have devised a variety of symbols to recognize these. Some agencies award a pin, and then add bars up to a given number, later presenting a different pin for additional hours of service. Others, following the military, put a stripe on a uniform or sleeve.

Whatever the award may be, it should be given at a public ceremony and reported in the press. This is the volunteers' extrinisic remuneration for service. Their intrinsic remuneration is their satisfaction in giving service. The extent of this is really only known by the individuals, although it can be partially measured by the volunteers' continued willingness to serve. Whatever the awards may be, they should be a sincere expression of appreciation of a job well done.

Summary

Volunteering is an important part of community living today, both for the individual and for the agency. As people find less and less satisfaction in their highly mechanized paid work, they look for other means to express initiative and creativity. In the inflated monetary condition of society, recreation and leisure service agencies cannot fully achieve their purposes without the help of volunteers to augment the meager resources allotted to them. Full community life, therefore, depends to a large extent on the quality of services given by volunteers; consequently, it is the responsibility of the professionals in the field to make the maximum use of volunteers. To do this, professionals must exercise their capacities to make wise selections, be creative in volunteer training, and use their insight to make placements that will benefit both the agency and the volunteers. The **Volunteer Services Staff Handbook** of the City of Tucson's Park and Recreation Department (see Figure 14.8). is an example of the way one agency communicates its philosophy, policies and procedures regarding volunteers to its staff.

Figure 14.8 A sample of staff handbook for volunteer services.

___

WHY VOLUNTEER?

Parks and Recreation is utilizing volunteers to provide for two basic needs. The first is to enhance Department programs. Providing new skills and methods of presentation, the variety of voluntarism offers an opportunity to raise the quality of the entire program, both as a supplement to existing activities, and as a new learning opportunity for participating volunteers, staff, and public. The second need is that of the volunteer. Voluntarism in itself is a program. It fulfills the desire of people to share what skills, enthusiasm, and time they can. It is a growing field; the demand for volunteers increasing with both limits placed by budget stress, and with the realization of the value of volunteer work. Volunteers are not "just free labor"! They serve a vital role, providing an exciting input of energy, talent, and experience.

GOALS OF VOLUNTEER SERVICES

1) To give volunteer and community a stimulated interest and satisfaction in creative activities, and intellectual and leisure pursuits.
2) To provide opportunity for people to be of service to someone and to attain a feeling of achievement.
3) To provide a stimulating atmosphere for volunteer help in a growth-oriented program.
4) To enhance programs for Parks and Recreation.
5) To provide variety and flexibility.
6) To give volunteer, staff, and community a time of pleasure
   . . .

PROMOTE LAUGHTER

RECRUITMENT

Two Primary Sources:
1) Volunteers drawn from existing programs or at existing sites.
   a) Those people who are volunteers for existing programs may be registered with Volunteer Services and receive recognition for their service.

b) Staff on site may recruit, receiving support and materials from Volunteer Services. Staff is invaluable here, being in contact with, and knowing the area people.

2) Volunteers drawn from Volunteer Services.

a) Volunteer Services provides a recruitment and orientation program. Both existing and new volunteers will be invited to orientation and volunteer action.

b) Volunteer Services will provide continuing workshops and study plans to enable volunteers to achieve expanding goals, as well as recognition for service given.

REQUESTING A VOLUNTEER

1) Determine if real need exists.

a) Has enough interest in the program been voiced to merit need for a volunteer?

b) Have *staff* skills and activities been reviewed?

2) Fill in a Request Card.

a) Available through Volunteer Services and Field Supervisors, the "Request for Volunteers" card is Volunteer Services' effort to provide exact service for specific requests. Giving clear and detailed information is the first step to providing the best volunteer. In addition, it will allow preparation to run smoothly; the volunteer will have a definite course for action, and staff will know how to inform public, and best prepare the site.

b) Give advance notice of at least two to three weeks.

MEET WITH VOLUNTEER

1) Staff member to be in charge will be asked to meet volunteer.

2) During meeting, discussion will cover service needed, area of responsibility, materials, and location organization. At this time, an evaluation technique will also be set.

SITE PREPARATION AND THE VOLUNTEER

Staff Responsibility:

1) Local publicity should be well developed.

2) A staff member to be in charge must be chosen, (and all staff should be informed of program). Never ask a volunteer to start or conduct activity without having paid staff member present!

3) Provide a safe place for personal articles while volunteer in service.

4) Have facility and materials ready (if it pertains—have class organized and ready to start).
5) Show your appreciation!
   a) By making volunteer welcome!
   b) By introducing to staff and site participants.
   c) By inviting comments, and answering questions.
   d) By informing volunteer of park activities.

Volunteer Services will be responsible for volunteer recognition in the
form of workshops, promotions, and rewards.

SERVICE TIME AND EVALUATION

1) Volunteer will give "Service Appointment" card to staff in charge
   for hours of service to be charted on the back. After service is
   complete, the card will be returned to Volunteer Services via Field
   Supervisor.
2) If volunteer calls, informing of inability to attend, or does not
   appear at the site, inform Volunteer Services as soon as possible.
3) If problems arise concerning the volunteer, notify Volunteer Services.
4) At completion of service, or at set intervals determined at earlier
   meeting, evaluation of program will be held; a combination of
   volunteer, staff and Volunteer Services.

BILL OF RIGHTS FOR VOLUNTEERS

1. THE RIGHT TO BE TREATED AS A CO-WORKER
       not as "just free help,"
       not as a "prima donna."
2. THE RIGHT TO A SUITABLE ASSIGNMENT
       with consideration for personal preference, temperament, life
       experience, education, and employment background.
3. THE RIGHT TO KNOW AS MUCH ABOUT THE ORGANIZA-
   TION AS POSSIBLE
       its policies,
       its people,
       its programs.
4. THE RIGHT TO TRAINING FOR THE JOB
       thoughtfully planned and effectively presented.
5. THE RIGHT TO CONTINUING EDUCATION
       follow up to the initial training,
       information about new developments.

6. THE RIGHT TO SOUND GUIDANCE AND DIRECTION
    by someone who is experienced, well informed, patient, and thoughtful.
7. THE RIGHT TO PROMOTION AND A VARIETY OF EXPERIENCES
    through advancement to assignment of more responsibility.
8. THE RIGHT TO BE HEARD
    to have a part in planning,
    to feel free to make suggestions.
9. THE RIGHT TO RECOGNITION
    in the form of promotion and awards or some tangible evidence, through day-to-day expressions of appreciation.
10. THE RIGHT TO A PLACE TO WORK
    an orderly, designated place, conducive to work and worthy of the job to be done.

ACKNOWLEDGEMENT

This Code was the result of meetings of the Altrusa Club of Melbourne and was designed to raise standards in volunteer service for the community and country.

CITY OF TUCSON
PARKS AND RECREATION DEPARTMENT

REQUEST FOR VOLUNTEERS

1. Location: _____

2. Address: _____   3. Phone: _____

4. Type of Program or Class: _____

   Number of Participants Expected: _____ Age Group: _____

5. Type and Number of Volunteer(s) Requested (Be specific): _____
   _____
   _____
   _____

6. Schedule Reference: Beginning Date: _____ Ending Date: _____

   Day(s): _____ Time: _____

7. Staff in Charge: _____

8. What Type of Preparation Will Be Made? _____

CITY OF TUCSON
PARKS AND RECREATION DEPARTMENT

VOLUNTEER SERVICES—SERVICE APPOINTMENT

1. Location: _____

2. Address: _____   Phone: _____

3. Staff in Charge: _____

4. Schedule: Starting Date _____   Ending Date _____

   Day(s): _____   Time _____   Total Hours _____

5. Assignment:

   A. Description: _____

   B. Preparation Made: _____

   C. Preparation Needed: _____

   D. Participants Expected: _____

6. Comments: _____

REFERENCES

Frances Arje, "The New Volunteer Venture," **Nursing Administrator,** Vol. 16, No. 6, November–December, 1962.

Edith L. Ball, **Developing Volunteers for Service in Recreation Programs.** (Arlington, Va: National Recreation and Park Association, 1958.)

Max Kaplan, **Leisure: Lifestyle and Lifespan.** (Philadelphia, Pa.: W.B. Saunders Company, 1979).

Richard Kraus and Barbara Bates, **Recreation Leadership and Supervision.** (Philadelphia, Pa.: W. B. Saunders, 1975), Chapter 13, "The Recreation Volunteer."

Toni Merrill, **Activities for the Aged and Infirm.** (Springfield, Ill.: Charles C. Thomas, 1967), Chapter VII, "Volunteers."

National Information Bureau, **The Volunteer Board Member in Philanthropy.** (New York: 1968).

National Recreation and Park Association, "Volunteerism: Special Issue," **Parks and Recreation,** Vol. 10, No. 12, December 1975.

Gerald O'Morrow, **Administration of Activity Therapy Service.** (Springfield, Ill.: Charles C. Thomas, 1966), Chapter VIII, "Volunteer Services."

Jane Mallory Park, **Meaning Well Is Not Enough: Perspectives on Volunteering.** (South Plainfield, N.J.: Groupwork Today, Inc., 1983).

Arthur Pell, **Recruiting, Training and Motivating Volunteer Workers.** (New York: Pilot Industries, 1972).

Eva Schindler-Rainman and Ronald Lippitt. **The Volunteer Community: Creative Use of Human Resources,** 2nd ed. (La Jolla: California: University Associates, 1977).

Ben Solomon and Ethel M. Bowers, **You Can Be A Leader.** (Claremont, California: Leadership Press, 1981).

James Tanck, **College Volunteers.** (Washington, D.C.: National Program for Voluntary Action, U.S. Government Printing Office, 1969), No. o-36-896.